5£0

The *NEW*
HANDBOOK
of
ATTRACTING BIRDS

ILLUSTRATED BY

H. R. WHITEMAN
AND
LAMBERT GUENTHER

The *NEW*

HANDBOOK

of

ATTRACTING BIRDS

THOMAS P. McELROY, JR.

INTRODUCTION BY

ROGER TORY PETERSON

Second Edition, Revised and Enlarged

NEW YORK · ALFRED A. KNOPF

1960

L. C. catalog card number: 60-14466

© ALFRED A. KNOPF, INC., 1960

THIS IS A BORZOI BOOK,
PUBLISHED BY ALFRED A. KNOPF, INC.

First published October 16, 1950, reprinted July 1951.
This edition completely revised and enlarged, reset, and printed from new plates.
October 1960

TO HANNAH

INTRODUCTION

by

ROGER TORY PETERSON

A GARDEN without birds would seem as sterile as a pond without fish. Although we have heard of someone who wrote to the National Audubon Society requesting information on berries that birds would *not* eat, 999 home gardeners out of 1,000 regard the birds as much a part of the garden as the petunias, nasturtiums, and tulips. The imaginative gardener sows his borders not only with red, pink, and yellow hollyhocks but also with red cardinals, rosy purple finches, and yellow evening grosbeaks. The advantage of birds is that they are not strictly seasonal. Cardinals grace the shrubbery the year round, and the finches and grosbeaks brighten the bare branches when all plant life is dormant.

It is a logical development that many garden clubs now include a bird chairman just as they have a conservation chairman. To their dismay, horticulture sometimes comes into conflict with bird protection; certain toxic pesticides are almost as lethal to the birds as they are to insects. The gardener deplores this, for by and large, everyone wants to have the birds around and the more the merrier.

But how to achieve this? There are ways to double a bird population, even triple it. It is significant that in England where the countryside has been modified by centuries of human use, the highest densities of birds, often as many as fifteen nesting pairs per acre, are to be found in gardens and on estates, not in wild country. On our newer continent many birds are adapting and seem to prefer the security of man's tidy (but not too tidy) acres. Barn swallows and phoebes have long ago forsaken their cliffs and ledges for barns and bridges, and the chimney swift now rarely nests in hollow trees in the ancestral manner. Cardinals, mockingbirds, house wrens, yellow warblers, robins, chipping sparrows, and at least three dozen other songbirds have drastically modified their way of life. By accepting man's environment, they are quite certainly more numerous today than they were before the land was settled. The cardinal and the Carolina wren are actually extending their ranges decade by decade, favoring farms and gardens in their spread northward. The evening grosbeak, helped in its winter survival by a bountiful supply of sunflower seeds at a thousand feeding shelves, is now breeding east to northern New England.

I know of one enterprising ornithophile, Herbert Mills, who operates a feeding station for hawks. He keeps a large supply of moribund mice in his refrigerator for just that purpose. At this unique feeder in southern New Jersey it is possible to see several evening grosbeaks feasting on sunflower seeds while they ignore a red-tailed hawk devouring a mouse at the other end of the board.

Except for Mr. Mill's method of luring hawks (it is somewhat of a secret), Tom McElroy discusses, in this book, just about every technique of attracting birds whether one owns a 50-by-fifty lot, a small farm, or a large estate. He tells us just how to proceed if we want hummingbirds about, or cardinals, or pheasants.

It can be argued that feeding birds on the window shelf is an artificial thing and therefore has little conservation significance. But need we justify it on such grounds? Is not our pleasure reason enough? Whereas the same birds might survive well enough in some thicket in the neighborhood, is it not better to see them every day? Don't believe for a moment that we pauperize birds by doling out the feed. The chickadee that helps itself to the suet will also investigate every insect-infested twig or cranny in the neighborhood.

There is no question, however, that putting out bird boxes, food plants, protective cover, and water has conservation significance, for it increases the carrying capacity of the land. An acre that harbors two breeding pairs of birds can be made to support five — an increase of 150 per cent. A hundred acres as intensively managed could mean an increase of 600 individuals. Build-ups even greater than this are possible.

The thing to remember is that birds are looking for security just as we are — a proper place to raise a family, enough to eat, in short, a good standard of living. And they also like variety, just as we do. Broken countryside, with plenty of "edge," harbors far more birds than solid woods, monotonous orchards, or extensive fields.

At the Roosevelt Memorial Sanctuary at Oyster Bay, Long Island, a small plot of only twelve acres, comparable in size to many a modest country place, the bird population was raised within a period of ten years to a density of more than twelve nesting pairs per acre. Water was piped in; the heavy forest canopy was broken up by cutting out some of the trees and letting in the sunlight. Around these "edges," thickets of shrubs and vines were planted. Grassy lawns and brush piles helped make the spot more favorable for a greater number of species. Dead and crippled trees were left standing for the pleasure of woodpeckers and nuthatches. The same principles that brought results at Oyster Bay can be applied to land almost anywhere.

Our wildlife forms, we must not forget, fit into very definite habitat niches, and frequently, as we create one environment we destroy another and the bird life that goes with it. However, in many cases it is a matter of making two blades of grass grow where one grew before, and hence two insects upon which two birds can feed instead of one. Even such simple tricks as drawing in the tops of bushes with a wire or cord works wonders. The resulting clumps of leaves and twigs offer such excellent places for hiding nests that few birds can ignore them.

In a large area the wildlife technician prefers to use only native species when building up the food and cover. But in a garden or small plot exotic varieties are quite all right.

Balanced planting should take care of the needs of birds throughout the year: shrubs with soft fruits that birds can feed to their fledglings in June; wild cherries and dogwoods attractive to passing flocks in late summer and early fall; and, most important of all, birches and other trees that carry their seeds through the critical deadline between winter and spring.

This book will prove to be of greatest use in the East and Midwest. It will not tell you how to weave a decoy stork's nest for a Rhine Valley roof or how to erect a stork pole. Nor will it advise on Merganser and Scoter boxes for use in Finland, or on the dimensions of boxes for olivaceous flycatchers and bridled titmice of Arizona canyons. But if you live in North America north of the Gulf States and east of the Rockies, you will find these nineteen chapters very comprehensive.

Mr. McElroy is particularly well qualified to be our guide in matters of bird management, for he left a teaching career to act as director of the famed Pequot-Sepos Wildlife Sanctuary at Mystic, Connecticut. Now he is doing a distinguished job at the National Audubon Society's Aullwood Sanctuary and Nature Center at Dayton, Ohio. This change of locale from New England to the Midwest has added to his broad understanding of the basic needs of birds. Like most modern field biologists, he recognizes that the problem of wildlife management has a unity. He is aware of the intricate chain that starts with energy from the sun and proceeds through water and soil to the plants and animal life. The relatively new life-science that we call ecology is more readily understood by the person who has manipulated his garden or his farm so as to make it more attractive for birds.

PREFACE

THIS BOOK is written for everyone who would attract and enjoy the bird life of our land. It endeavors to recognize all facets of interest, whether they are based on aesthetic, recreational, or economic reasons. Also, and perhaps most important, it is hoped that through the medium of this book the reader will have a better appreciation and understanding of the birds' place in an ever-changing outdoor environment.

The basic principles of attracting birds are quite consistent and positive. Food and water plus adequate cover are necessary requirements for an increased bird population. Although the fulfillment of the requirements may vary somewhat according to geographical locations, the essentials of enticing more birds to a given spot remain the same. For this reason, the use of this book is applicable to any locality. Primary consideration, however, has been given to attracting birds in areas east of the Mississippi River exclusive of the semitropical species found in Florida and the coastal states.

Attracting birds need not be an end in itself. I sincerely hope that those using this book may find sufficient inspiration to help them discover new and challenging experiences in the field of conservation.

Acknowledgments: This book is based on personal experiences and observations; however, I extend my sincerest appreciation to Roger Tory Peterson, John H. Baker, and William B. Stapp for their suggestions regarding certain portions of the text. I am also indebted to Mr. Louis Ripberger of Richmond, Indiana, for permission to use his designs for the construction details of the hopper feeder and weather-vane feeder included in Chapter 4.

THOMAS P. McELROY, JR.

CONTENTS

ILLUSTRATIONS

The *NEW*
HANDBOOK
of
ATTRACTING BIRDS

CHAPTER I

BIRDS IN
OUR ENVIRONMENT

BIRDS HAVE APPEALED to the affections and respect of mankind ever since history has been recorded. From the early ages of Greek mythology down through the centuries until modern times the prowess and beauty of birds have been glorified in the historical and cultural aspects of our living. Birds have been the source of inspiration for popular motifs in art and music. Their colors, form, and flight have been used as symbols to adorn the emblems, stamps, coins, and flags of many nations. Through these means, and for many other reasons of an aesthetic or economic nature, birds have added generously to the happiness of many generations.

Today more than during any other period in our history we are beginning to understand and appreciate the economic importance of birds and their relationships to our future welfare. New and intelligent approaches to the subject are being made through our schools and colleges. The efforts of such organizations as the National Audubon Society, the Wildlife Management Institute, and the National Wildlife Federation contribute measurably to the molding of public sentiment regarding all aspects of conservation. We are becoming acutely aware of the relationships in our outdoor

[3]

environment and the part birds must play in maintaining the delicate balance in nature.

The Bird Community

RELATIONSHIPS. The environment in which we live is amazingly intricate. The song of a cardinal in your backyard may well be the culmination of a long series of fortuitous happenings in this small niche of nature's vastness. For it is not by choice alone that the cardinal happens to be there. Circumstances spanned over eons of time, including the birth and the dying of innumerable generations and forms of life, have molded a small ecological area capable of perpetuating his highly specialized pattern of life.

We can but speculate upon the form and sequence of these circumstances. How could we possibly know, for example, what chain of events led to the germination of the first grapevine — so vital to the building of the cardinal's nest — in this specific area? Perhaps the seed was carried there by a cedar waxing. Or was it deposited through the scat of a fox or raccoon? And what series of happenings, both chemical and biological, took place within the soil to germinate the wind-blown seed of the sycamore about which the vine is now entwined?

We do know the processes of nature are so balanced that the chosen habitat of the cardinal provides food and cover for survival during all seasons of the year. There is a succession in the ripening of wild fruits and weed seeds that assures a continuous and varied food supply. The bark of the wild grapevine, tiny rootlets, and the geum plant provide an abundance of nesting materials. Tangles of briers, vines, shrubs, and trees provide home sites and protective cover. This biological niche becomes the home of the cardinal.

The cardinal is not alone in his chosen site. He is part of a dynamic community composed of plants and animals which are dependent upon each other for survival. He contributes to the community and benefits from the contributions of his numerous and diverse neighbors. The procession of dynamic change within the living community is a series of continuous physical and biological happenings that provides for the survival of all inhabitants. Soil fertility is maintained, energy is stored, and the population of species is controlled. The community is balanced to the liking of the cardinal and his neighbors. This equilibrium is the pattern of nature. No one individual or species stands alone an entity unto itself. Rather, each individual or species contributes to and is dependent upon, either directly or indirectly, all inhabitants of the community.

Success in attracting birds to a specific area will be somewhat proportionate to our understanding of these relationships. While our gardens, fields, marshes, and woodlands may be looked upon and treated as individual communities, they are basically a part of a larger and more involved society. The hawk may nest in the woodland but do most of his feeding over fields and marshes. The redwing may nest in the marsh but seek the shelter of the pine forest for roosting when the nesting season is past.

INFLUENCING FACTORS. The number and variety of birds attracted to your area will be determined, in part, by certain physical and biological factors. As in the case of the cardinal, each species is attracted and is adjusted physically and psychologically to living in a specific type of environment. The herons, for example, are accustomed to living in a wetland habitat. Accordingly, their legs are adapted for wading and their bills for the capture of aquatic foods. Many warblers feed upon insects abundant in our treetops. They are quick of flight. Their bills are small and sharply pointed. Meadowlarks and bobolinks are associated with grasslands; woodpeckers and vireos with trees. We can readily see how birds are so closely related to plant habitats that their abundance and distribution are directly affected by the varying factors influencing these habitats. In most cases, the presence or absence of birds in an area is directly attributable to a combination of factors rather than to any one determining condition.

The distribution of birds is greatly influenced by varying combinations of physical elements. Of all the physical conditions affecting birds, either singly or in combination, certainly air temperature is one of the most decisive. The physiology of birds is such that they are adjusted to living within a certain temperature range. Vegetation on which they depend is also adapted to respective temperature medians. The birds in your gardens, fields, and forests, and the plant life that provides them with food and cover are tolerant of local air temperatures.

Variations of air temperature within a bird community often influence normal activity. The arrival and departure of migrant birds can be hastened or slowed by temperature extremes. Nesting activities are similarly influenced by heat and cold. During abnormally cold periods more constant brooding will be required to maintain egg development. When heat is excessive, young birds may require frequent shading by their parents.

Sunlight is equally influential in determining the distribution and activities of birds. The lengthening number of daylight hours in springtime is thought to be a factor in stimulating migration and reproduction. Similarly, fewer hours of daylight in the fall would tend to culminate activities and influence the start of southern migrations. Even locally you can notice how certain species prefer the maximum light of open areas while others seek the protective shade of the forests.

Rain, snow, wind, and severe storms all have direct effects upon what we may consider normal activities within the bird community. Certain species may be depleted by storms during migration or when nesting in concentrated numbers. Extended periods of rain can take a severe toll of young nestlings. Disastrous results among warblers and other insect-eating species may result from unseasonal "cold snaps" that delay the hatching of insects. Snow and ice can be equally injurious to the seed-eating species.

There are certain biological conditions within any area which serve as natural controls upon bird populations. The abundance or scarcity of food is surely one of the most effective. The metabolism of birds is such that they require comparatively large amounts of food. Mass movements of normally permanent residents may be instigated by food shortages. This is one of the prime factors accounting for the sporadic influx of certain northern species during the winter months. Evening grosbeaks, pine siskins, and redpolls may suddenly appear at your feeders when there is a scarcity of food in their more northern feeding grounds. Conversely, an abundance of food will attract and support a more dense bird population.

The vegetation of an area is of major importance in the production of food, not for birds alone, but either directly or indirectly, for all inhabitants of the community. Vegetation is the architecture and the industrial center of the natural community. It provides home sites and landscaping; the green plants are manufacturers of all energy used by all inhabitants of the community. Plants absorb energy from the sun and, through various processes, use this energy in conjunction with water, carbon dioxide, and minerals to produce the fats, carbohydrates, proteins, and other substances necessary for the continuation of life. Animals, of course, are a vital part of this phenomenon, for it is they who release the carbon and keep the cycle functioning.

Life within the outdoor community progresses amid a never-ending struggle for survival. There is competition for territory and for food. There is predation of mammals upon birds, birds upon mammals, mammals upon mammals, and birds upon birds. Fortunately, all activities within the birds' environment are not so harsh. There are strong social relationships among individuals of numerous species. The terns and swallows are notable examples.

Mankind is not always tolerant of nature's processes. However, the more we understand about all the activities within our environment, the greater will be our appreciation and enjoyment of the birds about us.

Birds and Man

Birds contribute extensively to the welfare of human society. Their efficiency in consuming enormous quantities of pestiferous insects and weed seeds is a matter of record. We recognize their value as a source of sport and recreation. The aesthetic appeal enriches the lives of countless numbers of people. Yet, as important as these facts may be, there is still another factor — one not so easily recognized or understood — that is of greater importance and significance. *Birds are a vital link in the chain of events necessary to support all life, including mankind.*

As indicated earlier in this chapter, all forms of life — bacteria, insects, plants, birds, and mammals — function as dependent parts of a dynamic environment. The total vitality and life-producing capacity of this environment will be proportionate to the strength of its individual components. We cannot deplete or eliminate species of life forms without the danger of starting a chain reaction that could transform the entire area.

The particular role that birds play in maintaining a balanced or functioning community, and the manner in which it benefits man, is one of many facets. Certain species feed almost entirely upon insects. While this is without doubt an important factor of control, it is by no means exclusive or final. Birds are but one repressive agent along with weather conditions, disease, parasites, and other factors that keep our insect population within reasonable bounds.

We are quick to credit birds with the consumption of great quantities of weed seeds and wild fruits. There is no denying that they do consume tons of seeds yearly, but the results of this action are difficult to evaluate. Perhaps the real value here is not in the actual destruction of seeds consumed, but in the "thinning out" or lessening of competitive quantities. Seeds that remain to germinate are more likely to produce healthy productive plants. Other seeds and fruits are carried and dropped. Thus, the span of preferred food plants is extended. Birds, then, inadvertently, help the continuation of their own food supply.

Hawks and owls, along with other bird and mammal predators, serve the wildlife community as one means of controlling over-population. Certain species, such as the red-tailed hawk, marsh hawk, barn owl, and long-eared owl, feed mainly upon the fast-multiplying rodents — rats, mice, voles, and shrews. The slow, the diseased, and the crippled individuals are subject to constant predation. Thus, the community remains vigorous and healthy.

Vultures and gulls survive in the role of scavengers. They help keep our land and waters free of decaying litter.

Man, for many generations past, despite his part in well-known instances of greed and depletion, has looked sympathetically upon birds both from the economic and the aesthetic points of view. But, being aware of the increasingly faster pattern of living in America today, should not man now look upon them from the ecological viewpoint? Should he not be concerned with how birds, and all other forms of natural resources essential to his survival, will fit into the pattern of expanding urbanization and rapidly increasing human populations? For it is not with birds alone that we are concerned; it is with the understanding and the protection of a living environment that will continue to support man himself.

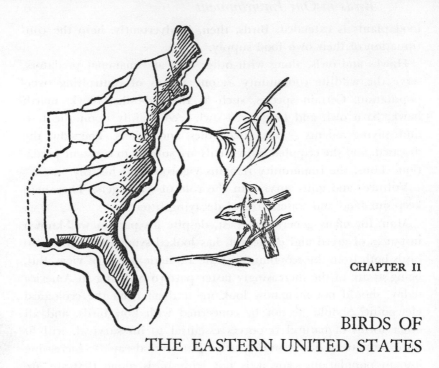

CHAPTER II

BIRDS OF
THE EASTERN UNITED STATES

THE TOPOGRAPHY of the eastern half of our country varies greatly. There are forested mountains, vast expanses of farmlands, inland water areas, cities, suburban developments, and thousands of miles of coastal shore lines. Within the confines of these diversified land masses are innumerable smaller biotic communities — swamps, marshes, lakes, islands, streams, fields, brushlands, woodlands, and gardens — that provide homes for the great variety of eastern bird life. Also, amid millions of people within these extensive areas live those of us who would attract birds to our feeders, birdbaths, and hedgerows.

One can easily recognize that many factors influence the number and variety of birds to be found on a single premise. The bird life in the spruce forests of Maine or New Hampshire will differ greatly from that along the coastal shores of New Jersey or Virginia. Birds of the mountains and birds of the lower valleys will not be the same; similarly, birds in your backyard will differ somewhat from those living in your neighbors' field or woodland. This variation in bird distribution is the result of a combination of biological, physical, and geographical factors.

Roger Tory Peterson's *Field Guide to the Birds* lists over 400 species of birds peculiar to eastern North America. Some species — the Kirtland warbler, for example — are definitely limited in range and distribution; others, such as the robin and red-eyed vireo, are widely spread throughout the East. The extent of a species's range is determined by a great many conditions of which quite a number are not precisely known. We do know that birds instinctively require specific types of habitats. Also, we recognize that certain species are more tolerant and adaptable to climatic changes than others. The density of a stand of evergreens may be the deciding factor as to whether is is acceptable by long-eared owls. The leaf canopy of a hardwood forest and the amount of undergrowth beneath will be determining conditions that influence the populations of thrushes, vireos, flycatchers, and ovenbirds.

The number and variety of species in a given area will not remain constant year after year. If natural plant succession is allowed to take place, the bird life will change as variations develop in the plant cover. An uncultivated field may appeal to meadowlarks, red-winged blackbirds, or Henslow's sparrows. As shrubs and young trees begin to predominate, these species will be replaced by brush-loving varieties — chats, cardinals, catbirds, thrashers, towhees, and others. This will be followed by another change as the trees begin to mature and the shrubs are shaded out. Species like vireos, goldfinches, least flycatchers tanagers, and blue jays will then be most common. As a forest, the area will attract woodpeckers, chickadees, thrushes, crows, and others preferring a dense woodland habitat.

This form of transition will, of course, vary from one environment to another and according to geographic locations. The process will be slow and gradual; however, changes will be noticeable over relatively brief periods — often from one nesting season to the next.

The manner in which an area is managed will have much to do with determining the bird life within its borders. The lack of continuity in farming procedures will cause fluctuation and diversification among nesting varieties. Life within a forest will change in the event of grazing or timber harvesting. Man's influence upon environment and wildlife populations is often harsh and sudden compared to natural succession. Yet it is upon man and his conceptions of land use that the future of our resources must depend.

The relative abundance of bird species within the eastern United States cannot, in most cases, be accurately indicated in figures. Certainly there is greater variation from one species to another. The Kirtland warbler is estimated at approximately 500 breeding pairs; whereas estimates on the number of English sparrows calculate them in the millions. Ornithologists believe our most abundant nesting bird (in the eastern United States) is either one of two species — the red-eyed vireo or the red-winged blackbird.

The nesting range of the red-eyed vireo extends from central Florida and the Gulf Coast northward to the Gulf of the St. Lawrence and central Manitoba. The predominant vegetative cover of this vast land area is the deciduous forest — the favorite habitat of the red-eyed vireo.

This species of *Vireonidae* is so widely spread that every hardwood area, from shaded lawns and farm woodlots to extensive forest ranges, becomes a summer home for one or more pairs. One can rarely go into the woods from mid-May until July without hearing the incessant song of the redeye.

We normally think of the redwing as a bird of the cattails — a bird of swamplands and marshes. Yet within the past decade it has proved to be one of the most adaptable of all songbirds. Throughout the Midwest it nests abundantly in hayfields, pastures, and weed patches, often far removed from any wetland. The large concentrations of redwings during the migration seasons, and during the wintering season in the southern United States, are creating serious problems for farmers and rice-growers. These flocks sometimes contain hundreds of thousands of birds — a potentially devastating menace to any field of grain.

Our bird populations change considerably with each spring and fall migration. While quite a number of species are classified as permanent residents — woodpeckers, chickadees, titmice, and cardinals, for example — the majority of varieties are apt to be with us only on a seasonal basis. The southward flights in the fall bring in species that have summered in the northern states and Canada. Many of these stay about our gardens, fields, and woodlands, and become a part of our winter populations. The most abundant winter birds in the eastern part of our country include:

American Crow	Horned Lark
American Goldfinch	Mockingbird
American Robin	Mourning Dove
Black-capped Chickadee	Purple Grackle
Blue jay	Red-winged Blackbird
Cardinal	Slate-colored Junco
Cowbird	Song Sparrow
Downy Woodpecker	Starling
Eastern Meadowlark	Tree Sparrow
English Sparrow	Tufted Titmouse

In the spring and summer we experience our greatest influx of both numbers and kinds. Many are with us for only a short period, as they travel to more northern nesting grounds. Others stay to nest and increase our summer totals. The abundance of summer species is more difficult to estimate. It is generally agreed that the more populous varieties would include:

American Robin	Mourning Dove
Barn Swallow	Red-eyed Vireo
Cowbird	Red-winged Blackbird
Eastern Meadowlark	Song Sparrow
English Sparrow	Yellow Warbler
Mockingbird	

Bird distribution, in most instances, is not a static procedure, nor is it limited by strictly defined boundaries. It is an ever changing process with the ranges of certain species in a gradual state of fluctuation. It is not unusual for bird watchers in New Enlgand to see cardinals, mockingbirds, tufted titmice, and Carolina wrens. These species are gradually spreading northward. At the same time, the dickcissel is disappearing in the Northeast. The great black-backed gull, normally associated with the coast of New England, has extended its range southward along most of the Atlantic sea-coast. The western kingbird is frequently observed in our eastern states, while the Baltimore oriole and red-headed woodpecker are progressing westward.

Migration is another factor that will, in part, affect the number and variety of species that can be observed in your particular area. We are prone to think of the terms "migration routes" and "fly-ways" as designations for specific travel lanes that birds follow in their northward and southward movements. While this is basically true, the actual lanes are somewhat theoretical and without definite boundaries. The time and speed of migrations and the routes followed are so varied from one species to another that our flyways are of a rather indefinite pattern.

In the United States, where the principal topographic lines run north and south, birds have a tendency to follow major river valleys, mountain ranges, and coast lines. Many eastern migrants follow the general direction of the Atlantic coast; others are guided by the ridges of the Appalachian Mountains. Still other concentrations follow the Ohio and Mississippi valleys. There are, of course, many lesser travel routes leading into these major flyways.

The many uncertain factors of bird distribution and bird abundance add much to the fascination of attracting birds and of bird study.

CHAPTER III

WAYS OF ATTRACTING BIRDS

Food, Water, and Cover

SUCCESS IN attracting birds can be measured by our ability to *provide them with what they want.* This simple statement is the key to acquiring and maintaining a constant bird population. It is equally applicable in the city or country — in a small town garden or a large country estate. Actually, the wants of birds are such that they can be provided for easily by anyone interested in having bird neighbors. Birds select a home site for its ability to provide them with the basic essentials for survival. They desire a continuous supply of natural food, plenty of water for drinking and bathing, and appropriate cover for nesting and protection from their enemies. If these conditions do not exist naturally, they must be provided if any appreciable bird population is to be built up in a given area. Birds cannot exist without them.

We know that all species do not have the same specific requirements regarding food preferences, amounts of water, and cover types. There are obvious differences among the needs of humming-birds, finches, and waterfowl. Areas of relatively uniform cover, regardless of the type, will attract a limited number of species — those with similar nesting and feeding habits. Therefore, varied type of terrain offers many advantages. Swampy meadowlands will prove ideal for redwings and meadowlarks. The dense wooded areas will be preferred by the vireos and thrushes, while the more open areas will be the favorite of song sparrows, field sparrows, catbirds, thrashers, and many others. Pond and stream areas will support aquatic-feeding species that cannot be found elsewhere. Every species has a preference for a definite type of habitat. The larger the variety of habitat groups within an area, the larger the number and variety of species which can be found. Even within the confines of the small garden, a diversification of vegetation — lawns, hedges, shrub borders, and shade trees — will attract a larger number and variety of birds than a garden with comparatively uniform plantings.

Birds are ever in search of food. Their normally high body temperatures demand an almost constant supply of energy. This is particularly true during the critical winter months when ice and snow often cover much of the already depleted supply of natural food. Birds can endure extreme cold if they have sufficient food to maintain normal body temperatures. There are two methods of supplementing this much needed food supply: balanced planting and artificial feeding. Planting is an essential part of any program designed to attract birds. All planting should be done as a part of a previously developed plan that provides seeds and fruits in all seasons of the year, nesting sites, and protective cover. It is one aspect of bird attraction which will pay great dividends, particularly if it is maintained over a period of years.

An extensive planting program will change the physical and biological aspects of the bird community. This, of course, is what we want it to do. We are striving for an increased and balanced food supply, adequate protection, and sufficient cover to attract and support a maximum bird population. This point should be remembered when the planting plan is being developed. This is the time to decide the size and type of area which are ultimately desirable. Thought should also be given to the birds preferred and their particular habitat requirements. A well-planned program should produce good results with a minimum of management.

Of all the ways of attracting birds, certainly none gives more pleasure than winter feeding. It affords an excellent opportunity for close observation and the satisfaction of providing a supplementary supply of food. A couple of well-placed feeders in early autumn will soon find steady customers among the permanent residents like the chickadees, white-breasted nuthatches, and downy woodpeckers. These will soon be followed by a variety of visitors from farther north, including such species as juncos, fox sparrows, white-throated sparrows, purple finches, and many others. Most species will show a preference for one or more kinds of food offered. A little experimentation and observation will soon indicate the kinds preferred. Species attracted will be somewhat in proportion to the variety of available food.

Water is a necessity in any environment planned for the attraction of birds. It is one of the three essentials — food, water, and cover — necessary to support bird life. Birds need it both for drinking and bathing. Extended areas without water will be practically void of any bird population.

Normally, birds get their water supply from ponds, brooks, swamps, rain puddles, melting snow, dewdrops, and similar sources. Land without at least one of the more staple sources of supply will of necessity have to rely on artificial means. Providing water for birds can be as simple as filling a shallow pan or as elaborate as erecting an ornate fountain. The actual method used isn't so important as having a fresh supply of water always available. Water that can be kept "live" or moving will have an added appeal.

In the course of a year, a constant supply of fresh water will attract a greater variety of birds than any other one effort we can make in their behalf. Spring and fall migrants especially will be attracted to water where they can drink, bathe, and refresh themselves for the long flights ahead. This is often the time that "new species" can be observed — species that otherwise would likely pass through the area unnoticed.

Nesting Facilities

When home grounds are improved to provide for the wants of birds, the need for adequate nesting facilities cannot be overlooked. The majority of species desire to nest in natural places such as trees, shrubs, vines, briers, and on the ground. Accumulative records show, however, that there are now more than fifty species of American birds which will accept man-made nesting devices. The former and larger groups of species can be helped only by providing adequate cover. The latter group, the cavity nesting species, can be increased in number and variety by providing nesting boxes. However, a certain amount of natural cover will be necessary, and boxes should be placed in the respective habitats of the species desired.

Birds can often be encouraged to build in a desired location by making quantities of natural nesting material available. In spring, birds cannot resist the temptation of cotton, feathers, wool, horsehair, twigs, yarn, and straw that have been laid out for their choice.

Other Methods of Attracting

DUST BATHS. Game birds and some species of songbirds enjoy taking dust baths. This is probably a favorite way of removing lice and other parasites from their feathers. To prepare a dust bath, select a sunny corner in your garden and remove the sod from an area about two feet by three feet. Spade the exposed soil and keep it fine and loose. It may have to be loosened occasionally, especially after heavy rains. Birds known to use a dust bath include the pheasant, ruffed grouse, quail, mourning dove, brown thrasher, and the various sparrows.

MUD. Robins, wood thrushes, phoebes, cliff swallows, and barn swallows all use mud as one of their main nest-building materials. An easily accessible supply of mud will encourage these birds to build locally. Perhaps you have a remote corner in a flower bed which can be kept exceptionally wet and muddy by a few minutes daily use of the garden hose. Another method of providing mud for nest building is to sink an old garbage-can lid flush with the ground. Fill this with a clay-type soil and mix with water until it is of molding consistency.

ROOSTING SHELTERS AND BOXES. Providing shelters and boxes specifically designed for roosting is one phase of bird attraction that is often neglected. However, this method of bird attraction is quite important during the cold winter months. Nesting boxes left in place throughout the winter provide some roosting protection, but specially designed roosting boxes are considerably more appealing and efficient. They will be used readily by many birds, particularly the cavity-nesting species. Construction designs for roosting shelters and boxes can be found in Chapter 9.

SOUND. For years ornithologists have used squeaking sounds to attract birds for close observation. This is done by sucking on the back of one's hand, allowing just enough air to enter the mouth between the lips and skin to produce a squeak or "kissing" sound. This resembles a bird in distress. Birds are curious and socially cooperative regarding certain phases of territory defense. For these reasons birds will often approach to within a few feet of the sound's origin. This method is particularly effective when dense foliage would otherwise prevent close observation. Best results are obtained if the observer is partially hidden.

DECOYS. Decoys, such as those used by hunters, can be used as an effective means of attracting waterfowl for close observation and photographic purposes. They are best used in the lee of a pond or lake known to be frequented by waterfowl.

While any of the previously mentioned methods would probably result in attracting a few birds of certain species, the combined use of all methods would produce much better results. Such a correlation of all methods would assure a constant bird population the year round. It would also provide for the needs of an increased number of birds representing a larger number of species. Complete details for the methods described will be found in succeeding chapters.

FEEDING SONGBIRDS

Theories about Feeding

MOST EVERYONE concerned with attracting birds is interested in winter feeding. It is one practice that produces immediate and noticeable results; birds quickly accept the supplementary food supply and are easily attracted to areas affording close observation. It is one conservation measure that adds to human enjoyment — one that often helps fulfill the need for companionship and inspiration.

Sometimes there is concern as to the value, or harmful effects, of

[22]

a supplementary feeding program. In the case of songbirds attracted to feeding stations about one's lawns and gardens, there is little reason for concern about the program's value so long as feeding is continuous. Extra feed for wintering birds does not make them indifferent to their natural food supply; birds will leave well-stocked feeders to feast upon weed seeds, insects' eggs, and grubs. Thus, the results of attracting an increased number of birds may be exceedingly beneficial.

The scattering of feed on the ground continuously in the same place should be avoided. Concentrations of birds feeding continually at the same location may be subject to diseases transmitted through droppings. This is more likely to be true with waterfowl and game birds than with songbirds. Most songbirds, including the ground-feeding species, can be attracted to man-made feeders that will keep the food dry and sanitary. The hopper-type feeder seems to be the best device for keeping grain in good condition until eaten.

An extensive feeding program will undoubtedly increase the winter bird population beyond the number that could be normally cared for by the natural food supply of the adjacent area. Necessity, therefore, requires that once such a feeding program is started, it should be continued unabated until an adequate supply of natural food is again available. The results would be disastrous if the supplementary food supply was suddenly discontinued after concentrated numbers have become dependent upon it.

Feeding According to Seasons

The feeding of birds is normally associated with the winter season. It is then that the need is greatest. The natural food supply is at a minimum, and the birds demand more food for energy and warmth. During unseasonable or prolonged periods of ice and snow an abundance of accessible food will save many birds from actual starvation or from becoming easy prey for predators.

There are advantages in starting the winter feeding program early. During the early fall months many birds are migrating; some will be content to stop and make their winter home at a feeding station already supplied with food. They will have ample opportunity to adapt themselves to the surrounding environment before the more critical months. Also, the migration period affords us the only opportunity to observe certain species. Extra provisions available at an early date will tend to make the natural food supply last longer.

All feedings should be continued until the insects and early fruits of spring are abundant. During the late winter and early spring, birds often need help most. Natural foods face depletion from constant winter foraging, and the new season's supply is not yet available. During this period early spring migrants are sometimes cut off from their usual foods by late and unseasonable storms. Supplementary feeding at this time will be most welcome and serve a very useful purpose.

Feeding during summer months is largely a matter of personal choice. Actually it is not needed, for during this period, insects, seeds, and fruits are most abundant. Many species of birds, however, will welcome an easily accessible hand-out that offers them a change in diet. Such a practice often enables the provider to observe at close range the habits of otherwise shy species. In addition, this supplementary provision may be influential in encouraging a larger number of birds to nest locally. Those who choose to feed in summertime must remember that birds are scattered for nesting. Large concentrations of a single species such as appeared in the winter cannot be expected.

Species Attracted by Winter Feeding

In general terms, the species of birds attracted by winter feeding can be divided into two groups. One group would be classified as permanent residents — that is, the species that reside in one locality the year round. A second grouping would include the winter visitors, species that come from farther north but spend the winter months locally. In addition to the above two groups, occasional summer residents that did not yield to normal migrating instincts can usually be found around most feeding stations. If feeding is started early enough in the fall, birds such as various thrushes often stop for an easy meal during their flight southward. The rare or unexpected visitor helps make winter feeding a thrilling experience.

Species classified as permanent residents vary accordingly to geographical location and the type of local terrain. Form the northern boundary of our country east of the Rocky Mountains, south through Kansas, Missouri, Pennsylvania, and northern New Jersey, the black-capped chickadee will probably be the first to discover newly placed feeders. South of this area the noticeably smaller Carolina chickadee will be an equally early and regular patron of any offered sunflower seeds, suet, or peanut butter. From southern New York southward and west to the Plains, the cardinal and tufted titmouse will become avid customers. Other permanently residing species such as the white-breasted nuthatch and downy woodpecker can be found throughout the eastern half of the United States.

As colder weather approaches, the more northern species will be on the move in search of a winter home that promises them ample provender during the cold winter days ahead. Then will come the flights of tree sparrows, white-throated sparrows, and juncos. These species usually appear in large numbers, and will spend the entire winter in the vicinity of a favorite feeding station. Other visiting members of the sparrow family include the song sparrow, the white-crowned sparrow, and the fox sparrow.

In the southern section of the United States song sparrows can be considered permanent residents. They migrate from the more northern states, leaving a few of their number behind. These, in company with those from still farther north, will partake freely of supplementary food offerings during the entire winter. It should be remembered here that the song sparrow, and other species normally associated with summer that choose to spend their winters in the North, are frequently not the same birds that spend the summers locally. For example, I have banded song sparrows in southern Connecticut in mid-January which have been retrapped in the interior of Canada during the following nesting season.

In the Northeast the white-crowned sparrow is most likely to visit the feeders in late fall and early spring during its migration. The fox sparrow winters thoughout the eastern section of our country, but usually not in concentrated numbers.

Other species that provide color and excitement for those who feed birds in the winter are the less frequent visitors. Redpolls and pine grosbeaks are not uncommon in the northern states. Evening grosbeaks, red crossbills, and white-winged crossbills, although erratic in their migratory movements, can be expected as far south as Virginia and Kentucky. Snow buntings leave their summer home in the Arctic tundra and winter in the open country in the northern states and along coastal waters to North Carolina. Snow buntings and horned larks often frequent the same winter feeding grounds together.

The few summer stragglers will also add excitement to any feeding station. Robins and bluebirds can be expected at any time. The partially migratory meadowlark is not an infrequent visitor, particularly along coastal waters. Such species as catbirds, towhees, purple grackles, and mockingbirds are frequently reported wintering far north of their normal range.

The species mentioned above are those that can usually be expected about the average feeding station. Many other species that have not been mentioned here partake readily of offered food. The variety of birds seen, the hope of attracting the unusual species, and similar challenging experiences and suspense add enjoyment to this conservation activity.

What to Feed

In regard to food preference, the species attracted by an artificial food supply can be divided into two general classes: insect-eating birds such as the woodpeckers, brown creepers, and warblers, and seed-eating birds like the sparrows and juncos. The first class prefers animal food, and the second vegetable food. A definite grouping cannot be made, as some species, including the blue jays, chickadees, and nuthatches, eat both types. The following list of foods has been proved satisfactory over a long period of years by the many people maintaining bird-feeding stations.

SUET. Beef suet is a favorite of all insect-eating birds. Chickadees, nuthatches, tufted titmice, brown creepers, and blue jays are extremely fond of it. Suet is practically the only food that will attract woodpeckers consistently. Juncos, white-throated sparrows, and tree sparrows will feed on it during extremely cold spells. It often provides the extra needed warmth for the occasional summer resident. Suet, when chopped in tiny pieces, will often attract wintering warblers to our feeding trays. Myrtle warblers, wintering in our eastern coastal states, are particularly fond of suet bits. In the Florida area other warblers, including the orange-crowned, yellow-throated, and palm, will come to feeders for bits of suet.

PEANUT BUTTER. This is a favorite of the chickadees, quite often being preferred to suet. It is eaten quite readily by tree sparrows, juncos, and numerous other species, particularly during unusually cold weather. The peanut oil helps provide the extra warmth and energy needed to combat low temperatures.

Brown creepers are attracted to peanut butter, but prefer not to leave trees in order to feed. The peanut butter should be spread on rough-barked trees for them. The nuthatches like this also, as they normally find much of their natural food under the bark of trees.

SUNFLOWER SEEDS. Every feeding station should have an abundant supply of sunflower seeds, as they are one of the favorites of many seed-eating species. Chickadees, titmice, nuthatches, and cardinals are exceptionally partial to these large seeds. Purple finches, gold-finches, evening grosbeaks, and crossbills will eat them in great quantities. Chickadees and finches will pick the seeds directly from large sunflower heads. Other species, such as the cardinal, prefer the seeds supplied in loose form.

HEMP.   Most seed-eating birds prefer hemp to any other seeds offered them. These seeds have an oily texture that makes them extremely nourishing as a winter food. Hemp is an excellent ingre-dient for any seed mixture, but it is comparatively expensive. This often prevents its use in large quantities.

MILLET.   There are several kinds of millet, all of which are eaten avidly by the seed-eating species. It is the best of the small grains, being a particular favorite of the juncos, sparrows, and goldfinches. It is a good bulk filler for any seed mixture, and has the added advantage of being inexpensive.

BUCKWHEAT.   The best customers are game birds, mourning doves, and blue jays, although buckwheat is eaten to some degree by most songbirds. Only a small percentage of buckwheat should be in-cluded in mixtures intended for songbirds.

CRACKED CORN.   The finer sizes are acceptable to the seed-eaters, particularly tree sparrows and juncos. It is not preferred over millet and hemp, but does make a good filler when mixed with these seeds. Experience has shown that feeding cracked corn alone does not at-tract the number or variety of birds that a good seed mixture will draw.

NUT MEATS.   Their price and preparation exclude them from gen-eral use. When they are provided, however, nut meats will be ac-cepted readily by blue jays, chickadees, cardinals, nuthatches, and titmice. Nut meats should not be included in any mixture of seeds to be kept over a long period of time, as they often become rancid and sour, thereby spoiling the entire mixture.

DOG BISCUIT.   Finely ground dog biscuit makes a good substitute for nut meats. Birds known to eat it include the chickadee, white-breasted nuthatch, blue jay, snow bunting, junco, and tree sparrow.

CHAFF. Chaff and sweepings from a barn floor include many grass and weed seeds. If scattered about the edges of open areas, they will be found frequently by horned larks and snow buntings. Sparrows and juncos will scratch out the seeds. The sweepings can be made more enticing by adding a little cracked corn or millet.

RAISINS. Raisins make a good substitute for the wild fruits normally eaten by birds. They are accepted by catbirds, mockingbirds, hermit thrushes, and robins. Catbirds seem to prefer them cut into smaller pieces.

DRIED BERRIES. Wild berries are the natural summer and fall favorites of many species, and are quite acceptable in the winter even though they are dried. The berries of dogwoods, viburnums, mountain ash, bittersweet, and bayberries will prove favorites.

FROZEN FRUITS. Certain wild fruits and berries can be frozen during the height of the fruiting season and kept for winter feeding. Pokeberries, a fruit preferred by many species, freeze well and are a welcome addition to any winter food supply. Packages kept in the family freezer should be conspicuously labeled as poison. Other wild fruits that freeze well include the berries of brush honeysuckle and the viburnums.

ORANGES. Baltimore orioles and rose-breasted grosbeaks are particularly fond of oranges. Cut the orange in half and secure them to posts or trees, or put them in your feeders. Catbirds, blue jays, and flickers also find oranges to their liking.

BANANAS. Once discovered, bananas will be eaten consistently by scarlet and summer tanagers. Partially peel and place in the open where they can be easily seen.

WHITE BREAD. White bread, broken in pieces and scattered about the lawn, is a sure way of attracting purple grackles. It is also eaten by starlings, sparrows, redwings, robins, and other species.

There isn't any foundation for the belief that white bread is injurious to wild birds. Definite experiments have proved that it is less nourishing, however, than whole grains, and that a constant diet of white bread alone can produce ill effects in birds and animals. But there need be no hesitancy about supplying your bird neighbors with an occasional meal of bread or crumbs.

CRUMBS. Crumbs of bread, doughnuts, and other pastry are acceptable to most birds. They can be made more palatable by browning them in some sort of shortening.

SALT. Sometimes eaten by finches and siskins.

GRIT. When the ground is covered with snow, an accessible supply of grit will be welcomed by birds. It is an essential part of their digestive process. Clean sand or fine gravel can be added to the seed mixture or made available in separate containers. Finely crushed clam or oyster shells are available in most feed stores. These are high in calcium and make a good addition to any supplementary diet.

OTHER FOODS. Rabbit food (pellet form), cooked spaghetti, boiled potatoes, fatty meats, apple peelings, and numerous small grains are acceptable foods for many wintering birds.

Wild Bird Food Mixtures

SEED MIXTURES. There are numerous mixtures of wild-bird food on the market. Many of these are expensive. They are often padded with seeds eaten only as a last resort, and this tends to make waste and add to the initial cost. To reduce this waste and expense, anyone planning to use a relatively large amount of food can combine his own ingredients in a more practical mixture. It is impossible to compound a mixture that can be considered ideal for all sections of the East. This is easily understood when we realize that certain birds have a decided preference for specific kinds of seeds. A recommended formula (by volume) for the average area in the eastern United States follows:

Sunflower seed	25 per cent
Hemp	25 "

Millet (small yellow)	20	"
Millet (large yellow or white)	20	"
Buckwheat	5	"
Fine cracked corn	5	"

MAKING THE BEST MIXTURE FOR YOUR AREA. Perhaps the best way of ascertaining just what mixture is best for your particular location is through the use of a testing tray similar to the one illustrated. The tray is divided into six or more compartments, and a separate grain (equal amounts by volume) is placed in each compartment. If chickadees, nuthatches, titmice, and cardinals are the predominant species about your station, the sunflower and hemp seeds will show the greatest rate of consumption. If tree sparrows, white-throats, and juncos are most abundant, the smaller grains such as millet and cracked corn will be consumed most rapidly. Thus, by observing the comparative rate of consumption of each grain, a mixture can be compounded (by volume) that will be most practical for your particular bird population.

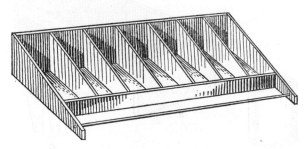

FIGURE 1. TESTING TRAY SHOWING A SEPARATE COMPARTMENT FOR EACH GRAIN TO BE TESTED.

The testing tray should be permanently located the same as any other feeder. When the testing is finished, you can continue to use the tray as a regular feeder. If the testing is continued periodically throughout one complete feeding season, a more accurate formula can be determined.

SUET MIXTURES. There are many ingredients that may be added to melted suet to make delicacies that will be favorites of many wintering species. The addition of any or all of the following will make an acceptable suet mixture: millet, sunflower seeds, raisins, corn meal, oatmeal, rice, cracked corn, chopped peanuts, and cooked noodles or spaghetti. A favorite recipe can be developed for any locality after a little experimentation with the ingredients suggested above.

Note. When purchasing suet, have your butcher grind it for you. It will melt quicker and more thoroughly with less heat.

Suet mixtures are usually used to make molded cakes for use in specific types of feeders. They can also be poured directly into coconut shells and other form-type feeders. They are sometimes used as a dip for pine cones and evergreen boughs to be hung in trees.

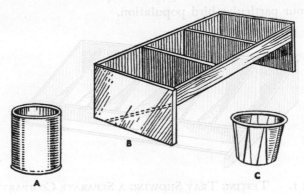

FIGURE 2.   SUET MOLDS.

A. Tin-can mold for use with feeder E, page 35
B. Wedge mold for use with feeders F and G, page 35
C. Soufflé cup for direct use in feeder A, page 35

The above illustration shows three of the most popular suet molds. Mold A is made by cutting both ends from a tin can. Mold

B is made of wood, and will form three wedge-shaped suet cakes at one time. The finished cakes can be easily removed from this mold if each compartment is lined with aluminum foil before filling. Mold C is a soufflé cup that can be purchased from most any paper-supply company.

Bird Feeders

Factors influencing the methods of making food available for birds are: feeding habits of various species, the type of food being offered, protection of food from inclement weather, and the protection of birds from their enemies.

Most of the sparrows and juncos are by nature ground feeders. They welcome seeds scattered about the ground in sheltered areas. They will also patronize most types of feeders if they are not placed too high. If feeding is done on the ground, put out just the amount of food that will be consumed in one day. A fresh supply of food daily will eliminate the possibility of contamination and prevent unnecessary waste. Also, feed left on the ground overnight may attract mice and rats. Species such as snow buntings, horned larks, and quail are definitely ground feeders. The trunk-clmbing species including woodpeckers, nuthatches, and brown creepers prefer their suet on trees or posts that resemble the natural sources of their food. The nuthatches and woodpeckers will feed quite readily from suet logs or suet boxes placed on window sills, or as part of a larger feeder, but the brown creepers are more hesitant about leaving trees to obtain food.

All grain food needs to be protected from the elements. Excessive dampness will cause it to get soggy and sometimes sour. It should be protected from becoming covered during snow and ice storms, for this is when birds need it most.

Trees or shrubs near feeders afford birds easy escape from predacious hawks and cats. Most evergreen trees and hedges provide excellent cover.

There are many devices for feeding birds. From this large number, the following sketches and descriptions are presented as being representative of those that have proved most efficient and satisfactory through extensive use by many conservationists. The designs are essentially basic and simple in detail. Construction details are given for designs preferred by the writer.

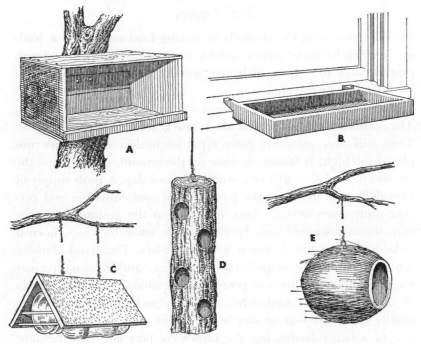

FIGURE 3.   STARTING FEEDERS.

A. TREE BOX.   A wooden box with a two- or three-inch strip nailed across the lower edge of the opening makes an easily constructed and practical feeder. Place on the trunk of a tree or post, four or five feet from the ground, facing away from the prevailing winds. A piece of tar paper tacked on the roof will help make the box weatherproof.

B. WINDOW SHELF.   This is a practical way of getting birds to start feeding at your window. Keep the tray clean and replenish with fresh food daily. Once the birds become used to feeding at your window, the tray can be replaced with a glass window feeder.

C. QUART-JAR FEEDER. This is an excellent way to provide sunflower seed for the smaller birds, such as chickadees, nuthatches, and purple finches. The small crossbars will keep out the ravenous blue jays. It is best used when suspended by two wires.

D. SUET AND PEANUT-BUTTER LOG. A small log with drilled holes makes a very practical and attractive way of serving suet and peanut butter. Sassafras and white ash are good woods to use, as the rough bark affords easy footing and adheres well to the sapwood. If suspended by a wire from the limb of a tree, woodpeckers, chickadees, brow creepers, and several other species will soon prefer to obtain their suet and peanut butter in this fashion.

E. COCONUT FEEDER. A coconut shell can be filled with ground suet, melted suet, peanut butter, or a combination of melted suet and seeds. This is a particularly good feeder for titmice, chickadees, nuthatches, and woodpeckers.

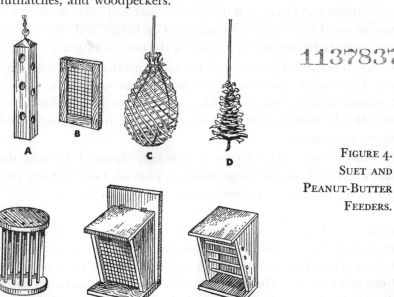

1137837

FIGURE 4.
SUET AND
PEANUT-BUTTER
FEEDERS.

A. SUET STICK.   These can be bought commercially or made in your own workshop. Holes are drilled in square pieces of soft pine to hold the small soufflé cups illustrated and described on page 35. If you make your own, buy the cups first and, with an expansion bit, drill the holes so the filled cups will fit snugly.

B. PEANUT-BUTTER RACK.   A piece of ¼- or ½-inch hardware cloth is tacked to a wood frame. Spread the wire with peanut butter. The rack is most practical when nailed to the end of another feeder.

C. ONION OR FRUIT BAG.   A coarse-mesh onion or fruit bag obtainable from any grocery store makes a good container for serving generous amounts of suet. Fill the bag with large pieces of suet and suspend from the limb of a tree.

D. PINE CONE.   Large, open pine cones make an attractive way of providing suet and peanut butter. Fill and hang from branches, small end up.

E. SUET FEEDER.   This feeder is made of ¼-inch dowel sticks and two circular end pieces. It is designed to hold suet cakes made in the tin-can mold illustrated on page oo. The height and diameter of the feeder is determined by the size of the can used for a mold.

F. SUET FEEDER.   This is one of the most practical of all suet feeders. The slanting front causes the suet to rest against the ½-inch hardware cloth so that it is within reach of the birds. This feeder may also be used to hold the suet cakes made in the wedge mold shown on page oo.

G. SUET FEEDER.   This feeder is especially designed to hold the suet cakes made in the wedge mold on page oo. Commercially prepared suet cakes are also available for this type of feeder.

From ½-inch boards, cut all pieces to size and shape as illustrated. By nailing through the back section, fasten the two sides and bottom in place. Next, cut a piece of ½-inch hardware cloth to fit the front and tack fast. The two front strips, nailed in place, will cover the rough edges of the hardware cloth. The back edge of the roof should be angled with a block plane or saw so that it fits uniformly against the back section. The roof is fastened with hinges and hook and eye.

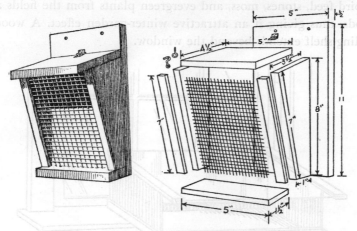

FIGURE 5.   CONSTRUCTION DETAILS OF SUET FEEDER.

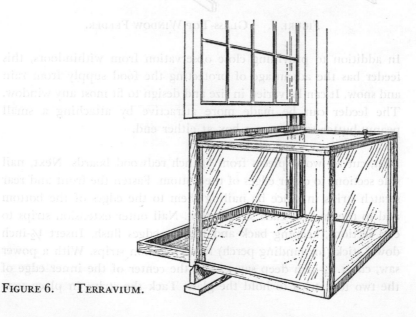

FIGURE 6.   TERRAVIUM.

This is probably the most elaborate type of feeder yet devised. It is a framed glass box that extends within the room through a partly raised window. The terravium is designed to contain, in addition to bird feed, stones, moss, and evergreen plants from the fields and woods, thus giving it an attractive winter-garden effect. A wooden feeding shelf extends beyond the window.

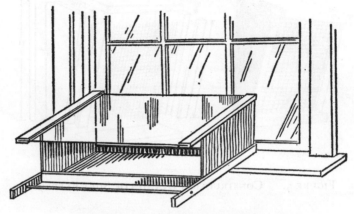

FIGURE 7.   GLASS-TOP WINDOW FEEDER.

In addition to providing close observation from withindoors, this feeder has the advantage of protecting the food supply from rain and snow. It can be varied in size and design to fit most any window. The feeder can be made more attractive by attaching a small peanut-butter rack or suet box at either end.

First, cut all wood pieces from ½-inch redwood boards. Next, nail side sections to outer edges of the bottom. Fasten the front and rear scratch strips in place by nailing them to the edges of the bottom and to the ends of each side section. Nail outer extension strips to end sections, keeping back and bottom edges flush. Insert ½-inch dowel stick (for landing perch) into extension strips. With a power saw, cut a ¼-inch deep saw cut in the center of the inner edge of the two top strips to hold the glass. Tack the strips in place temporarily and check to see if glass fits properly. The strips may be moved slightly to gain desired fit. A back section is not needed for this feeder, as it fits against the window. Mount on sill with shelf brackets.

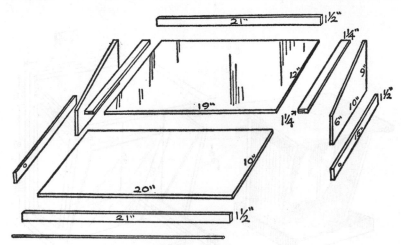

FIGURE 8.   CONSTRUCTION DETAILS OF GLASS-TOP
WINDOW FEEDER.

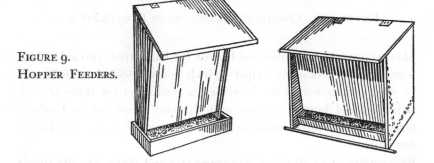

FIGURE 9.
HOPPER FEEDERS.

The "self-feeding" feature of hopper feeders keeps the task of replenishing the food supply at a minimum. It is usually more efficient, or at least more economical, when filled with one type of seed. When it is filled with a mixture, blue jays often scratch away other seeds until the last sunflower seed is gone. Larger sizes of this feeder are most practical for feeding game birds. They are particularly effective when placed under a lean-to shelter.

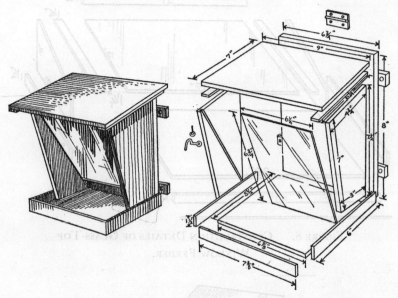

FIGURE 10.   CONSTRUCTION DETAILS OF HOPPER FEEDER.

MATERIALS: ½-inch redwood boards for back, roof, two sides, bottom, and two mounting strips; ¼-inch boards (½-inch boards may be used if dimensions are increased accordingly) for three scratch strips around bottom section and the two strips for roof edges; glass for front; hinge, hook, and eye for fastening roof; small finishing nails.

PROCEDURE: Cut all pieces to proper size and shape. On the inside of each side section, make a ¼-inch deep saw cut on the diagonal from the upper front corner to the lower rear corner. This will make grooves to hold the glass front. By nailing through the back, fasten the two sides and bottom in position. Finish nailing bottom to end sections. Next, nail the scratch strips around the bottom and the two mounting strips across the back. Hinge the roof in place. Before inserting the glass, drive a small brad or staple across each groove one inch from the bottom. This will provide stops for the glass and leave an opening for dispensing the food.

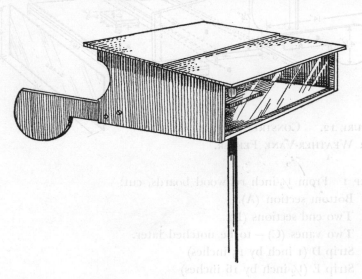

FIGURE 11.
WEATHER-VANE FEEDER.

This feeder is ornamental as well as very practical. It is so designed that it swings with the wind, keeping the opening away from the driving rain or snow. The feed stays dry and the birds are protected while feeding.

There are many designs for weather-vane feeders. They can be purchased in most garden centers and hardware stores, or they can be easily made in your own workshop. The feeder illustrated above has many advantages; it is light in weight, simply constructed, easily mounted, and made of durable redwood.

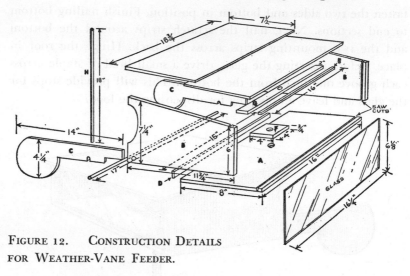

FIGURE 12.   CONSTRUCTION DETAILS
FOR WEATHER-VANE FEEDER.

STEP 1   From ½-inch redwood boards, cut:
   Bottom section (A).
   Two end sections (B).
   Two vanes (C) — to be notched later.
   Strip D (1 inch by 15 inches)
   Strip E (½-inch by 16 inches)

STEP 2   Make a ¼-inch deep saw cut (to hold glass) ½-inch in
from outer edges of sections A and B as illustrated. Drill $1\frac{3}{16}$-inch
hole in center of bottom (A). Drill ⅜-inch hole (to hold dowel
perch) in each end section, ¾-inch in and up from lower front
corner.

STEP 3   Nail end sections (B) to outer edges of bottom (A). Put
dowel perch in place at the same time.

STEP 4   From ¾-inch pine or hardwood, cut bearing block (F) and
bearing board (G). Drill a $1\frac{3}{16}$-inch hole in the center of each.
Nail a piece of tin or other metal over the top of the hole in the
bearing board (G). Fasten securely, as this acts as a bearing for the
vertical rod (H) supporting the feeder.

STEP 5   Nail bearing block (F) over hole in bottom (A). By nailing through the two end sections (B), fasten the bearing board (G) in place, keeping all holes in alignment. The rear edges of the board (G) should be flush with the top edges of the end sections (B).

STEP 6   Notch vanes (C) so they fit over the dowel perch and floor (A). Fasten vanes by nails or two 1/8-inch bolts. Nail scratch strip (D) to front edge of floor (A).

STEP 7   Insert glass.

STEP 8   Cut two pieces of redwood siding to length for roof and nail in place. Place retaining strip (E) against top edge of glass and nail fast to underside of roof.

STEP 9   For the vertical supporting rod (H), cut an 18-inch piece from a 3/4-inch dowel stick. In the center of one end, drive a large domed upholstery tack (or a dome-of-silence) to act as a bearing. Insert vertical rod.

STEP 10   The feeder can be mounted by wood screws (through lower portion of vertical rod) to a wood post, or by inserting the vertical rod into a 1-inch steel pipe of the desired height.

CHAPTER V

ATTRACTING WITH WATER

WATER IS AN ESSENTIAL PART of any bird community. In addition to the more obvious needs for drinking and bathing, water, either directly or indirectly, affects the lives of all birds according to its relative abundance. The presence or absence of water has a direct effect upon the vegetation wherein birds build their homes, find their food, and seek protection. Arid areas with sparce plant coverage have comparatively small bird populations; areas with abundant rainfall support a more compact and varied vegetative cover and a higher bird density.

The relationship of birds with water varies according to groups and species. For the herons, kingfishers, grebes, loons, most ducks, and numerous other species of shore and water birds, it supports their main source of food. The prothonotary warbler and the tree swallow frequently build their nests in hollow stubs along the water's edge and feed upon the insects of this water-land habitat. For island-nesting gulls, terns, and shore birds, water provides a protective barrier isolating them from most predators.

Songbirds require generous amounts of water for drinking and bathing. This is especially true during the hot summer months when the natural supply may be at a minimum. It follows, therefore, that birds will be attracted to areas affording an abundant supply of water. It is with this point the remainder of this chapter is mainly concerned.

Water for Drinking and Bathing

You are indeed fortunate if you have a brook or pond within the confines of your bird-attracting area. A small stream or pond affords an excellent opportunity to provide birds with natural drinking and bathing pools. These pools, like artificial baths, must conform to a few basic principles if they are to be used readily. Shallow water, no more than two or three inches deep, with edges cleared of all grass, weeds, and similar growth, is necessary. An edging about two feet wide covered with gravel and sand makes an ideal beach and provides easy entrance into the pool. Sandbars extending into the shallow water are equally attractive.

If these natural water conditions do not exist within your preferred area, the only alternative is to provide water by means of artificial baths and fountains. This, of course, has the advantage of attracting birds to any chosen spot for close observation.

Essentials of Birdbaths and Fountains

Birds are rather a discriminating lot when it comes to bathing. Just any receptacle filled with water and put out for them will not suffice. True, the basic requirements for a safe and acceptable birdbath are quite simple, but none the less essential.

Regardless of the type or style of bath being provided, the important thing to remember is to keep the water quite shallow. Birds have an inherent fear of deep water. A bath that gradually slopes to a depth of two and one-half inches in the center is most practical. A rough bottom enables the birds to obtain a foothold. In a smooth birdbath, coarse washed sand or gravel may be added.

The sizes of birdbaths may vary according to the facilities available and the discrimination of the builder. Small baths, such as earthen pie plates and flowerpot containers, are satisfactory, but usually can accommodate only a single bird at a time. Larger ones, two or more feet in diameter, will provide drinking and bathing facilities for several birds at the same time.

The sound of dripping or trickling water has a special appeal to birds. They are attracted by water that is kept alive and moving. If your budget and facilities permit, this can be accomplished by using a small jet fountain attachment on the end of a pipe connected to the household water supply. It can be accomplished more simply by suspending a drip bucket over your bath or pool.[1]

CARE OF BIRDBATHS. Birdbaths require a reasonable amount of care. They need to be kept clean and filled with fresh water daily. Most types of baths can be kept cleaned by the use of a stiff brush or by scouring with sand and a piece of burlap. Larger pools are sometimes affected by numerous growths of algae. This condition can be minimized by adding about one ounce of copper sulphate to approximately every fifty gallons of water. To get extra years of use from your birdbath, remove and store it before freezing weather unless it is equipped with a heating device. Terracotta and cement baths will often chip or crack when exposed to repeated freezing and thawing.

LOCATION. All bathing facilities should be so located as to avoid depredation by cats. Birds with wet feathers are easy prey for the prowling feline. Place the bath a distance of ten or fifteen feet from any low shrubbery or other means of concealment. The visual protection thus afforded by an exposed bath or pool eliminates any hesitancy the birds may have concerning its safety.

Any bathing or drinking device will prove doubly attractive if, within a safe distance, there are some shrubs or trees that provide protective cover when danger threatens. This same cover will serve the birds as a lookout when they are approaching the water and

[1] See pages 49 and 50 for illustration and construction details.

as a place for drying and preening when they have finished their baths. Overhanging tree limbs aid them in approaching and leaving the water.

Types of Baths and Fountains

When selecting a birdbath or fountain, you should consider its effect upon the appearance of your garden. There are several basic types of baths to choose from, whether you are buying or building. The choice depends largely on the matter of time and mechanical ingenuity of the builder. The following types are basic in design and principle. Many variations can be made in these designs without any loss of appeal to the birds.

FIGURE 13.   EASILY ACQUIRED BIRDBATHS
flowerpot saucer; pedestal-type bath; trash-can lid and tile pipe.

FLOWERPOT SAUCER.   Using a large flowerpot saucer is one of the simplest ways of providing drinking and bathing facilities for birds. It can be placed on a stump, post, tripod, or on the ground. It has the disadvantage of normally accommodating but one bird at a time.

PEDESTAL-TYPE BATH.   These can be acquired at most any garden nursery or hardware store. They are a safer type of bath for use in areas frequented by cats. The high-fired terracotta type is most durable.

TRASH-CAN LID.   Place lid on a section of tile pipe and weight it down with a stone as shown in the preceding illustration. The bath will be more attractive if painted with a flat paint. While the inside is still tacky, cover it with a layer of washed and dried sand. Dump out the excess that doesn't adhere to the bottom. This will roughen the bottom of the bath.

> *Note.* Most trash-can lids are galvanized. To get good paint adhesion and avoid peeling, before painting wash the lid thoroughly with vinegar (do not rinse) and allow to dry.

CEMENT BATHS.   The use of cement provides opportunity for a wide range of types and designs. Numerous molds or forms, varying in size and design, can be made from wood, tin, or clay. Such baths can be used on a pedestal or on the ground. They can be mounted in rock gardens or on top of a low pile of stones that have been artistically decorated with moss, ferns, and flowers.

A formula for mixing a good cement consists of four parts of sand to one part of dry cement. Enough water should be added to form a soft mortar that can be easily shaped with a trowel.

FIGURE 14.   DESIGNS FOR CEMENT BIRDBATHS.

The cement-type designs suggested above have the advantage of an easy approach to the water and a gradual increase in depth.

STONE AND CEMENT.   A neatly arranged pile of stones with a cement basin on top makes an attractive and durable birdbath. The crevices between the stones can be filled with soil, moss, low-growing ferns, and a variety of rock-garden plants.

STONE-CHISELED.   A bath chiseled in a flat-topped boulder will last indefinitely and is not nearly so difficult to construct as appearance would indicate. A stone chisel and about a 2-pound hammer are used to chip a depression. It should have a depth of zero at the edge, and slope gradually to a maximum depth of 2½ inches at the center or back end.

FIGURE 15. STONE-TYPE BIRDBATHS
stone and cement; stone-chiseled.

GROUND POOL WITH DRIP BUCKET. Bird-banders have contrived a very unique and simple method of keeping the water within their traps in motion. This same principle can be applied to drinking and bathing devices. A bucket filled with water is suspended over the bathing pool. A small nail hole in the side of the bucket about ½ inch above the bottom (with nail inserted from the inside) permits the water to drip slowly into the pool below. Placing the hole on the side of the bucket makes it less likely to become clogged by flecks of dirt that will accumulate on the bottom. A board cover will keep out most dirt. This arrangement may be too rustic for the formal garden. The results, however, are so satisfactory that its use is warranted wherever possible.

FIGURE 16.   THE SOUND AND ACTION OF MOVING WATER
MAKE THIS AN IDEAL BIRDBATH.
a drip bucket is suspended over a natural-looking ground pool.

The sound and action of moving water are particularly attractive
to the spring and fall migrants. The warblers, vireos, and flycatchers
are easily attracted by it, yet are rarely observed about the more
conventional types of baths. Water so arranged as to provide this
sound and motion will undoubtedly attract increased numbers and
species that otherwise would not be observed. It will be the favorite
birdbath in your garden.

STONE FOUNTAIN.   A stone fountain with three or four cement bathing pools at different levels presents a more elaborate type of ac-
commodation, but is one of the most efficient and attractive baths
that can be built. It combines sound, action, and ample bathing
space.

The stone part of the fountain should be built of rough field-
stones and cemented together for permanency. Ample openings allowed between the stones permit the adding of soil for planting.
The cement bathing pools should conform in principle to those de-

FIGURE 17. A STONE FOUNTAIN
is one of the best and most efficient
bird-attracting devices for any garden.

scribed previously in this chapter. Water is piped to the top of the
fountain and allowed to trickle into the uppermost basin. The
overflow from this basin goes to the one underneath. This is repeated until the ground-level pool is reached. A drainage ditch or
pipe is then needed to carry the overflow. The effect of a woodland
spring can be achieved by planting the crevices with wild flowers,
mosses, and ferns.

FIGURE 18.   A FOUNTAIN OR JET SPRAY
will greatly increase the effectiveness of
conventional baths.

FOUNTAIN SPRAY. Small mist sprayers that will fit in the center of your birdbath are now available commercially. They connect directly to your water outlet or garden hose by means of small plastic tubing. They keep the water within the bath active and fresh. Water consumption is very low — as little as ⅓ gallon per hour.

> *Note.* A fountain spray similar to the one illustrated can be obtained from Beverly Specialties Co., 10331 S. Leavitt St., Chicago 43, Ill.

Birdbaths in Winter

Birds will continue to use a bath throughout the winter for both drinking and bathing when it is kept free from freezing. This can be accomplished by the use of a thermostatically controlled acquarium heater or by the installation of a light bulb in the vertical stand of a pedestal-type birdbath.

FIGURE 19.   TWO WAYS OF KEEPING YOUR BIRDBATH ICE-FREE
*for winter use: thermostatically controlled aquarium heater;
light bulb installed in pedestal.*

AQUARIUM HEATER.   Electrical aquarium heaters can be obtained in almost any pet shop. Submerse the heater in the water (heating unit and lead-in wire are waterproof) and weight it down by attaching a small lead fishing sinker. Plug it into an extension wire or electrical outlet leading from your house.

LIGHT BULB IN PEDESTAL.   A light bulb installed in the hollow pedestal of the conventional commercial birdbath is a simple and efficient means of providing heated water. If the pedestal is too narrow, or otherwise inaccessible for installation purposes, remove the basin and place over a section of 4- or 6-inch tile pipe for winter use. The tile pipe has ample space for installing the heating bulb. If desirable, a trash-can lid can be used for the basin section (see page 47).

> *Note.* Extension cords constantly exposed to the weather or buried beneath the ground should be of a durable weatherproof type. Check with your local electrician or electrical supply house about the type best suited for your area and purpose.

CHAPTER VI

ATTRACTING
BY PLANTING

BIRDS ARE DEPENDENT upon plants for cover and food. Trees, shrubs, vines, weeds, grasses, and other types of plant life combine into varying habitat forms so arranged as to provide a favorable place of retreat, shelter, protection from predators, and nesting sites. Plants are the source of all bird food, either directly or ultimately so. From the smallest bacteria, important in the decomposition of organic materials, through the largest trees of our forests, all plants are significantly involved in a biological and physical cycle of life-producing events. Birds, therefore, like all animals, are in one way or another dependent upon plants for their existence. This being so, a planting program that provides these necessities of life is one of the greatest attributes of any bird-attracting endeavor.

Fortunately, many of the plants that provide food and cover for birds are also of ornamental value to mankind. Planned planting will not only provide the essentials for an increased and varied bird population but will, at the same time, enhance the beauty and aesthetic values of our gardens, estates, and farmlands.

Start with a Plan

The results of any project are apt to be most satisfying if they have been based on a predetermined plan. This is certainly true of any extensive planting effort designed to attract birds. Your plan need not follow any set pattern. Designs and details can be quite flexible so long as they result in food, protective cover, and nesting sites for birds. These three essentials will become the measuring unit for the success of your planting endeavor. You will, of course, want to be continually conscious of the resulting landscaping effect.

You will find it most advantageous to put your plan on paper. Through the use of notes, sketches, and scaled drawings, a thorough and orderly plan can be developed — one that can be easily followed and executed. Perhaps you have a year's list of the birds observed within your selected area — winter visitors, migrants, permanent residents, and nesting species. Ultimately, such a list would be most helpful in evaluating the success of your planting program. If you do not have such a list, this would make a good starting point.

Start your plan on paper by taking a survey of what you now have. This can be done in the form of notes and scaled drawings. Include the trees and shrubs you want to keep and decide which ones, if any, are to be moved to new locations. These will serve as the foundation for the addition of your new plantings.

One of the most important guiding factors in the development of a planting program for birds is an understanding of the variety and habits of species normally found within the selected area. A knowledge of their arrival dates, food preferences, and nesting habits will be extremely helpful in the selection and arrangement of preferred plants. This information can be found elsewhere in this book.

Planting for Cover and Nesting Sites

Frequently, our first thought in planning to attract birds by planting is to consider only fruit-bearing trees and shrubs that will supply generous amounts of food. While an adequate food supply is always essential, it is equally important that birds have sufficient environmental protection and nesting sites. With most songbirds, food and cover are so closely related to survival that one is of little value without the other. There are, fortunately, numerous dual-purpose plants that provide both food and cover.

Shelter and nesting sites can be provided by a single plant, such as an evergreen tree or a rose bush, or by varying combinations of several plants. Tangles of briers and honeysuckle or thickets of multiflora rose afford good concealment and places of escape for birds that are being pursued. Thick stands of evergreen trees furnish good protection from ice, snow, and rain. They are especially attractive to owls and make excellent roosting shelters for many birds. In the more formal type of garden, hedges of privet, barberry, and arborvitae provide similar protection for numerous species of songbirds. This type of emergency cover gives birds a sense of security and enables them to exist in the presence of many natural enemies.

The requirements for nesting sites vary according to the individual species. Each desires a different type of location for its nest. Most species will not adapt themselves to an immediate change in local environment. For example, song sparrows that normally nest in the low briers and shrubbery of open terrain will not nest in treetops once the open areas have reverted to woodland. This makes it necessary for us to adapt the environment to the nesting habits of the birds we wish to attract.

In a woodlot, ovenbirds and towhees will nest on the ground. Red-eyed vireos, redstarts, and wood thrushes will nest in the low undergowth, while still other species will nest in the higher trees. Dead trees in a woodlot provide homes for cavity-nesting species such as the woodpeckers, chickadees, titmice, and crested flycatchers. Meadowlarks and bobolinks prefer the open grasslands. Old pastures with thickets of briers, shrubs, and young trees make an excellent nesting area for brown thrashers, yellow-breasted chats, goldfinches, and many other species. Bushy fencerows and hedges are favorite nesting spots for many birds. Swamplands of reeds and cattails will be welcomed by marsh wrens and red-winged blackbirds. In the garden, hedges and corners of various shrubs will provide homes for catbirds, cardinals, mockingbirds, song sparrows, chipping sparrows, robins, yellow warblers, and other species tolerant of mankind as close neighbors. Considering all this diversity in nesting requirements, we should avoid large expanses of uniform cover. Within reason, the more variety we have in cover, the more variety we shall have in the species attracted.

Planting for Food

A natural food supply must be available at all seasons of the year if we are to maintain a constant bird population. Soft fruits rich in vitamins and carbohydrates, such as early cherries and blueberries, will be welcomed by songbirds during the nesting season, as fruit constitutes a large portion of the diet of many fledglings. In the fall, migrating flocks patronize areas offering them ample provender for their flight southward. Late winter and early spring are critical seasons of the year for many birds, as there is frequently a scarcity of seeds and fruits during this period. Trees and shrubs that produce fruits which persist throughout the winter, such as the juniper, bayberry, hackberry, and flowering crabapple, are a necessary part of any planting program.

This year-round food supply should include enough variety to appeal to the largest possible number of species. Annuals, such as the sunflower, buckwheat, millet, and Sudan grass, are good food-producing plants for seed-eating sparrows, juncos, and finches. Food patches, such as those described in Chapter 11, "Attracting Game Birds," will be patronized by many songbirds.

Our larger trees are an important source of bird food. The samaras of the elm are early spring favorites of the finches. The winged seeds of ashes, maples, tulip trees, and box elders are eagerly sought by many species, including the pine and evening grosbeaks. Goldfinches, pine siskins, and redpolls seek the small seed-bearing cones of the birches and alders. The larger cones of the conifers are favorites of the crossbills and others. Nuthatches, woodpeckers, and jays are fond of the acorns and nuts of oaks and beeches. Trees bearing fruits favored by many species include the mountain ash, mulberry, red cedar, wild cherry, flowering crab, hackberry, and hawthorn.

Chart A

SPRING	SUMMER	FALL	WINTER
American elm			
American holly			American holly
Barberries			Barberries
		Birches	Birches
	Black Cherry	Black Cherry	
	Blueberries		
Box elder		Box elder	Box elder
	Buckthorn	Buckthorn	
	Buffalo berry	Buffalo berry	
Cotoneasters		Cotoneasters	Cotoneasters
	Elderberries		
Flowering		Flowering	Flowering
crabapples		crabapples	crabapples
		Flowering	
		dogwood	
Hackberry		Hackberry	Hackberry
			Hawthorns
Honeysuckles	Honeysuckles	Honeysuckles	Honeysuckles
Mountain ash		Mountain ash	Mountain ash
	Mulberries		
		Oaks	Oaks
	Pin cherry		
Red cedar	Red cedar	Red cedar	Red cedar
	Serviceberry		
	Shrub dogwoods	Shrub dogwoods	
		Shrub hollies	Shrub hollies
Snowberry	Snowberry	Snowberry	Snowberry
Viburnums		Viburnums	Viburnums
Virginia creeper		Virginia creeper	Virginia creeper
		Wild grapes	Wild grapes

In addition to the trees, there are many varieties of shrubs and vines which produce fruit that is eaten avidly by birds. Many of these varieties also provide excellent cover and nesting sites. Outstanding among the shrubs are the viburnums, dogwoods, and honeysuckles. Grapes are fall favorites of birds and other wildlife species. Trees, shrubs, and vines that will supply protective cover, ample nesting sites, and an all-year food supply can be selected by consulting the lists in the next chapter. The above chart will help you select plants that will furnish food on a seasonal basis.

Planting and Care of Stock

The young trees, shrubs, and vines used for planting are known as planting stock. There are two sources of supply for this stock. The native species may be obtained by transplanting young plants found in the fields and woodlands. Desired exotic species can be supplied by most nurseries.

Fortunately for the budget, many of the native plants of woods and fields are among the most useful and attractive species available. While resorting to a nursery for all planting stock would be easier, there are advantages in using some local wild-growing species. Unlike imported plants, they do not have to adapt themselves to local weather conditions and growing seasons. Also, certain desirable native trees and shrubs are often difficult to obtain from commercial nurseries. There are, however, some advantages in procuring nursery stock. Most nursery plants have been started as seedlings and have been transplanted two or three times. This process involves the pruning of roots and proper cultivation to produce a balanced root growth. This tends to produce a smaller and more compact root system, enabling the plants to be more easily moved and with less danger of injury. Plants growing in the wild are more difficult to transplant because they have had to compete with all surrounding vegetation. They often must send their roots long distances for food and water, resulting in a less compact and balanced root system than that of well-cultivated nursery stock.

TRANSPLANTING. One need not be an experienced nurseryman to transplant native stock. Adherence to a few basic principles will assure reasonable success. A well-shaped, healthy plant with a compact root system has the best chance of survival. Plants intended for use in sunny spots should be selected from stock growing in open fields, meadows, and fencerows. Plants moved from dense woodlands will grow best in shaded areas.

The best time to transplant trees and shrubs is spring and fall. During these seasons the life of most plants is dormant and they can be moved then with the greatest surety of living.

Most trees and shrubs should be dug in such a manner that they retain a compact ball of earth around the roots. The size of the earth ball will depend on the size of the plant and the extent of its root system. A tree 2 inches in diameter should retain all the roots in a ball at least 3 feet across. When trees and big shrubs are being dug, the larger roots must often be cut or pruned. It is often advantageous to root prune during the growing season. This can be done by cutting a narrow trench around the plant with a sharp shovel and pruning shears. The remaining roots will produce more food-carrying fibers until you are ready to move the plant in the fall or spring. Small deciduous trees and evergreen seedlings can be transplanted successfully without much of the original soil.

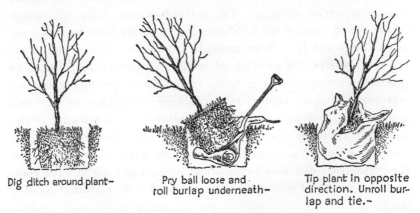

Dig ditch around plant—

Pry ball loose and roll burlap underneath—

Tip plant in opposite direction. Unroll burlap and tie.—

FIGURE 20.   METHOD OF REMOVING TREE OR SHRUB WITH BALL OF EARTH.

PLANTING SUGGESTIONS

1. When possible, buy nursery plants from a local nursery.

2. Dig holes large enough to avoid crowding the roots.

3. Reset plants in soil the same day they are dug. If necessity requires holding them over for a day or two, the roots should be kept moist by covering them with wet moss, straw, or loose dirt.

4. Reset plants at their original depth.

5. Pack good topsoil firmly about the roots.

6. If the roots have been badly injured, prune after planting.

7. Water generously after planting.

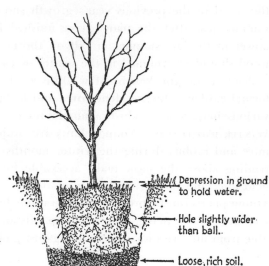

FIGURE 21.
METHOD OF PLANTING
TREE OR SHRUB.

Depression in ground
to hold water.

Hole slightly wider
than ball..

Loose, rich soil.

Care after Planting

CULTIVATION. The cultivation and fertilizing of new plantings will stimulate rapid growth. Turn the soil under periodically to avoid compacting and weed competition. Fertilizing will tend to promote weed growth, also. This can be controlled by mulching around the plants.

PRUNING. Trees and shrubs planted for the benefit of birds need pruning periodically to maintain maximum cover and food production. Thick-growing, bushy shrubs provide the best cover. Thick, bushy growth can be developed by cutting away the tall, vigorous top-growth. A new growth of wood is forced, producing a thicker and more productive shrub.

A maximum food crop can be acquired by sacrificing the weaker parts of the plant and by root pruning. The cutting of the larger roots tends to produce more food-providing fibers. It lessens the production of wood and increases fruitfulness.

Shrubs that bloom in the spring or early summer from buds on the wood of the previous year's growth should be pruned in the summer just after the plants have finished flowering. Those that flower in the late summer or fall on the present year's growth of wood should be trimmed in the winter or early spring.

Pruning for the benefit of wildlife need not be done as for a formal garden. Thickets, fencerows, and hedges can be trimmed at various heights to produce a maximum of varying cover.

WINTER PROTECTION. Young plants are subject to depredation by mice and rabbits during the winter months. Young branches protruding above the snow make accessible forage for rabbits. Both field mice and rabbits will girdle plants by eating the tender bark. Young plants can be protected from rabbits by circling with a small section of wire fencing. Commercial paints and wrappings are available from nurseries for protection against girdling.

Using Insecticides and Herbicides

LANDSCAPING WITH HERBICIDES. Through the process of natural succession, most open land in the eastern states will revert to woody plants — shrubs and young trees. For the purpose of attracting birds and other forms of wildlife, the landowner may wish to retain such an area or woodland border in shrubs. This, of course, would mean eliminating young trees that otherwise would eventually predominate. This can be done through the continuous use of an ax, but a more feasible and less laborious method demands the use of herbicides.

Through the use of commercial brush-killers, basically 2,4,5T, undesirable species can be eliminated. Basal applications are preferable for reasons of safety. Directions for using the 2,4,5T solution usually call for an oil base such as kerosene. The solution is most effective when applied directly to the base of the tree. This can be done with a paint brush or a small hand sprayer. Foliage spraying is also effective, but there is always the danger of wind-drift spray reaching desirable plants and wildlife foods. If the plants are small enough, they can be eliminated by dipping the foliated tips in the solution. For a complete kill, more than one application may be necessary in some cases.

Landscaping with herbicides eliminates resprouting, which often occurs when the plant is cut with an ax or clippers.

Effects of spraying. The federal government, state agencies, and farmers are now using DDT and other recently developed insecticides as a means of insect control. How does this affect our birds and other wildlife? This is a question frequently asked of today's conservationists and wildlife technicians.

The continuously increasing use of chlorinated hydro-carbons and numerous other forms of pesticides is a profound threat to American wildlife. The real danger is in the extensive, and sometimes indiscriminate, use by governmental agencies — federal, state, and local. For example, millions of pounds of DDT are used each year by these agencies, resulting in positive records of serious damage to bird life.

Certainly, those of us who are interested in attracting birds have little cause for the extensive use of DDT or any of its allies. We may continue to spray our roses or save our favorite garden tree from blight. However, it behooves us all to be vitally concerned about the current use of insecticides and its relation to the future welfare of our wildlife.

CHAPTER VII

PLANTS
ATTRACTIVE
TO BIRDS

THE PLANTS included in this chapter were selected as a result of personal observation and experience in planting, information based on plantings in public and private sanctuaries, and U. S. Department of Agriculture data. The plants listed were chosen because of their proved attractiveness to birds either for food, for nesting sites, or for cover.[1]

The lists are not intended to be all-inclusive, as there are many other plants of special value to birds. Specific growing ranges have been purposely avoided because certain physical and geographical factors often provide exceptions for any designated boundaries. Such factors as soil types, amount of annual rainfall, elevation, proximity to the seashore, and whether or not the area has been glaciated, are often influential in determining if a plant will grow in a specific location. Your local nurseryman can advise you about doubtful garden varieties. For extensive farm and estate plantings, check with your County Agent and Soil Conservation Service Administrator.

1 Additional information on what to plan for specific purposes can be found in Chapters 6, "Attracting by Planting"; 10, "How to Attract Hummingbirds"; 11, "Attracting Game Birds"; 12, "Attracting Waterfowl"; 13, "Birds in the Small Garden"; 14, "Birds on Farms and Estates." Also, see Bibliography.

[64]

Trees

AMERICAN ELM. *Ulmus americana;* native.

Food Value: The blossoms, buds, and winged nutlets are particularly attractive to finches and pine siskins. The elm attracts many insects, which in turn attract many of the smaller insect-eating birds.

Cover and Nesting: Provides the ideal site for the swinging nest of the Baltimore oriole. Many other species will build in its forked limbs and branches. Its height (to 120 feet) provides protective perches for singing and foraging.

Landscape Value: The American elm is considered one of the most graceful and beautiful of all trees. It is neat in appearance and growth habits and is used extensively for shade trees in lawns, parks, and street plantings. Subject to Dutch elm disease.

Soil Preferred: Prefers a moist, rich soil in full light. Once established, it will tolerate a variety of soil conditions.

Birds Attracted: Purple finches, goldfinches, pine siskins, rose-breasted grosbeaks, and myrtle warblers. The insects attract vireos, warblers, and others.

AMERICAN HOLLY.   *Ilex opaca;* native.

Food Value: Red berries are an important source of winter and early spring food. Particularly attractive to mockingbirds and thrushes.

Cover and Nesting: Exceptionally good. Evergreen foliage provides good cover. Used extensively by early-nesting species.

Landscape Value: Very attractive and ornamental at all seasons of the year. Can be used as single tree or as a hedge planting. Used for Christmas decorations.

Soil Preferred: Characteristic of moist woods. Will do well in most garden soils from northern New Jersey southward.

Birds Attracted: Known to attract nearly fifty species including mockingbirds, thrushes, catbirds, robins, bluebirds, brown thrashers, towhees, and woodpeckers.

BIRCHES.   *Betula alba, B. lenta, B. lutea, B. populifolia;* native.

Food Value: The seeds in the small cones are favorites of wintering finches and pine siskins. The birches are particularly attractive to birds because of the insects found on them.

Cover and Nesting: The birches are often favorite nesting places for vireos and redstarts. Decayed limbs and trunks provide homes for chickadees, woodpeckers, and other cavity-nesting birds.

Landscape Value: The bank of a pond or stream provides a naturalistic setting for the yellow birch. The white bark of the gray and white birches provides an interesting contrast for any landscape planting. The black birch is largely a forest tree.

Soil Preferred: The gray and white birches prefer a dry soil in the sun. The black birch prefers partial shade, but will adapt itself to most soil conditions. The yellow birch likes partial shade and moist soil.

Birds Attracted: The seeds attract purple finches, goldfinches, blue jays, juncos, titmice, and others. The insects attract vireos, warblers, and other insect-eating species.

BLACK CHERRY.   *Prunus serotina;* native.

Food Value: The soft purple-black fruits provide an excellent food supply during late summer and fall. They are eaten avidly by both songbirds and game birds.

Cover and Nesting: The black cherry is not a favorite nesting tree, but has been known to be used by robins, kingbirds, and scarlet tanagers. It is of little use in providing protective cover.

Landscape Value: Not outstanding as a lawn tree. The blossoms are rather attractive. The fruit clusters are quite showy and will aid in distracting birds from cultivated fruits.

Soil Preferred: This rather fast-growing tree will adapt itself to almost any type of soil condition. Prefers full sun for shaping and fruiting.

Birds Attracted: The wild cherries, *Prunus sp.*, are known to attract more than eighty species of birds. The black cherry is a favorite of many, including cedar waxwings, robins, catbirds, mockingbirds, and thrushes.

Box Elder. *Acer negunde;* native.

Food Value: The winged seeds persist throughout the winter, making them a valuable source of food for seed eaters. Seeds are also favorites of squirrels and chipmunks.

Cover and Nesting: Usually wide-spread and open. Not of particular value.

Landscape Value: Not especially attractive. Sometimes used for shade trees in arid areas.

Soil Preferred: Not particular as to soil or shade conditions.

Birds Attracted: A favorite of evening grosbeaks. Also liked by purple finches and game birds.

Cornelian Cherry. *Cornus mas;* exotic.

Food Value: Fruits are a fall favorite and have a greater attraction value than is generally realized. A recommended plant for any planting program.

Cover and Nesting: Fine thick foliage provides good cover and nesting sites when planted in the open or as part of a border planting.

Landscape Value: Yellow blossoms appear early in the spring. Especially attractive as an understory tree for mixed hardwoods. Good for background or border plantings.

Soil Preferred: Does best in an acid soil. Will tolerate shade, but fruits best in the open.

Birds Attracted: Has special appeal to fall migrants including robins, bluebirds, thrushes, catbirds, towhees, and many others.

FLOWERING CRAB. *Malus floribunda;* exotic.

Food Value: The small applelike fruits are an excellent source of winter food. They persist well into the winter and are preferred after they have been softened by frost.

Cover and Nesting: The larger trees provide good nesting sites. The foliage is dense enough to provide protective cover.

Landscape Value: Very attractive for lawn planting. The tree bears an abundance of rose-colored blossoms in May. The fruit is very showy, being bright red in color.

Soil Preferred: Does best in an open, sunny, well-drained location.

Birds Attracted: The fruit is a winter favorite of the mockingbirds. Eaten readily by wintering finches, crossbills, and grosbeaks. The fallen fruits are eaten by the ruffed grouse and other game birds.

FLOWERING DOGWOOD. *Cornus florida;* native.

Food Value: Offers one of the most attractive food supplies for fall migrants as well as local species. The small clusters of red berries are eaten avidly after softening by the first frost.

Cover and Nesting: Will be accepted readily for nesting by robins, vireos, and occasionally other species. Provides a fair amount of cover.

Landscape Value: One of the loveliest of our flowering trees. In May the foliage is preceded by beautiful large white blossoms. It grows in graceful form and presents an attractive crimson and orange picture in fall foliage. An ideal tree for either a small lawn or estate planting.

Soil Preferred: Should be planted in the open to produce a well-shaped tree. Will tolerate shade, but will not fruit as well. Not particular about moisture or soil conditions.

Birds Attracted: Ninety-four species, including ruffed grouse, bob-whites, flickers, downy woodpeckers, kingbirds, catbirds, brown thrashers, robins, thrushes, Eastern bluebirds, cedar waxwings, red-eyed viroes, purple finches, white-throated sparrows, and song sparrows.

HACKBERRY. *Celtis occidentalis;* native.

Food Value: Furnishes an abundant supply of food, which clings until spring. Makes a good food supply for wintering birds and early spring migrants.

Cover and Nesting: Furnishes only fair amount of cover and desirable nesting sites.

Landscape Value: Frequently attacked by a fungus growth causing a thickly bunched formation of small twigs known as "witches' brooms." Best suited for remote area or thicket planting.

Soil Preferred: Will grow in almost any soil condition and will stand shade.

Birds Attracted: Forty-seven species, including cardinals, brown thrashers, cedar waxwings, robins, flickers, towhees, hermit thrushes, and mockingbirds.

HAWTHORNS. *Crataegus sp.;* native.

Food Value: There are many varieties of the native *Crataegus* all of which bear fruits liked by birds. *C. coccinea, C. cordata,* and *C. crusgalli* are outstanding varieties producing fruits that persist well into the winter.

Cover and Nesting: The thick, thorny, horizontal branches offer good protective cover and nesting sites. This combined with their food-producing qualities makes them excellent plants for attracting bird life.

Landscape Value: Very popular as garden plants. They bloom in a profusion of white, pink, or red flowers, which are followed by decorative, small, applelike fruits. The fall foliage is a brilliant red or orange.

Soil Preferred: Not particular as to type of soil, and will thrive in open woodlands or sunny areas.

Birds Attracted: Thirty-nine species including robins, purple finches, bobwhites, hermit thrushes, pine grosbeaks, and ruffed grouse.

HEMLOCKS. *Tsuga canadensis; T. caroliniana;* native.

Food Value: The small winged seeds are a good source of fall and winter food.

Cover and Nesting: Makes excellent winter cover for both game birds and songbirds. Used for nesting by warblers, thrushes, robins, jays, and several other species.

Landscape Value: Hemlocks are among the most attractive of all our native evergreens. They grow quite rapidly and tall. Can be trimmed as evergreen hedge.

Soil Preferred: Moist rich soil on cool slopes. Does well in ravines along streams. Shade tolerant.

Birds Attracted: More than a dozen species including chickadees, pine siskins, crossbills, juncos, and warblers.

MOUNTAIN ASH. *Sorbus americana,* native; *S. aucuparia,* exotic.

Food Value: The clusters of red berries of *S. americana* and the large orange berries of *S. aucuparia* are a good source of bird food for the fall and winter months.

Cover and Nesting: Not a tree of dense foliage, so only of fair value for cover and nesting.

Landscape Value: Ornamental trees with attractive summer foliage and brilliantly colored fruits in the fall.

Soil Preferred: Not particular as to type of soil. Drought-resistant and will tolerate shade.

Birds Attracted: A favorite of robins, Bohemian and cedar waxwings. Also eaten by red-headed woodpeckers, brown thrashers, evening and pine grosbeaks, Baltimore orioles, and others.

MULBERRY. *Morus alba,* exotic; *M. rubra,* native.

Food Value: Bears fruit in early summer during the nesting season and provides a soft, juicy fruit for nestlings. Eagerly sought by virtually all songbirds.

Cover and Nesting: The trees grow to a height of fifty feet and furnish good cover and nesting sites.

Landscape Value: Grows in a rather graceful, weeping shape. The leaves vary in form and are a glossy, light green. Should not be planted over walks or driveways, as fruit drops freely.

Soil Preferred: Both species prefer a rich, moist soil and will tolerate only partial shade.

Birds Attracted: Many species, including mockingbirds, catbirds, robins, yellow-billed cuckoos, wood thrushes, cardinals, and half a hundred others.

NORWAY SPRUCE. *Picea excelsa;* exotic.

Food Value: The cones of this evergreen contain seeds sought by wintering finches.

Cover and Nesting: This is an excellent shelter tree. Many species of birds will nest in its dense foliage.

Landscape Value: One of the most attractive evergreens, particularly when small. Make good windbreaks and can be planted as a hedge, as they will stand severe pruning.

Soil Preferred: Not particular as to soil, shade, or moisture conditions.

Birds Attracted: Purple finches, crossbills, grosbeaks, ruffed grouse, and others.

OAKS. *Quercus sp.;* native.

Food Value: Acorns are a staple fall and winter food for birds and other wildlife.

Cover and Nesting: Young oaks provide nesting sites for robins, thrushes, doves, vireos, and others. Large oaks are attractive to jays, wood pewees, woodpeckers, and hawks.

Landscape Value: Oaks are good ornamental trees. Used extensively for shade trees in lawns, park areas, and along city streets.

Soil Preferred: Our eastern oaks thrive best in rich, loose soil. Avoid compact clay types.

Birds Attracted: More than sixty species, including jays, grosbeaks, nuthatches, woodpeckers, game birds, and waterfowl.

RED CEDAR. *Juniperus virginiana;* native.

Food Value: The blue berries are attractive to wintering finches, cedar waxwings, and myrtle warblers. Provides food for early spring arrivals, such as robins, bluebirds, and phoebes.

Cover and Nesting: The dense foliage makes excellent cover and provides ideal nesting sites for many species.

Landscape Value: An ideal evergreen for landscaping. Should not be planted near apple orchards, as they serve as host to cedar-apple rust.

Soil Preferred: Dry, light, sandy soil in full sunlight.

Birds Attracted: Over fifty species, including myrtle warblers, robins, flickers, cardinals, phoebes, kingbirds, blue jays, chickadees, cedar waxwings, and thrushes.

RUSSIAN OLIVE. *Elaeagnus angustifolia;* exotic.

Food Value: Berries are good winter food acceptable to many species.

Cover and Nesting: Rather open plant when grown singly. Furnishes good cover and nesting sites when planted in hedge form.

Landscape Value: Its silver-gray foliage and attractive berries make it a showy shrub. Often used for tall border or hedge plantings. Grows to a height of thirty feet.

Soil Preferred: Not particular as to soil types, but prefers sun.

Birds Attracted: Robins, thrushes, waxwings, and more than thirty other species.

SHADBUSH. *Amelanchier canadensis;* native.

Food Value: The dark purple-red berries in midsummer are sought by nearly fifty species. Particular favorites of orioles, waxwings, and thrushes.

Cover and Nesting: Being a rather small tree, it furnishes only fair cover and nesting locations.

Landscape Value: The white flowers in May are very attractive. The tree is small and decorative.

Soil Preferred: Not particular as to soil conditions and will grow in shade or sun.

Birds Attracted: Over forty species, including thrushes, orioles, cedar waxwings, woodpeckers, cardinals, robins, red-eyed vireos, mourning doves, scarlet tanagers, brown thrashers, and others.

Sour Gum. *Nyssa sylvatica;* native.

Food Value: The bluish-black berries often last well into winter. Provides good food for game and songbirds.

Cover and Nesting: Provides good cover and nesting. Hollow cavities also attractive to other wildlife, such as raccoons, opossums, and squirrels.

Landscape Value: Beautiful foliage and brilliant fall colors. Branches are horizontal and crooked. Fine for picturesque planting.

Soil Preferred: Deep, moist, swamp soil.

Birds Attracted: Thrushes, waxwings, woodpeckers, mockingbirds, blue jays, robins, pheasants, ruffed grouse, wood ducks, and mallards.

White Pine. *Pinus strobus;* native.

Food Value: One of the most valuable evergreens. Provides food for songbirds, ruffed grouse, bobwhites, squirrels, and deer.

Cover and Nesting: Provides good protective cover and is preferred for nesting by purple finches, pine siskins, crossbills, and several species of warblers. A good roost for owls.

Landscape Value: Large, attractive evergreen. Can be used as background planting where height is desired.

Soil Preferred: Not particular as to soil or moisture conditions. Matures best in sunlight.

Birds Attracted: A large variety, including woodpeckers, waxwings, pine siskins, red-breasted nuthatches, ruffed grouse, wood ducks, horned grebes, warblers, and owls.

WHITE SPRUCE. *Picea canadensis;* native.

Food Value: Seed-bearing cones attractive to songbirds. Favorite of finches, woodpeckers, and crossbills.

Cover and Nesting: Provides excellent cover and ideal nesting sites for many species.

Landscape Value: Most attractive when small. Should be planted where eventual height will not be objectionable.

Soil Preferred: Prefers wet, rich soil and will tolerate shade. Suffers from drought.

Birds Attracted: More than twenty-four species, including purple finches, crossbills, woodpeckers, chickadees, and wood thrushes.

WILD RED CHERRY. *Prunes pennsylvanica;* native.

Food Values: The small red cherries distract birds from cultivated fruits during midsummer. The fruits are a favorite of many species.

Cover and Nesting: Provides only fair cover and nesting sites.

Landscape Value: A fast-growing tree. Attractive foliage and flowers.

Soil Preferred: Not particular as to soil and moisture conditions. Better shape and more abundant fruit if planted in full sunlight.

Birds Attracted: Approximately eighty species of song and game birds, including white-throated sparrows, white-crowned sparrows, towhees, goldfinches, gray-cheeked thrushes, song sparrows, and grouse.

Shrubs

ARROWWOOD. *Viburnum dentatum;* native.

Food Value: Produces clusters of blue-black fruit of good quality. Sought by migrating birds in early fall.

Cover and Nesting: A large bushy shrub, providing good cover and nesting sites.

Landscape Value: Grows to a height of fifteen feet. Thick foliage of coarse-toothed leaves that turn purple and red in autumn. Good for mass planting.

Soil Preferred: Likes moist soil and is tolerant of shade. Fruits best in full sun.

Birds Attracted: Fruit known to be eaten by thirty-five kinds, including thrushes, bluebirds, flickers, catbirds, phoebes, brown thrashers, and ruffed grouse.

ASIATIC SWEETLEAF. *Symplocos paniculata;* exotic.

Food Value: Fruits are good fall food. Birds eat them eagerly even before fully ripened.

Cover and Nesting: Provides only fair cover and nesting. Most popular for its food value.

Landscape Value: Attractive when planted singly. Fruits are a beautiful sapphire-blue color.

Soil Preferred: Likes a well-drained soil in full sun.

Birds Attracted: Nearly all songbirds, including waxwings, robins, thrushes, vireos, and brown thrashers.

BAYBERRY. *Myrica carolinensis;* native.

Food Value: One of the best food-producing shrubs in the Atlantic coastal states. The gray waxy berries persist throughout the winter and are favorites of many species.

Cover and Nesting: A low shrub providing only fair cover and opportunities for nesting. Chief value is for food.

Landscape Value: Used as a soil binder in sandy coastal areas. Not particularly attractive as a landscaping shrub.

Soil Preferred: Sandy soil. Will not tolerate shade.

Birds Attracted: More than eighty species, including cardinals, myrtle warblers, flickers, downy woodpeckers, meadowlarks, phoebes, Carolina wrens, catbirds, hermit thrushes, and bluebirds.

BLACK ALDER.   *Ilex verticillata;* native.

Food Value: Provides excellent food for fall and winter months. Particular favorite of migrating hermit thrushes.

Cover and Nesting: Provides fair cover in mass plantings. Not a favorite for nesting.

Landscape Value: Bright red fruits in fall and winter. Often planted as a winter ornamental shrub.

Soil Preferred: Grows best in very wet soil in either sun or shade.

Birds Attracted: An exceptional favorite of the hermit thrushes and ruffed grouse. Also eaten by cedar waxwings, bluebirds, and brown thrashers.

BLACK HAW.   *Viburnum prunifolium;* native.

Food Value: These shrubs usually fruit very well, producing an abundance of blue-black fruits that persist throughout the winter months.

Cover and Nesting: Large shrub with dense foliage that provides good cover and nesting sites.

Landscape Value: Has attractive foliage, flowers, and fruit. Can be planted singly as a small tree (it grows to twenty feet) or can be used in mass plantings.

Soil Preferred: Not particular as to soil or moisture conditions. Will grow in sun or shade.

Birds Attracted: Liked by more than thirty species of songbirds, including pileated woodpeckers, yellow-billed cuckoos, olive-backed thrushes, brown thrashers, and cedar waxwings.

BLACK HUCKLEBERRY.   *Gaylussacia baccata;* native.

Food Value: This is an exceptional summer favorite, but fruits last for only a comparatively short time.

Cover and Nesting: Provides only fair cover and is not generally preferred for nesting.

Landscape Value: Attractive autumn foliage. Fruits eaten by man.

Soil Preferred: Sandy, acid soil. Sunlight required for fruiting.

Birds Attracted: Forty-six species, including pine grosbeaks, towhees, robins, catbirds, hermit thrushes, chickadees, and bluebirds.

BUCKTHORN. *Rhamnus cathartica;* exotic.

Food Value: The shiny black fruits provide good summer and fall food. Help distract birds from cultivated fruits.

Cover and Nesting: The masses of twigs and spines provide both good cover and nesting sites.

Landscape Value: Can be used best in hedges or backgrounds. Serves as host to oat rust. Should not be planted in areas growing oats.

Soil Preferred: Prefers a sandy, well-drained soil in either shade or sunlight.

Birds Attracted: Ruffed grouse, purple finches, waxwings, brown thrashers, and others.

CHOKEBERRY. *Aronia arbutifolia, A. melanocarpa;* native.

Food Value: Both varieties proved fruits for fall and early winter feeding. Also sought by various mammals.

Cover and Nesting: Not particularly valuable for cover or nesting owing to its low height — three to four feet. Sometimes used for nesting by field sparrows and song sparrows.

Landscape Value: The red berries of *A. arbutifolia* are very attractive. Both species have colorful fall foliage. Good for front-edge plantings along shrub borders.

Soil Preferred: Quite tolerant of soil conditions but does best in low, moist areas.

Birds Attracted: Birds partial to the chokeberry fruits include the chickadees, cedar waxwings, meadowlarks, and grouse.

CORALBERRY. *Symphoricarpos orbiculatus;* native.

Food Value: The coral-colored berries persist from late summer through the entire winter. Good for wintering sparrows, thrushes, and grosbeaks.

Cover and Nesting: Provides good cover in mass plantings. Liked by song sparrows and chipping sparrows for nesting.

Landscape Value: Ideal shrub for steep banks and front of shrub borders. Best in mass plantings.

Soil Preferred: Likes limestone or clay and is indifferent as to sun or shade. Wet or dry soil.

Birds Attracted: Both song and game birds, including pine and evening grosbeaks, robins, towhees, brown thrashers, pheasants, and ruffed grouse.

ELDERBERRY. *Sambucus canadensis, S. pubens;* native.

Food Value: An excellent food for late summer and fall. The small juicy fruits are eagerly sought by virtually all songbirds. Should be a part of any planting program.

Cover and Nesting: Provides good cover in mass plantings, and nesting sites for a few species.

Landscape Values: Makes good mass planting for borders or roadsides. Blossoms and fruit are showy.

Soil Preferred: A wet soil in either sun or shade. Fruits best in full sun.

Birds Attracted: One hundred and eighteen species, including woodpeckers, kingbirds, grosbeaks, bluebirds, thrushes, towhees, mockingbirds, and white-crowned sparrows, are known to eat the fruits.

GRAY DOGWOOD. *Cornus racemosa;* native.

Food Value: A very fine food plant for late summer and fall. Provides an abundance of fruit, particularly when planted en masse.

Cover and Nesting: Group and hedge plantings make acceptable cover. Single plants give little protection.

Landscape Value: White berries and red stalks make this an attractive shrub for ornamental use. Will spread from root sproutings.

Soil Preferred: This is one dogwood tolerant of most soil conditions. Will stand some shade.

Birds Attracted: More than twenty species have been observed eating the berries. Included were chats, purple finches, crested flycatchers, woodpeckers, and grosbeaks.

Highbush Blueberry. *Vaccinium corymbosum;* native.

Food Value: Common market blueberry. Provides excellent summer food for nearly 100 species of song and game birds.

Cover and Nesting: A rather dense shrub, providing fair cover. Occasionally used for nesting by chipping sparrows, song sparrows, and low-nesting warblers.

Landscape Value: A well-shaped shrub with beautiful fall foliage.

Soil Preferred: An acid, moist soil in either sun or shade.

Birds Attracted: Over ninety species, including tufted titmice, orchard orioles, hermit thrushes, cedar waxwings, towhees, kingbirds, and ruffed grouse.

Highbush Cranberry. *Viburnum trilobum;* native.

Food Value: The fruits are a staple winter food of the ruffed grouse. Fruits ripen in September and October and persist throughout the entire winter.

Cover and Nesting: Furnishes a good shrub type of cover for nesting and roosting, and for travel lanes in hedges and windbreaks. Highly recommended by the U. S. Soil Conservation Service.

Landscape Value: The creamy-white clusters of flowers in spring, the scarlet leaves in the fall, and the translucent red berries throughout the fall and winter make this one of our handsomest shrubs.

Soil Preferred: Survives best in fertile, well-drained to wet soil. Avoid dry, unproductive soils.

Birds Attracted: Avidly eaten by ruffed grouse and pheasants. Eaten sparingly by some songbirds.

Inkberry. *Ilex glabra;* native.

Food Value: The glossy black berries remain until late winter on shrubs to eight feet in height. A good source of food for wintering songbirds.

Cover and Nesting: Provides good cover when bunched. Uses sparingly for nesting.

Landscape Value: An evergreen shrub easily adapted to garden conditions.

Soil Preferred: A well-drained soil and partial shade.

Birds Attracted: Bluebirds, catbirds, robins, chickadees, tufted titmice, hermit thrushes, mockingbirds, and bobwhites.

JAPANESE BARBERRY. *Berberis thunbergi;* exotic.

Food Value: The great quantities of red berries are preferred in late winter after they have been softened by cold weather. A good emergency food supply.

Cover and Nesting: One of the best shrubs that can be planted for this purpose. Provides good cover and is used for nesting by many species.

Landscape Value: Used extensively for dense hedges and borders. Trims well to a uniform shape. The foliage and berries make it an attractive year-round shrub.

Soil Preferred: Not particular as to soil conditions.

Birds Attracted: Catbirds, chipping sparrows, hermit thrushes, juncos, song sparrows, tree sparrows, and others.

MAPLELEAF VIBURNUM. *Viburnum acerifolium;* native.

Food Value: A small shrub that provides a staple fall and winter food for ruffed grouse and songbirds. Also eaten by deer.

Cover and Nesting: A low shrub providing cover for ground-nesting species such as the towhee and ruffed grouse.

Landscape Value: Good for low mass plantings. Attractive fall coloring.

Soil Preferred: Prefers a light, dry soil in either shade or sun.

Birds Attracted: Bluebirds, cedar waxwings, flickers, robins, thrushes, bobwhites, ruffed grouse, and many others.

MULTIFLORA ROSE. *Rosa multiflora;* exotic.

Food Value: Produces an abundance of fruit that persists throughout the winter. Good food supply for both song and game birds. An exceptional favorite of wintering bluebirds, robins, and cedar waxwings.

Cover and Nesting: Excellent as an escape cover to avoid predators. Provides ideal nesting sites for many species.

Landscape Value: Highly recommended by the U. S. Soil Conservation Service for live fences, soil-erosion control, hedges, and windbreaks. Has dense clusters of attractive white flowers.

Soil Preferred: Adaptable to almost all well-drained soil, from nearly barren to rich.

Birds Attracted: Bluebirds, robins, cedar waxwings, white-throated sparrows, juncos, tree sparrows, catbirds, bobwhites, pheasants, and many others.

NANNYBERRY. *Viburnum lentago;* native.

Food Value: Furnishes a staple winter food for ruffed grouse and pheasants. Also eaten by songbirds, gray squirrels, and rabbits.

Cover and Nesting: A large thicket-forming shrub furnishing good cover and nesting sites.

Landscape Value: Good for mass plantings. Has creamy-white flowers and drooping clusters of black berries.

Soil Preferred: Thrives in full sun to half-shade in almost any soil condition.

Birds Attracted: Ruffed grouse, pheasants, rose-breasted grosbeaks, cedar waxwings, flickers, robins, catbirds, hermit thrushes, and others.

RED-OSIER DOGWOOD. *Cornus stolonifera;* native.

Food Value: A good source of fall and winter food for both song and game birds. Also eaten by deer.

Cover and Nesting: Furnishes only fair cover. Red-winged blackbirds and yellow warblers have been known to use it for nesting.

Landscape Value: Has bright red branches that are very attractive in winter. Good for stream-bank plantings. Both flowers and berries are white.

Soil Preferred: Moist to wet soil in full sun. Will tolerate partial shade.

Birds Attracted: Nearly 100 species of song and game birds are attracted to the various dogwoods, this being one of the favorites.

SHRUB LESPEDEZA. *Lespedeza bicolor;* exotic.

Food Value: Provides first-quality food for quail and is used ex-

tensively for this purpose in the Southeastern states. Also eaten
by songbirds.

Cover and Nesting: Provides good cover in the summer, but is
rather open in winter when the leaves are off.

Landscape Value: Has been used successfully for soil-erosion control
and revegetation. Good cover for unproductive land.

Soil Preferred: Adaptable to almost any soil condition in the open.
The growth rate is most rapid in rich soil.

Birds Attracted: Bobwhites, pheasants, and songbirds.

SIEBOLD VIBURNUM.   *Viburnum sieboldi;* exotic.

Food Value: One of the better viburnums. Red and black fruits are
eagerly sought in late summer and fall.

Cover and Nesting: Provides fair cover and nesting sites. Grows to
a height of thirty feet.

Landscape Value: An excellent ornamental viburnum. Does well
when planted singly or in group plantings. Flowers and fruits
are exceptionally attractive.

Soil Preferred: Prefers a rich, well-drained, garden soil.

Birds Attracted: Especially attractive to hermit thrushes. Also eaten
by other thrushes, catbirds, robins, waxwings, towhees, thrashers,
mockingbirds, and several other songbirds.

SNOWBERRY.   *Symphoricarpos racemosus;* native.

Food Value: The white pealike fruits last throughout the winter
and supply winter food for ruffed grouse, pheasants, bobwhites,
and songbirds.

Cover and Nesting: Provides desirable cover when used in mass
plantings. Not particularly valuable as a shrub for nesting.

Landscape Value: Good for underplantings or in front of shrub
borders. Planted mainly for the showy white berries. Most effective in mass plantings.

Soil Preferred: Grows naturally in a limestone soil, but this is not
necessary for planting. Sun or shade.

Birds Attracted: Thirty-three species, including towhees, robins, pine and evening grosbeaks, cardinals, cedar waxwings, and thrushes.

TATARIAN HONEYSUCKLE. *Lonicera tatarica;* exotic.

Food Value: One of the most popular food plants for birds. The fruits ripen in the spring and are a good source of food for nestlings.

Cover and Nesting: Mature shrubs provide good cover and nesting sites. It is most valuable, however, as a food-producing plant.

Landscape Value: Well suited for mixed-shrub plantings or for screens and backgrounds. Has fragrant, attractive flowers and decorative red fruits.

Soil Preferred: Indifferent as to soil and moisture conditions. Fruits best in full sun.

Birds Attracted: Brown thrashers, catbirds, robins, cedar waxwings, purple finches, and white-throated sparrows.

WILD BLACKBERRY. *Rubus allegheniensis;* native.

Food Value: An exceptional favorite during late summer. Eaten avidly by nearly all species of songbirds.

Cover and Nesting: Provides good cover and nesting sites when growing in thick tangles. Cardinals, catbirds, brown thrashers, and song sparrows will nest in it readily.

Landscape Value: Not particularly adaptable for landscaping. Best used in areas remote from gardens and lawns. Fruit edible by man.

Soil Preferred: Adaptable to almost any soil condition.

Birds Attracted: Over 100 species, including cardinals, flickers, Baltimore orioles, kingbirds, tufted titmice, mockingbirds, song sparrows, and rose-breasted grosbeaks.

WITHE ROD. *Viburnum cassinoides;* native.

Food Value: Fruits last well into the winter and have proved to be desirable food for at least thirty-five species.

Cover and Nesting: A compact viburnum, especially when cultivated, affording good cover and nesting sites.

Landscape Value: One of the handsomest of our native shrubs. Clusters of creamy-white flowers, followed by an abundance of varicolored berries.

Soil Preferred: Moist soil and sunlight.

Birds Attracted: Rose-breasted grosbeaks, purple finches, pine grosbeaks, cardinals, catbirds, brown thrashers, robins, bluebirds, cedar waxwings, and others.

Vines

BITTERSWEET. *Celastrus orbiculatus,* exotic; *C. scandens,* native.

Food Value: Provides fall and winter food. Eaten readily by game birds and a few species of songbirds.

Cover and Nesting: Of little value if used alone. Should be mixed with other shrubs to aid in forming dense borders.

Landscape Value: Used on trellises and arbors. Planted for the decorative red berries.

Soil Preferred: Not particular as to soil conditions. Will tolerate shade.

Birds Attracted: Ruffed grouse, pheasants, bobwhites, bluebirds, robins, hermit thrushes, and red-eyed vireos.

COMMON MATRIMONY VINE. *Lycium halimifolium;* exotic.

Food Value: A good vine to supply fall and early winter fruits.

Cover and Nesting: Usually thick and somewhat spiny, affording good cover and nesting sites.

Landscape Value: Can be trained as a vine for wall covering or to an upright shrub form. Best used in mass plantings. The scarlet fruits are quite showy.

Soil Preferred: Any drained soil. Prefers sun.

Birds Attracted: Songbirds, fall migrants, and early winter arrivals.

GREENBRIER. *Simalx rotundifolia;* native.

Food Value: The blue fruits endure from one season until the next. A good source of emergency food during long periods of snow.

Cover and Nesting: Forms thick tangles used for nesting by catbirds, brown thrashers, and others. Provides excellent protective cover.

Landscape Value: Best used in remote areas. Will spread rapidly. Of little value for actual landscaping.

Soil Preferred: Will grow in any type of soil in sun or shade.

Birds Attracted: Nearly fifty species, including white-throated sparrows, flickers, mockingbirds, bluebirds, waxwings, grosbeaks, and finches.

HALL'S HONEYSUCKLE. *Lonicera japonica halliana;* exotic.

Food Value: The black berries persist well into the winter, providing food for both song and game birds. A particular favorite of wintering meadowlarks.

Cover and Nesting: Most of the green leaves cling throughout the winter, providing a dense protective cover. Provides good nesting sites by twining about shrubs and small trees.

Landscape Value: Used for covering walls, trellises, and road banks. Good soil binder in cases of hillside erosion. Spreads rapidly. Flowers are attractive and very fragrant.

Soil Preferred: Not particular as to soil or shade conditions.

Birds Attracted: Meadowlarks, white-throated sparrows, song sparrows, tree sparrows, flickers, bluebirds, goldfinches, and ruffed grouse.

VIRGINIA CREEPER. *Ampelopsis quinquefolia;* native.

Food Value: Provides an abundance of berries in late fall and winter which are eagerly sought by many species. One of the best food-producing vines.

Cover and Nesting: Hardy growths provide good cover and nesting locations.

Landscape Value: Good for wall coverings, trellises, and arbors. Early fall coloring.

Soil Preferred: Not particular as to soil conditions. Prefers full sunlight.

Birds Attracted: Thirty-eight species, including flickers, red-headed woodpeckers, yellow-bellied sapsuckers, olive-backed and gray-checked thrushes, red-eyed vireos, and scarlet tanagers.

WILD GRAPE. *Vitis sp.;* native.

Food Value: Provides a juicy fruit for fall and early winter feeding. Liked by a large variety of song and game birds. Fruits used for making jellies.

Cover and Nesting: Provides only fair cover and few nesting opportunities. Best used in natural tangles.

Landscape Value: Naturalistic plantings.

Soil Preferred: Not particular as to soil conditions. Will grow in shade or sun.

Birds Attracted: The combined species of wild grapes are known to attract eighty-seven kinds of birds.

Ground Covers

The use of ground covers in wildlife plantings is often overlooked. Their use along shaded garden paths, wooded slopes, and border plantings can be very attractive and provide food for birds and other wildlife. The following listed species are generally conceded to be the most attractive, both from the landscape point of view and food-producing qualities.

BEARBERRY *(Arctostaphylos)*

Normally found in Canada and along the northern border of the United States. Will survive farther south if transplanted. Prefers sandy loam in partial shade. Eaten by game birds and a few ground-feeding songbirds such as towhees and thrashers.

BUNCHBERRY *(Cornus canadensis)*

The smallest of our dogwoods — less than a foot in height. The clusters of red berries and foliage are similar to the flowering dogwood in appearance. Grows in colonies and is most abundant in the cooler forests of our northern states. A favorite of grouse, thrashes, and vireos.

CANADA MAYFLOWER *(Maianthemum)*

Commonly referred to as the wild lily-of-the-valley. Easily grown. Its presence in northern woodlands often indicates thin, acid soil over ledge. Has bright red berries in late summer and fall.

CROWBERRY *(Empetrum nigrum)*

Low evergreen with black berries. Its natural range extends southward from the subarctic to our northern states. Berries eaten by grouse and some songbirds.

PARTRIDGEBERRY *(Mitchella repens)*

A very attractive vinelike evergreen of our eastern woodlands. Bright red berries enhance its beauty in fall and winter. A staple source of food for upland game birds.

WINTERGREEN *(Gaultheria procumbens)*

Sometimes called teaberry or checkerberry. A native evergreen of northern woodlands and mountain areas south through Virginia and the Carolinas. Bright red berries persist throughout the winter. Berries and young foliage eaten by game birds.

Flowers

Many cultivated garden flowers produce an abundance of seeds that are especially attractive to a great variety of seed-eating songbirds. The seeds of certain species, like the *Amaranthus* and *Helianthus* groups, are so eagerly sought that special plantings are warranted.

If the flowers in the following list are permitted to seed, they will furnish food for many songbirds during late summer, fall, and winter.[1] Among the many birds attracted to flower seeds are finches, sparrows, buntings, juncos, doves, thrashers, towhees, and cardinals.

Astor, Chinese (*Callistephus chinensis*)
Bachelor button (*Centaurea cyanus*)
Bellflower (*Campanula*)
Black-eyed Susan (*Rudbekia*)
California poppy (*Eschscholzia californica*)
Chrysanthemum
Columbine (*Aquilegia*)
Cosmos
Forget-me-not (*Myosotis*)

---

[1] Flowers specially attractive to hummingbirds are not necessarily included in this list. See Chapter 10, "How to Attract Hummingbirds."

Love-lies-bleeding (*Amaranthus caudatus*)
Marigold (*Tagetes*)
Petunia
Phlox (*Phlox drummondi*)
Portulaca
Prince's father (*Amaranthus hypochondriacus*)
Scabiosa
Snapdragon (*Antirrhinum*)
Sunflower (*Helianthus*)
Sweet William (*Dianthus barbatus*)
Verbena
Zinnia

CHAPTER VIII

HELPING BIRDS
AT NESTING TIME

BIRDS ARE DRESSED in their most brilliant plumage during the spring nesting season. This is the time, too, when the air is filled with their songs of courtship — the time when they are busiest about our gardens catching myriads of insects to feed their new-born families. Surely, for both aesthetic and economic reasons, we want to attract as many nesting birds as possible to our gardens.

There are three things we can do to attract birds during the nesting season. They are: (1) provide natural nesting sites, such as trees, shrubs, hedges, and thickets; (2) provide nesting boxes for cavity-nesting species; and (3) furnish them with a variety of nesting materials. Better results will be obtained by devoting some time to each of these three projects rather than concentrating on any one of them.

Nesting Habits

We can do a much better job of encouraging birds to build on our premises if we know something of their normal nesting habits. In this respect birds can be divided into two general groups: (1) the cavity-nesting species, such as woodpeckers, wrens, bluebirds, tree swallows, chickadees, crested flycatchers, purple martins, and others; and (2) those that nest in branches of trees or shrubs or on the ground. The former group will accept man-made nesting boxes. In fact, the use of nesting boxes is the only way we can entice these

[90]

species to build in the well-groomed, formal garden. The latter group, which includes the majority of our songbirds, prefer to build an open nest in dense thickets, shrubbery, or trees.

A variety of trees and shrubs will provide nesting sites for more birds than a concentrated planting of any one kind. Certain individual plants and group plantings are more acceptable than others.

The following evaluation is presented as being representative of those habitats and plant groupings found about most gardens, farms, and larger estates. If they are not present, many of them can be developed through construction and planting programs. In each case, birds most likely to be attracted for nesting are included.

BARBERRY HEDGES. A hedge of common barberry is a favorite nesting area of chipping sparrows, song sparrows, and catbirds. If the hedge is not trimmed too severely, it will also be used by cardinals, brown thrashers, and mockingbirds.

MULTIFLORA-ROSE HEDGES. A hedge or fence of multiflora rose will have a high nesting density. Its mass of briers and dense foliage affords a maximum of seclusion and protection. Birds attracted for nesting include mockingbirds, cardinals, catbirds, thrashers, chats, and the various sparrows.

MIXED HEDGES AND BORDERS. A dense hedge or border containing a variety of shrubs, such as lilacs, forsythia, spiraea, barberry, and viburnums, will provide good home sites for several species of birds. A border of this type will attract song sparrows, chipping sparrows, catbirds, robins, cardinals, yellow warblers, and, if there is some deep shade nearby, perhaps a vireo or woodthrush.

EVERGREENS. Cedars, hemlocks, pines, and spruces furnish protective nesting cover in the early spring before deciduous trees and shrubs are in leaf. They are usually the first nesting sites of early-nesting robins and mourning doves. Evergreens are also liked by home-hunting jays, purple finches, a number of warblers, and chipping sparrows — the last usually nesting well out on the tips of thick branches. Owls will welcome the darkened interior of dense stands for daytime roosting. Long-eared owls will use them for nesting.

GRASSLANDS AND PASTURES.   A greater variety of birds nest in a grassland habitat than is generally realized. Fields and pastures of uncut grasses and weeds appeal to many birds, including meadow-larks, bobolinks, dickcissels, red-winged blackbirds, indigo buntings, quail, pheasants, and several species of sparrows.

ABANDONED FIELDS AND ORCHARDS.   Fields and orchards that have not been disturbed for a few years are ideal habitats for nesting birds. The open grass areas are used by the species mentioned above. Briers, shrubs, and young trees appeal to another group of birds, including cardinals, thrashers, robins, goldfinches, cuckoos, doves, and certain warblers. Old apple trees often contain knothole cavities — favorite nesting sites for bluebirds and crested flycatchers. Tall pear trees have a special appeal to kingbirds.

MARSHY AREAS AND POND BORDERS.   Wetland habitats provide homes for many birds. Common nesting species of marsh areas include a variety of ducks, grebes, and rails. Marshes are also the home of bitterns, short-eared owls, and Florida gallinules. Songbirds nesting about a marsh might include marsh wrens, yellow-throats, and sparrows — swamp, Lincoln, and Leconte's.

Vegetation along the borders of a small pond, such as one might have on a farm, always attract a large number and variety of song-birds. In addition to those species already mentioned, tree swallows and prothonotary warblers will be attracted to a hollow stub or stump overhanging the water.

STREAM BANKS.   A high, sloping bank along a stream or pond is the favored nesting site for bank swallows, rough-winged swallows, and kingfishers. The bank swallows nest in colonies, each pair placing its nest at the end of a burrow measuring 2 to 8 feet into the bank. Rough-winged swallows and kingfishers nest singly but use the same type of burrow.

SHADED LAWNS AND PARK AREAS. Birds nesting in the tall shade trees of lawns and parks include many species. Maples appeal to robins and cedar waxwings. The Baltimore oriole will invariably locate its nest in the long, graceful boughs of an elm tree. Locusts are often the favorite nesting tree for mourning doves and cuckoos. Oaks have acceptable home sites for blue jays, wood pewees, and scarlet tanagers. A dozen or more other species will nest in the shade trees of semi-open areas.

WOODLANDS. Many birds make their homes in the dense shade and cover of our woodlands. Among the most common nesting species are ovenbirds, thrushes, vireos, warblers, and grouse. Hawks, owls, and turkey vultures are apt to find the seclusion they prefer in deep woodland areas.

DEAD TREES AND STUBS. Regardless of the location, most dead trees and stubs will attract one or more of the cavity-nesting species. Those in wooded areas provide home sites for woodpeckers, chickadees, titmice, flickers, crested flycatchers, screech owls, and others. In open or semi-open areas they would attract wrens, bluebirds, flickers, crested flycatchers, titmice, tree swallows, and some of the woodpeckers. Those close to the water's edge would have special appeal to tree swallows, prothonotary warblers, and wood ducks.

Providing Nesting Materials

We can encourage birds to build in our gardens by providing them with an abundance of assorted nesting materials. These materials, such as short lengths of string, bits of cotton, and feathers, should be conspicuously placed so home-building birds can find them easily. Nesting-material containers can be made from half-inch hardware cloth or soft wood. Materials may also be placed in the crotch of a tree or hung over a clothesline. The use of containers prevents wind from scattering the materials. Avoid placing materials in a bird box or on its roof. This would indicate the box is already occupied. These containers can also be used as suet-holders for winter feeding.

FIGURE 22.   CONTAINERS FOR NESTING MATERIALS.

Robins, orioles, and vireos will appreciate short lengths of string, yarn, and shoemakers' flax. Avoid using pieces longer than 8 or 10 inches, as birds may become entangled in longer lengths. Bits of cotton will be sought eagerly by yellow warblers and goldfinches. Horsehair, normally used as lining in the nests of chipping sparrows and song sparrows, is becoming increasingly scarce. It can sometimes be found in the stuffing of old, discarded furniture. The long bristles from an old paint brush make an acceptable substitute material. Feathers are sought by both barn and tree swallows. They can be acquired in quantity from a local poultry market.

Materials Acceptable to Birds for Nest-Building

string	excelsior
knitting yarn	kapok
shoemakers' flax	cotton
raveled rope	bristles from old paint brush
thread	dried spagnum moss
pieces of soft cloth	feathers
raveled burlap	horsehair
stuffing from old furniture	dried grass
bits of fur	dental floss
wool	Spanish moss

Nesting Boxes

Woodpeckers, chickadees, nuthatches, wrens, bluebirds, and other cavity-nesting species are having increased difficulty in finding suitable natural cavities for nesting sites. Our policy of "clean" gardens, farms, and estates calls for eliminating dead branches and trees, and filling all cavities necessary to prolong the life and beauty of our favorite trees. The old fencerow, with its wooden posts that provided homes for many wrens and bluebirds, has been replaced by modern wire fencing. These practices, coupled with changes in environment brought about by our eagerness to harvest all available commercial timber, have made serious inroads on the population density of certain species.

Fortunately, many of these displaced species will accept man-made nesting boxes. Records of the U. S. Fish and Wildlife Service reveal that more than fifty species of birds have been known to use artificial nesting devices. The house wren, bluebird, and tree swallow are the easiest birds to attract. They will accept almost any type of nesting device, especially the house wren, but greater success can be attained by using properly constructed houses.

Commercial nesting boxes. Commercially manufactured bird houses can be purchased from almost any hardware dealer. These houses are sometimes made of tin, roofing paper, or other cheap materials nonresistant to heat. They often are difficult to open for cleaning, thus serving as a harbor for parasites.

Before you purchase a bird house, you would do well to answer these questions: Is the house designed for a specific kind of bird or is it just "for birds"? Does the house have provisions for drainage and ventilation? Can it be cleaned easily? Will it bake the nestlings during hot summer days?

Although some manufacturers are now producing well-built and properly designed bird houses, considerable savings can be realized by building your own, especially if a considerable number of them is wanted. Most practical bird houses are so simple in design that they can be built by anyone able to use a saw and hammer.

Features of a Good Bird Box

FIGURE 23A.

MATERIALS.   Use well-seasoned, durable woods, such as cypress, red-wood, white cedar, or western cedar. To prevent rusting and eventual loosening of boards, use only galvanized steel or brass hardware, including nails, screws, and hinges.

FIGURE 23B.

DIMENSIONS.   Build each box for a definite species. Use proper dimensions for size of entrance, height of entrance, and depth of cavity. Provide ample floor area. See Chapter 9 for the proper dimensions of specific boxes.

FIGURE 23C.

DRAINAGE.   Drill two or three ¼-inch holes in the bottom to drain off water that may enter during storms. Have the front and sides overlap the bottom for better weatherproofing.

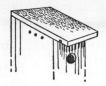

FIGURE 23D.

VENTILATION. Drill two or three ¼-inch holes in each side just under the edges of the roof for ventilation. Holes below the entrance will cause drafts. Roof extends over back, front, and sides for maximum protection.

FIGURE 23E.

EXIT CLEATS. Tack one or two small cleats below the entrance hole on the *inside* of the front section. This makes it easier for adult birds to get out of an empty box. Cleats also assist young birds when feeding and leaving the box.

FIGURE 23F.

DRIP LINE. About 1 inch back on the underside of the roof projection, cut a ⅛-inch deep drip line. This can be done easily with a table saw or hand saw. The drip line prevents water from following the underside of the roof.

FIGURE 23G.

OPENING. Boxes should be made so they can be opened easily for cleaning and observation. In this design, a nail inserted through each side hinges the front section. When closed, the front is fastened by an L screw inserted through a slot in the front and screwed into the bottom section.

PAINTING BIRD BOXES. Many people make the mistake of painting their bird houses brilliant colors, white and red being particular favorites. Although birds will occasionally nest in boxes of this kind, they will accept a home of modest colors — brown, dull green, or gray — more readily.

Boxes made of cypress, redwood, or western cedar need not be painted. These woods are extremely durable and will weather to a "natural" color through exposure. Boxes allowed to weather outdoors during the winter will be more acceptable in the spring. Bird houses made of white pine, white cedar, or spruce, should be painted or stained to eliminate the bright, new look. When painting new boxes, I prefer to add a little green paint and either some brown paint or oil stain to a generous amount of linseed oil. This mixture is stirred only slightly and applied generously to the inside and outside of the box and allowed to soak into the wood. Any excess can be wiped off with a cloth. The process should be repeated until the wood is well saturated and be done well in advance of the nesting season. The resulting mottled effect comes closest to duplicating natural nesting sites. Pine boxes treated in this manner have been known to last for twenty years.

Martin houses may be painted white. This helps them reflect the sun and is not objectionable to the martins.

Locating and Mounting Boxes

Bird houses often fail to attract the tenants for which they were intended. This difficulty can frequently be attributed to improper location of the houses. The choice of a good site — from the birds' point of view — is the most effective way to attract birds to our nesting facilities.

Most birds prefer to nest in open areas. While some cavity-nesting species, especially woodpeckers and chickadees, will nest in the deep woods, most birds desire to locate their homes in more sunny areas. Bluebirds, tree swallows, and wrens like a box mounted on a post along the edge of an open field, orchard, or garden. Flickers, and other members of the woodpecker family, like a box placed on the dead stub of an old tree. Old apple orchards, woodland borders, and semi-open pasturelands provide good locations for houses intended for crested flycatchers, titmice, screech owls, and most other house-nesting birds. Sparrow hawks and red-headed woodpeckers like a box placed rather high on a telephone pole or dead tree stub.

As a rule, greatest success will be attained by placing boxes on a post or pole located in partial or full sunlight. Boxes placed high in the dense foliage of a shade tree evidently do not impress birds as being safe and are usually avoided.

The average flower garden or lawn should contain a limited number of nesting boxes. Most birds of the same species do not like to nest close to one another. In a small area you will attract more tenants by putting up one house for each of a few species than by attempting to attract a family to every post and tree within the vicinity. Tree swallows and martins are exceptions to this rule. Martins are colony-nesting birds and like a house that will accommodate eight or more pairs. Individual boxes for tree swallows may be placed near one another, as these birds are quite sociable.

Nesting boxes may be erected during either the fall or early spring months. If the boxes are weatherproof and put up in the fall, they will serve as roosting shelters. New boxes should be put up in the fall and allowed to weather over the winter. All boxes need to be thoroughly cleaned before the beginning of the nesting season.

Points to Remember

There are definite standard features applicable to the building and placing of any bird house. These rules are based on experience involving the use of hundreds of differently constructed bird houses by public and private sanctuaries. They are listed briefly as follows:

Build every bird house for a specific kind of bird — not just "for birds."

Never build a box with more than one compartment, except for martins.

Build your boxes of wood. Do not use tin or other metals.

Always include provisions for drainage and ventilation.

Use brass or galvanized hardware.

Use dull colors for painting or staining — brown, green, or gray.

In a small area, put up only one or two boxes for each species.

Place boxes where they cannot be molested by cats, or use metal cat-guards.

Place boxes in the open. Avoid dense foliage and deep shade.

Clean boxes thoroughly after each brood of birds leaves the nest.

CHAPTER IX

HOMES FOR BIRDS

THE NESTING BOXES recommended in this chapter are for definite species. The dimensions and information are based on personal experiences and observations supplemented by the findings of the Fish and Wildlife Service of the United States Department of the Interior.

You will note that only one box design is recommended for each species. In each case, the design selected is a personal choice of the author — one that has been tested and proven satisfactory.[1]

Wrens

Wrens are the easiest of all birds to attract to man-made nesting devices. They will build in almost any type of box that will hold a bundle of nesting materials and afford some protection from inclement weather. It is better, however, to provide boxes specially designed for them. They will accept them more readily and will not be so likely to occupy boxes intended for other species.

In the East there are three species of wrens that can be attracted to our gardens by nesting boxes — the house wren, Carolina wren,

[1] See *Features of a Good Bird Box*, page 96.

and Bewick's wren. Of the three, the house wren is the most widely distributed. The Bewick's wren nests southward and west from central Pennsylvania and Ohio. The Carolina wren is extending its range northward and is now becoming a permanent resident in the New England states.

There is considerable variation in recommended specifications and commercial wren boxes regarding the proper size and shape of the entrance. An oblong entrance is preferable. This facilitates nest building and the feeding of young birds. Houses that are intended specifically for house wrens should have an entrance $\frac{7}{8}$ inch by 2 or $2\frac{1}{2}$ inches. This is adequate for the house wren and will eliminate competition from English sparrows. If both the house wren and the Bewick's wren are prevalent, the height of the entrance ought to be increased to 1 inch. The larger Carolina wren needs an opening $1\frac{1}{2}$ inch in height.

Wrens will accept nesting boxes placed on posts, on the sides of buildings, or hung from the boughs of trees. Stationary boxes located in open areas provide the maximum opportunity for acceptance and occupancy.

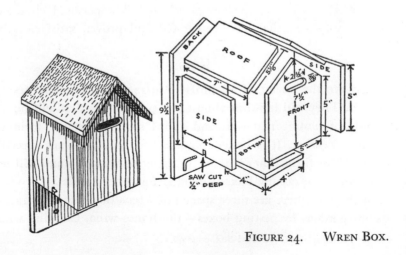

FIGURE 24.   WREN BOX.

Floor of box	4 by 4 in.
Depth of box	6 to 8 in.
Size of entrance	
House wren	⅞ by 2½ in.
Bewick's wren	1 by 2½ in.
Carolina wren	1½ by 2½ in.
Entrance above floor	4 to 6 in.
Height above ground	6 to 10 ft.
Boxes up by	March 1

CONSTRUCTION DETAILS. The dimensions given in the above illustration are for a box intended for house wrens. With the exception of the entrance hole, the same measurements may be used for boxes planned for Bewick's wrens or Carolina wrens.

All sections of the box are cut from ½-inch redwood boards. The first step in assembling the box is nailing the back, and then the front, to the sides. On the side with the saw cut, only one nail is inserted from the front and one from the back. These two nails serve as hinges so this side can be opened easily for cleaning and observation purposes. The bottom is then put in place and nailed through the front, back, and opposite side. An L screw inserted through the saw cut and screwed into the bottom holds the hinged side in place. The box can then be opened or closed by turning the L screw a ¼-turn. The roof sections can now be nailed in place. The final step is to drill ¼-inch holes for drainage, ventilation, and mounting.

Bluebirds

In many areas the bluebird population has decreased alarmingly owing to the lack of natural nesting cavities. Putting up boxes for bluebirds, therefore, becomes a worthy conservation endeavor.

The favorite habitat of bluebirds is open or semi-open areas — fencerows, orchards, abandoned fields, and sizeable gardens. They are birds of the country and can seldom be attracted to nest within the confines of our larger cities.

Homes intended for bluebirds are often invaded by English sparrows. These alien birds can best be discouraged by placing the box rather low (5 feet) on a post in the open and as far away from buildings as space permits. Fencerows, garden borders, and roadsides are good locations for boxes. Bluebirds nest early and usually rear two broods a year. Boxes should be cleaned and ready for occupancy by mid-March.

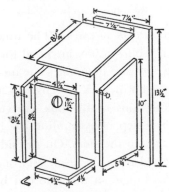

FIGURE 25.   BLUEBIRD BOX.

Floor of Box[2]	4½ x 4½ in.
Depth of box	8½ in.
Diameter of entrance	1½ in.
Entrance above floor	6 in.
Height above ground	5 to 10 ft.
Boxes up by	March 1

CONSTRUCTION DETAILS. This box was designed by the author to fulfill the need for a bluebird box that was practical, durable, and easily maintained. It incorporates such desirable features as:

A simple method of opening which eliminates all commercial hinges.

Adequate drainage and ventilation.

2 Some published specifications call for a bottom 3¼ inches square with an entrance hole 6 inches from the bottom. A cavity of these dimensions acts as a trap for tree swallows, as they cannot get enough wing span or "jump" to reach the exit.

A drip line on the roof extension.

A roof that covers all top joints assuring maximum weatherproofing.

Constructed of ¾-inch redwood for maximum insulation and durability.

A slightly recessed bottom so that all outside drainage is carried beyond the floor line.

To assemble, first nail the two sides to the front with the two hinge nails as illustrated. Insert the bottom and recess it slightly so that the front and two sides extend down beyond it about ⅛ of an inch. Nail the bottom in place through the two sides, leaving the front swing free. Next, nail the back and then the roof in position, making sure that no nails are driven into the front section. Fasten the front down with the L screw as illustrated and drill ¼-inch holes for drainage, ventilation, and mounting.

Tree Swallows

Tree swallows like a box in the open, preferably along the borders of pastures, meadows, swamplands, or ponds where they can find an abundance of flying insects. The boxes should be placed on a post 6 to 15 feet in height and away from all shade trees. Unlike most songbirds, tree swallows will tolerate neighbors of their own kind. They will nest amicably in boxes 50 feet apart. However, if space permits, better results will be obtained by spacing the boxes two or three times that distance.

Tree swallows will often occupy houses intended for bluebirds. In fact, the bluebird box illustrated previously in this chapter makes a good tree-swallow home. A more acceptable box planned specifically for tree swallows has been designed by Henry E. Kinney of Massachusetts. The Kinney design is a rather radical departure from the conventional one-hole nesting box. It is planned to speed up the feeding of young birds and provide maximum protection during periods of rain and cold. In addition to the main entrance hole 1½ inches in diameter, the front section contains three additional 1-inch holes. This permits the parent birds to feed the fledglings without taking time to enter the box. Continued use of this box during the past ten years has proven that this design increases the percentage of survival among nestlings, especially during seasons with an abundance of cold, wet weather.

The male tree swallow protects the nesting site quite zealously and is usually found on or near the selected box. The T perch is added as a place for him to stand guard.

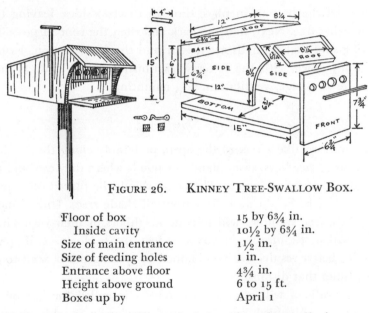

FIGURE 26.   KINNEY TREE-SWALLOW BOX.

Floor of box	15 by 6¾ in.
Inside cavity	10½ by 6¾ in.
Size of main entrance	1½ in.
Size of feeding holes	1 in.
Entrance above floor	4¾ in.
Height above ground	6 to 15 ft.
Boxes up by	April 1

CONSTRUCTION DETAILS.   Use ¾-inch boards and cut all pieces to the shape and size illustrated. Start assembling by nailing the two sides to the floor, keeping the back edges flush. Next, nail horizontal cleats, ½-inch square by 6¾ inches long, to the front section — one on the inside and one on the outside, 1 inch below the main entrance. The front can then be put in place and nailed through the sides and floor. The back is hinged to the rear edge of the floor. The roof sections can be nailed in place and the back hooked to the roof by means of a hook and eye. Tack the T perch to one side as shown.

> *Note.* The curved sides can be cut with a jig saw, band saw, or a hand-coping saw. The holes can be made with a drill saw or an expansion kit. Use another board for backing while drilling. This will keep the front from splitting.

Woodpeckers, Crested Flycatchers, Nuthatches, Titmice, and Chickadees

The woodpecker family, crested flycatchers, nuthatches, titmice, and chickadees will nest in man-made houses properly designed for their use. While all of these species have been known to nest in boxes made of boards, they have a definite preference for the log type of house that closely duplicates natural nesting cavities.

The downy, hairy, and red-headed are the three species of woodpeckers most likely to be attracted to your nesting boxes. Boxes are most acceptable to woodpeckers when placed on the dead stub of a tree in groves, semi-open woodlands, or an old orchard. Red-headed woodpeckers like boxes high on telephone poles or in an oak grove.

The best box for crested flycatchers is one made from a section of hollow log containing a natural knothole that can be used as an entrance. Old apple orchards often contain such hollow limbs. Place the finished box in a tree in a grove, woodlot, orchard, or pasture.

Nuthatches and titmice are both woodland birds with similar needs for nesting places. Both species normally nest in natural tree cavities or abandoned woodpecker homes. They have a preference for woodland borders but can be enticed to nest in garden areas that are not too open or sunny. Boxes may be placed on posts or trees.

Although there are two species of nuthatches, the white-breasted and the red-breasted, which may nest in your area, it is not necessary to design a box for each species. The white-breasted nuthatch, which is the more common and the larger of the two, will be the more likely inhabitant. Both species, however, have been known to nest in the log type of box. You will increase your chances of success in attracting the red-breasted nuthatch if the box is placed in an evergreen grove or forest.

The Carolina chickadee and the black-capped chickadee are woodland birds, which normally nest in abandoned cavities made by woodpeckers. If they can find a dead stub that is soft enough, they will sometimes dig their own nesting cavities. This is often done in woodlands containing an abundance of gray birch trees.

Chickadees will accept a log box quite readily. It should be placed on a dead stub or tree along a woodland border or in the partially shaded areas of gardens and orchards.

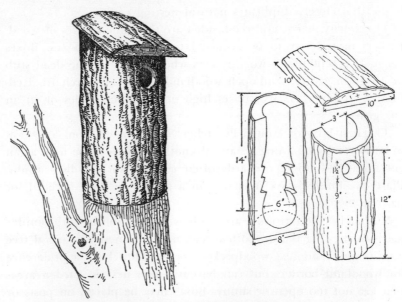

FIGURE 27.   HOLLOW LOG HOUSE — HAIRY WOODPECKER.

Note. Bird houses intended for woodpeckers need an inch or more of sawdust, fine chips, or dry, rotted wood in the bottom of the hollowed-out cavity so the birds may shape a nest for the eggs. Although this woody material is not necessary for all the woodland species mentioned, it is best to use some in all houses made of logs. The material is not objectionable to other species and it gives the woodpeckers a choice of boxes.

Species	Diameter of cavity	Depth of cavity	Diameter of entrance	Entrance above floor	Height above ground	Boxes up by
Downy woodpecker	4″	8″ to 10″	1¼″	6″ to 8″	6′ to 20′	April 1
Hairy woodpecker	6″	12″ to 15″	1½″	9″ to 12″	10′ to 20′	April 1
Red-headed woodpecker	6″	12″ to 15″	2″	9″ to 12″	12′ to 20′	April 1
Crested flycatcher	6″	8″ to 10″	2″	6″ to 8″	8′ to 20′	April 1
Nuthatches	4″	8″ to 10″	1¼″	6″ to 8″	8′ to 20′	April 1
Titmice	4″	8″ to 10″	1¼″	6″ to 8″	8′ to 15′	April 1
Chickadees	4″	8″ to 10″	1¼″	6″ to 8″	5′ to 15′	April 1

CONSTRUCTION DETAILS. Select a log of the proper length and diameter and cut off one end on a slant to allow the roof to slope toward the front. Next, saw the log in half lengthwise. With an expansion bit, bore the entrance hole in the front half before attempting to hollow out the inside. This will avoid the possibility of splitting the log. Fasten one half of the log in a vise or between two boards nailed to your workbench, and then, with a wood chisel and hammer, cut away the interior as illustrated. Do the same with the other half. The two halves may be fastened together by wire bands around the top and bottom of the house or by long wood screws. Cut the roof from a wood slab (a plain board may be used); fasten in the back with a hinge and in the front with a hook and eye.

Robins and Phoebes

The robin is one of our most widely distributed and adaptable birds. We usually think of the robin as a bird that nests in trees and large shrubs, but like many of the birds previously mentioned, it will also nest in man-made nesting devices.

Robins are not cavity-nesting species, but they will accept a shelf or bracket type of box with one or more sides open. Boxes placed under overhanging eaves of a shed, garage, or porch roof, or on an arbor in the garden, will be most acceptable.

Phoebes will accept the same type of shelf or bracket. Normally, they nest on rock ledges along a stream or ravine. Another favorite place is amid the roots and soil of a wind-downed tree. They frequently nest on beams under bridges and under the eaves of porches and low buildings.

The shelves will have a natural appearance and be more acceptable if they are stained a dull color or made of weathered lumber.

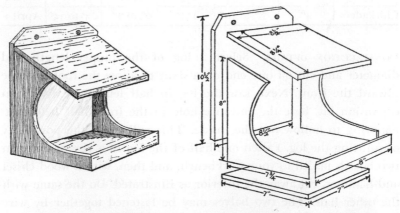

FIGURE 28.   NESTING SHELF FOR ROBINS AND PHOEBES.

Floor of box	7 by 7 in.
Depth of box	6 to 8 in.
Entrance	1 or more sides open
Height above ground	6 to 15 ft.
Boxes up by	March 1

CONSTRUCTION DETAILS. Cut all pieces to size and shape as illustrated from ¾-inch boards. The curved cuts on the two sides can be made with a band saw, jig saw, or a small hand-coping saw. Nail the sides and front piece to the bottom. Next, nail the back and then the roof into place. As the final step, drill two ¼-inch holes in the bottom for drainage.

Purple Martins

During the years that I have been studying birds, I have received more requests asking how to attract martins than on any other phase of bird-attracting. Many people interested in birds are desirous of having a colony of nesting martins about their gardens, but too often their efforts to attract them go unrewarded. They put up houses and find that they attract only starlings and English sparrows.

There isn't any magic formula that will guarantee success in attracting martins. However, there are two essential factors, if followed, that will provide the maximum enticement to migrating martins. They are (1) a properly constructed house and (2) a well-chosen location for erecting it.

I have had 100 per cent success in attracting martins to houses based on the design recommended by the U. S. Department of Agriculture. I believe this is the most practical and satisfactory martin house that has been designed, and would hesitate to recommend any other type. The illustrations and construction details that follow are based on this design. A few changes have been made in the methods of assembling in order to simplify construction.

The finished house should be erected in the open well away from all trees and buildings, on the top of a pole 15 to 20 feet in

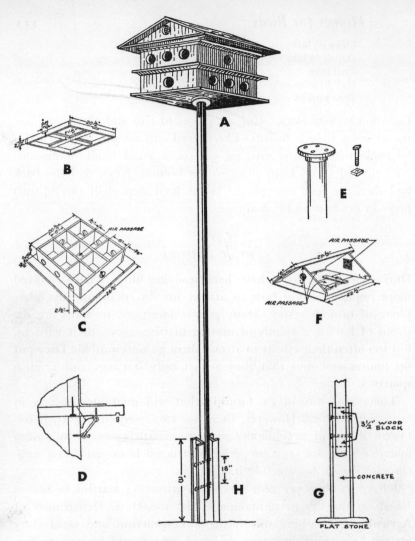

FIGURE 29.   MARTIN HOUSE SHOWING CONSTRUCTION DETAILS.

Floor of compartment	6 by 6 in.
Depth of compartment	6 in.
Diameter of entrance	2½ in.
Entrance above floor	1 in.
Height above ground	15 to 20 ft.

height. Martins feed in the air and return to the box in long, gliding swoops. Nearby obstructions would interfere with this normal flight pattern. Houses erected near a body of water offer an additional enticement. Light wires or phone wires located just beyond the approach pattern (100 feet or more) will be used extensively for resting, particularly by young martins just out of the box.

Martins are colony-nesting birds and, once established, will return to the same location year after year. For this reason, the supporting structure should be a permanent one. I prefer to use a 3-inch steel pipe with a threaded flange on top. This is mounted between two channel irons set in concrete (see illustration).

CONSTRUCTION DETAILS. I prefer to use redwood for all parts of the house with the exception of the foundation frame. For this I use ¾-inch oak for all pieces. Redwood is more durable than pine and is not so subject to warping. Paint the box white to reflect heat. Paint the roof and pole a dark green.

A. Completed martin house bolted to threaded flange on top of 3-inch steel pipe. Additional sections can be added to the house as the colony increases. The ½-inch steel bar (b) is for a ladder support to aid cleaning or dismantling. It also serves as a perch.

B. Foundation built of ¾-inch oak and fastened together with screws. The central cross is double thickness with the top piece notched into the outside frame. Center the flange (E) on the underside of the cross. Mark and drill corresponding holes. When bolting the flange to the foundation, use square-headed bolts and countersink the heads flush with the top side.

C. One of the nesting sections. The compartments are 6 by 6 by 6 inches, inside dimensions, and the bottom of the central compartment is left open as an air shaft. The compartment dividers are made of ½-inch boards. The bottom boards are nailed securely to the outside frame and dividers. This eliminates any need for iron L-braces as indicated in the original design. The bottom of the air shaft of the lower section should be screened to keep out sparrows, starlings, and wasps.

D. Porch detail of nesting section showing floor attachment by use of nails. The molding (m) fits about the top of the lower story; the screw eyes and hooks (s) fasten the units together; and the groove (g) is a ⅛-inch saw cut to prevent water from draining inward.

E. Threaded flange, to which the foundation frame is bolted, screwed on 3-inch steel pipe as supporting structure.

F. Roof section with one side removed to show central air shaft. Air also passes through a 1-inch slot under the eaves (screened to keep out wasps and sparrows) and through two screened holes in the ends. The actual roof is made of redwood siding notched on a table saw to give a flush fit with the slanting edges of the ends.

G. Positioning of 3-inch channel irons. Dig a hole 3 feet deep and 18 inches in diameter. Bolt the channel irons together against two 3½-inch blocks as illustrated. A 3-inch steel pipe has an outside diameter of 3½ inches. Use a level to get the channel irons in a true vertical position. Fill the hole with stones and concrete. Remove top block when concrete is set.

H. Mounting the pipe in channel irons. Insert the bottom bolt (½-inch by 5 inches) through the channel irons and pipe. Insert the top bolt through the channel irons only. This bolt acts as a stop when the pipe is pulled into position. The pipe can then be easily steadied while the top bolt is put through the channel irons and pipe.

The box can be put up in sections with a ladder resting on the bar (b).

Screech Owls and Saw-whet Owls

Of all the owls, the screech owl will accept man-made boxes most readily. Homes that are covered with bark or made of natural hollow logs are excellent. I have had the best results with the hollow-log type. Suitable logs can often be obtained from dealers in fireplace wood.

Screech owls frequent old orchards and open groves of trees and will accept boxes placed in these areas. Fasten the box rather high in a tree, preferably to the main trunk. If you live in the North-eastern section of our country, the same type of box and location may prove attractive to the saw-whet owl.

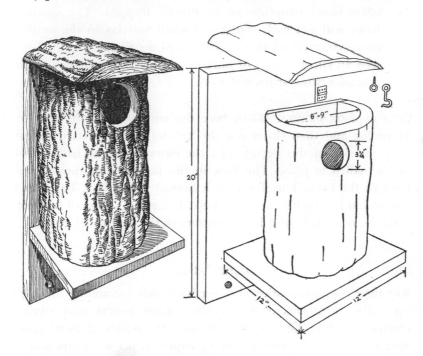

FIGURE 30.   LOG HOUSE FOR SCREECH OWLS AND SAW-WHET OWLS.

Diameter of cavity	8 to 9 in.
Depth of cavity	12 to 15 in.
Diameter of entrance	3¼ in.
Entrance above floor	9 to 12 in.
Height above ground	10 to 30 ft.
Boxes up by	March 1

Boxes not occupied by owls are used frequently by flickers, crested flycatchers, sparrow hawks, and nuthatches. Starlings and squirrels may also become competitors for these attractive homes.

Note. If you have a colony of purple martins nearby, I wouldn't advise encouraging sparrow hawks to nest in the same area. Normally, the sparrow hawk's main diet consists of small rodents and grasshoppers. However, a colony of martins offers many tempting meals already trapped. The sparrow hawk will pin both young and adult martins in the nesting compartments and then reach in and get them at will. I have seen an entire colony of purple martins destroyed by a single pair of nesting sparrow hawks.

CONSTRUCTION DETAILS. First, bore the entrance hole in your selected log and then chisel out the nesting cavity. Flatten or cut away the side of the log opposite the entrance so the back board can be nailed in place. The floor should be nailed to the log and through the back. The slab roof is hinged to the back board and fastened in front with a hook and eye. Put 2 or 3 inches of sawdust, shavings, or rotted wood in the bottom of the completed box.

Barn Owls

The most common nesting sites for barn owls are among the high supporting structures of barns, silos, water towers, and similar undisturbed buildings. They also nest in cavities of large trees. Sites meeting their specific nesting requirements are quite scarce, and for this reason, they will accept structures specifically designed for them.

The construction and erection of a home for barn owls is quite a major task. However, the owls' value as a means of rodent control makes our efforts exceedingly worth while when space and facilities are available.

Perhaps the simplest structure we can make consists of mounting a barrel-type house on top of a tall pole. Discarded light and telephone poles are good for this purpose. The house would probably be equally effective mounted in a large tree, but would be sub-

ject to occupancy by raccoons and squirrels. Metal guards can be
placed around poles, if necessary.

The house and structure plans that follow are based on those
used at the Aullwood Audubon Center near Dayton, Ohio.

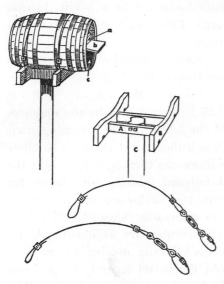

FIGURE 31.

HOUSE AND

MOUNTING STRUCTURE

FOR BARN OWLS.

SPECIFICATIONS AND CONSTRUCTION DETAILS. Exact specifications
cannot be given for this house and supporting structure, as they
will depend, for the most part, on the size of the barrel and the pole
selected. Some minimum measurements should be kept in mind.
The actual nesting cavity ought to be at least 18 by 18 by 18 inches,
preferably larger. Minimum diameter for the entrance hole is 6
inches. The height of the entrance may vary from 4 to 10 inches
above the surface of the nesting materials. A 4- to 6-inch-deep
mixture of rotted wood, shavings, and sawdust should cover the
bottom.

The barrel selected needs to be a heavy durable type — one that
will stand the extremes of wet and dry weather. Good oak barrels
may be obtained from a local co-operage firm or brewery.

In the accompanying illustration, one end of the barrel has been removed and replaced by a new partition (a) recessed about 8 inches. This partition should leave the top 6 inches open for an entrance. It can be fastened from the outside with nails or screws. About half the original end (c) is then put back in place. The two partitions (a and c) are then joined together by a board (b) that serves as a porch and landing area. This design affords maximum protection from inclement weather.

The size of the supporting structure is determined by the size of the barrel. All four pieces are cut from 2- by 8-inch pine planking. The two shorter pieces (A) will fasten to the pole (C) with lag screws, so their distance apart will be determined by the diameter of the pole at that point. Build the frame first by fastening parts B to parts A with lag screws. Notch the end of the pole to allow for the curve of the barrel. The frame can then be slipped over the end of the pole, squared, and fastened securely with heavy lag screws. With the pole resting on two sawhorses, the barrel can then be blocked into position in the cradle. Two $\frac{1}{4}$-inch cables, assembled with cable clamps and turnbuckles as illustrated, are placed over the barrel and secured in the notches in parts B. Tighten the turnbuckles to hold the barrel securely in position. Staple the cable to the top of the barrel to avoid any slipping. The completed house may then be painted a neutral color.

Erecting the completed structure will require the use of some tools and machinery. Companies specializing in the care and maintenance of trees usually have equipment capable of doing this type of work. Telephone or power companies may give you some friendly assistance.

Wood Ducks

With the cuting of our older forest trees, the natural tree cavities normally used by wood ducks as nesting sites are diminishing in number. Fortunately, wood ducks will accept man-made nest boxes, which, during the past few years, have contributed considerably to their increase in numbers.

Boxes erected in or near water are subject to constant dampness. For this reason, they should be made of durable wood and galvanized hardware. I have had excellent results in attracting wood ducks by using boxes based on a design used extensively by the Connecticut State Board of Fisheries and Game. The accompanying illustrations and specifications are based on this design.

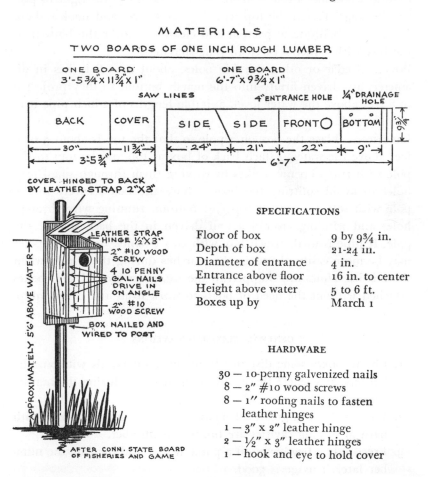

MATERIALS

TWO BOARDS OF ONE INCH ROUGH LUMBER

ONE BOARD
3'-5 3/4" x 11 3/4" x 1"

ONE BOARD
6'-7" x 9 3/4" x 1"

SAW LINES   4" ENTRANCE HOLE   1/4" DRAINAGE HOLE

| BACK | COVER | SIDE | SIDE | FRONT ○ | BOTTOM |

30" — 11 3/4"
3'-5 3/4"

24" — 21" — 22" — 9"
6'-7"

COVER HINGED TO BACK
BY LEATHER STRAP 2" X 3"

LEATHER STRAP
HINGE 1/2" X 3"
2" #10 WOOD SCREW
4 10 PENNY GAL. NAILS DRIVE IN ON ANGLE
2" #10 WOOD SCREW
BOX NAILED AND WIRED TO POST

APPROXIMATELY 5'6" ABOVE WATER

AFTER CONN. STATE BOARD
OF FISHERIES AND GAME

SPECIFICATIONS

Floor of box	9 by 9 3/4 in.
Depth of box	21-24 in.
Diameter of entrance	4 in.
Entrance above floor	16 in. to center
Height above water	5 to 6 ft.
Boxes up by	March 1

HARDWARE

30 — 10-penny galvenized nails
8 — 2" #10 wood screws
8 — 1" roofing nails to fasten
    leather hinges
1 — 3" x 2" leather hinge
2 — 1/2" x 3" leather hinges
1 — hook and eye to hold cover

FIGURE 32.   WOOD DUCK NESTING BOX.

CONSTRUCTION DETAILS

Box: The nesting box should be made of rough, unplaned lumber, preferably 1-inch stock. Use all galvanized nails, toe-nailed into boards to prevent drawing. Galvanized screws used in the corners will strengthen the box. *Do not* stain, creosote, or paint; leave a natural wood finish that will weather. Make the cover tight to prevent leakage. Fasten the top with leather hinges and hook-and-eye fastener to facilitate inspection and cleaning. Cover the bottom of the box with 4 inches of clean pine shavings.

Poles: Cedar or other durable poles, about 4 to 6 inches in diameter, are driven firmly into the marsh bottom so they project 6 to 8 feet above the water level. Suitable lengths of 2-inch pipe may also be used.

Erection: Place the box on a pole so that the top is about 5 or 6 feet above the water. Attach back of box at top and bottom to the pole with two 16-penny spikes by driving them through small lead holes to avoid splitting the board. Wire the box securely to the pole with soft #9 wire at top and bottom, running wire through holes and winding around a nail driven in the back side of the pole. If pipe is used, attach box with two U-bolts. Boxes and poles may be more easily placed in the marshes during the winter when there is ice. Holes are chopped in the ice, poles erected, and boxes attached without the need of boats to work from and carry equipment.

GENERAL RECOMMENDATIONS

1. Locate boxes some distance from shore on ponds with marshy borders, and where there will be open water during the nesting season.

2. Boxes will be of greatest benefit in areas where large trees with natural nesting cavities are limited in number.

3. Erect only a few boxes on a pond at first and increase the number later if usage is good.

4. Place boxes 50 to 100 yards apart.

5. In areas subject to flood, erect boxes above maximum flood level.
6. Fasten boxes securely to poles.
7. Stagger boxes — do not place in a straight line.
8. Do not have any light showing through bottom of box.
9. If boxes are erected on trees, be certain that branches do not obstruct the entrance hole.
10. Do not place entrance of box within jumping distance of raccoons and squirrels.
11. Rough lumber should be used in constructing boxes. If dressed lumber is used, tack a "ladder" of ¼-inch mesh hardware cloth between nesting material and opening to allow ducklings to climb out.
12. Boxes should not be placed where broods have little chance for survival.
13. Erect boxes not later than March 15 — earlier in the South.
14. Conduct a snapping-turtle trapping project in areas where these predators are abundant.
15. Inspect boxes annually to make any necessary repairs, clean out debris, and replace the shavings.

Shelters and Boxes for Roosting

Providing birds with protective shelters for winter roosting is one important phase of bird-attracting which is often neglected. As one might suppose, birds do seek the protection of tree cavities and dense foliage for roosting purposes. They will frequently use nesting boxes that have been left in place during the winter. Nesting boxes, however, are not nearly as satisfactory as structures specifically designed for this purpose. Unless nesting boxes are weatherproof, well cleaned, and have adequate drainage, they may do more harm than good. I have seen a whole brood of bluebirds frozen to the bottom of a nesting box after a night of cold, freezing rain.

Cavity-nesting species, especially, will accept roosting structures just as readily as they will nesting boxes. In fact, quite a number of the same species will roost together for added warmth and protection. The shelters of boxes may vary in size and design, but they should be waterproof and the inside perches staggered so that one bird does not roost directly above another. The entrance hole is placed near the *bottom* of boxes, rather than at the top. This allows the accumulated body heat to be retained within the boxes. All roosting facilities should be erected in a sheltered area and faced to the south away from prevailing winter winds. Use cat and squirrel guards around poles, if necessary.

The larger cavity-nesting species, such as the flicker and screech owl, prefer to nest singly. Nesting boxes make satisfactory roosting places for these birds.

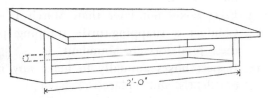

FIGURE 33.   ROOSTING STRUCTURES:
a shelter designed for use
against the side of
a building or under
the eaves of a roof;
roosting box for use
on pole or tree.

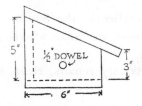

SPECIFICATIONS

Floor	8 in. by 8 in.
Back	9½ in. by 2½ ft.
Front	9½ in. by 22 in.
Sides	8 in. by 22-24 in.
Roof	9½ in. by 10 in.
Entrance	2½ in.
Dowel perches	⅜ in. by 4 in.

Construction Details

Roosting shelter. If available, use old, weathered, ¾-inch boards. If new lumber is used, stain with a wood preservative and allow to dry before erecting. Cut all pieces to size according to dimensions given in the illustration. First, nail the bottom to the back. Nail one end in place and insert the ½-inch dowel in the end hole. Nail the other end and then the roof in place.

This particular shelter can be made any length desired.

Roosting box. Construct in the same manner as you would a nesting box. Cut all pieces to size according to the listed specification. A deeper box may be made, if desired. Before assembling, determine positions for the ⅜-inch dowel perches. Drill ⅜-inch holes ½-inch deep; dip one end of each perch in wood glue and tap into holes with a hammer. Use galvanized nails to assemble the box and drive them in on a slant to minimize drawing and warping. Use weathered lumber, if possible. Otherwise, treat the box with a neutral-wood preservative. Do not paint.

CHAPTER X

HOW TO ATTRACT HUMMINGBIRDS

OF ALL THE BIRDS we may attract to our gardens, there is surely none other that wins our admiration and affections quite so completely as the hummingbird. Perhaps its diminutive size, the flashing gorget, or its aggressiveness strikes a quick and sympathetic response. Whatever the reason, the hummingbird has long been a favorite of birders everywhere.

The habits and requirements of hummingbirds differ considerably from those of other species. Their selection of nesting materials is quite specific; and the choice of food and the manner in which it is acquired are decidedly diverse. They are easily attracted by a supplementary food supply, but both food and feeders must be planned to meet their particular requirements. Undoubtedly, we will have greater success and enjoyment in attracting hummingbirds if we know more about them and cater to their specific needs.

The Ruby-throated Hummingbird

Ornithologists tell us there are approximately 500 different species of hummingbirds in the world, and all of these are found in the Americas. Of this vast number, only sixteen or seventeen species can rightfully be considered as part of our country's regular bird population. From this number, the ruby-throated hummingbird is the only one found east of the Mississippi River. The remaining varieties spend at least part of the year in the western or south-western parts of the United States. Fortunately for those of us who live in the East, the range of the ruby-throat covers a good portion of our country — from the northern borders of Maine south to Florida, and westward to Texas and the Plain States north to the Canadian border. It also summers throughout much of eastern Canada.

MIGRATION. A few ruby-throats are content to winter in southern Florida and Louisiana, but the vast majority of them continue on to Mexico, Central America, and Panama. Here they spend the winter with numerous varieties of other hummingbirds. With the coming of spring, they gather on the shores of the Ucatan Peninsula in preparation for their flight northward. On a given night, when conditions seem satisfactory, they will head out to sea on their non-stop flight of more than 500 miles across the Gulf of Mexico to the southern shores of the United States — a truly remarkable flight for a bird that weighs no more than ⅛ of an ounce.

The ruby-throat rests and feeds in our southern states, moving north with the warming of the land and the blooming of spring flowers. The male arrives in our gardens in late April or early May. The female follows in a week or ten days. They spread throughout the eastern United States and eastern Canada, going as far north as central Saskatchewan and the Gulf of St. Lawrence. With the coming of September, they begin their flight southward, gradually working their way to our southern coastline. Another nonstop flight of several hundred miles returns them to their winter home in another country.

NESTING. The male ruby-throat will defend his courting and nest-ing territory against all intruders most vigorously. He is pugnacious and fearless, and seems to enjoy a good scrap. No trespasser is too large or too ominous to deter his pressing attack. Even crows and hawks are subject to the rapierlike thrusts of his long, sharp beak.

Despite the ruby-throat's small size, his great speed and maneuverability make him a respected foe of all would-be intruders.

The courtship flight or air dance of the male ruby-throat is one of nature's most exciting displays. In long, swinging arcs, like the path of a huge pendulum, he flies back and forth, going higher and higher with each arc. As he passed, his gorget becomes an alluring glow of flashing red to his watching mate. One might think that such antics were the exemplification of a devoted and helpful mate. Such is not the case with the male ruby-throat. Once the courting period is over, the female assumes all the duties of nest building and rearing the young.

The nest is quite small, barely larger than a standard bottle cap, and is placed atop the horizontal branch of a tree. It is built of feltlike down gathered from ferns and other plants. The down is bound to the branch with spider webs and fine plant fibers. The outside of the nest is covered with lichens and bits of moss until it looks like just another knot on the tree branch. This expert job of camouflaging makes the finished nest extremely difficult to locate.

Two tiny white eggs are laid over a period of three to five days, and the young are hatched eleven to fifteen days later. The young remain in the nest approximately three weeks, during which time they subsist on a diet of partially digested insects — mostly tiny spiders and aphids. When they leave the nest, they are as large as their parents and soon ready to fend for themselves.

Plants Attractive to Hummingbirds

We have all noticed hummingbirds in our gardens, darting from one flower to another. They seem to be ever on the move, probing each blossom for its nectar and any tiny insects that it may have lured. Actually, the ruby-throat perches nearly as often as most other birds, dead twigs and phone wires being favorite resting places.

Certain flowers and colors have a special appeal to our eastern ruby-throats. They are particularly enamored by bright red and orange. Flowers with tubelike structures that retain an abundance of nectar are preferred. Fortunately, there are a great many flowers, both wild and cultivated varieties, that can be planted to make our gardens exceedingly attractive to hummingbirds.

In the spring we are suddenly aware of the male ruby-throat's arrival when we see him flitting about the early-blooming columbine. The orange-red blooms of the native variety are one of his favorites, and should be included in every garden planned to attract hummingbirds. The plant can be easily transplanted or grown from seeds. The Japanese flowering quince vies with the columbine for first honors. Its bright red flowers of early spring seldom fail to attract a number of male ruby-throats during their northern migration flight. These two flowers, columbine and flowering quince, along with azaleas, honeysuckles, larkspurs, weigelas, lilacs, and other early blooming varieties, may be instrumental in enticing some of these migrants to stay and nest within the confines of your garden.

As the summer progresses, numerous other flowers will prove equally attractive. Bee balm (*Monarda*) is one of the best. There are numerous varieties from deep red to near-white; all are good. Another favorite is the trumpet vine. It is a rapid-growing plant and thrives throughout the East. It is best planted about stone outcroppings, on fences, or on trellises. The trumpet vine should not be planted so that it can climb shingled or clapboard buildings. Its vigorous new growth will seek every joint and crevice. This often results in pulled shingles or boards, causing leakage and other damage.

All of the honeysuckles are liked by hummingbirds. Perhaps the preferred variety is the coral, or trumpet, honeysuckle, *Lonicera sempervirens*. Although not the most common of the honeysuckles, it is found in most all our eastern states. When in bloom, the flowers appear to be a miniature replica of those on the trumpet vine; however, they are a bit more delicate and colorful.

Other flowers particularly attractive to hummingbirds include petunias, nasturtiums, lilies, delphiniums, iris, cardinal flowers, scarlet sage, snapdragons, phlox, morning glories, and numerous additional species, many of which can be found in the list that follows.

There are also a number of trees which have a special appeal to hummingbirds. Outstanding among these would be the mimosa tree, *Albizzia julibrissin*. We usually think of this tree as being confined to our southeastern states. Actually, indications are that it will survive farther north than we might expect. I have seen fine, mature mimosa trees thriving well in Pennsylvania, New Jersey, and Connecticut. It is not unusual to see three or four ruby-throats about one tree at the same time, gathering nectar from the abundance of fragrant, pink blossoms. The horsechestnuts and buckeyes (*Aesculus sp.*) are also favored by hummingbirds, particularly the pink- and red-blooming varieties. The red buckeye, *Aesculus pavia,* native to the bottomlands of our southern states, is exceptionally good. If transplanted, it will also thrive in states considerably farther north than its listed range.

The plants included in the following list are all favorites of our eastern ruby-throat. The list is not intended to be a complete or all-inclusive one. Undoubtedly, there are other plants that may be equally attractive; this list, however, will serve as a reliable basis for planning hummingbird plantings.

PLANTS ATTRACTIVE TO HUMMINGBIRDS

azaleas (*Rhododendron sp.*)
beautybush (*Kolkwitzia amabilis*)
bee balm (*Monarda sp.*)
begonia (*Begonia sp.*)
cardinal flower (*Lobelia cardinalis*)
clematis (*Clematis texensis*)
columbine (*Aquilegia sp.*)
coral bells (*Heuchera saguinea*)
day lilies (*Hemerocallis sp.*)

flowering tobacco (*Nicotiana sanderae*)
foxglove (*Digitalis sp.*)
fuchsia (*Fuchsia sp.*)
geraniums (*Pelargonium sp.*)
gladiolus (*Gladiolus sp.*)
hawthorn (*Crataegus sp.*)
hollyhocks (*Althaea rosea*)
honeysuckle (*Lonicera sp.*)
horsechestnut and buckeye (*Aesculus sp.*)
Japanese flowering quince (*Chaenomeles japonica*)
larkspur (*Delphinium sp.*)
locust (*Robinia sp.*)
lupines (*Lupinus sp.*)
mimosa tree (*Albizzia julibrissin*)
orange tree (*Citrus sp.*)
petunias (*Petunia sp.*)
phlox (*Phlox sp.*)
pinks (*Dianthus sp.*)
royal poinciana (*Poinciana regia*)
sage (*Salvia sp.*)
scabiosa (*Scabiosa sp.*)
scarlet hamelia (*Hamelia erecta*)
scarlet runner bean (*Phaseolus coccineus*)
Siberian peashrub (*Caragana arborescens*)
snapdragon (*Antirrhinum sp.*)
spider plant (*Cleome spinosa*)
trumpet plant (*Campsis radicans*)
weigela (*Weigela sp.*)

Feeding Hummingbirds

Ever since the discovery that hummingbirds would accept an "artificial nectar" in the form of sugar water, thousands of people have been using this substitute food to attract them to their gardens. The hummers are quite fond of this sweet syrup, and will devour quantities of it daily. Until recently, the practice of feeding sugar water to hummingbirds was continued without any apparent reason for questioning its actual value. An extra food supply, always available, seemed to be an obviously sound conservation measure. However, studies and observations made during the past few years indicate that a continuous supply of sugar water may actually do more harm than good.

Sugar is 100 per cent carbohydrates — strictly an energy-producing substance. From the nutritional point of view, we know that proteins and minerals are essential to growth and survival. Experimental feedings in aviaries have proved that excessive amounts of sugar in the diet of hummingbirds will cause a critical enlargement of the liver. The greatest danger, it seems, would come during periods of drought when the natural food supply is at a minimum, or with young birds that become dependent upon the easily available sugar water. Actual accounts of young hummingbirds dying have been recorded, the cause of death being attributed to a continuous diet of sugar water. It would seem advisable, therefore, that those of us who are interested in attracting hummingbirds should resort to a safer and more nutritious food offering. Honey water is an acceptable substitute that meets these requirements quite precisely.

In addition to a high percentage of carbohydrates, honey contains substantial amounts of muscle-building proteins and minerals. It is a refined product of nectar — a natural hummingbird food.

To prepare the honey water for feeding, mix one part honey with three parts boiled water. Boiling the water kills bacteria and reduces the possibility of fermentation. Honey, in its natural state, will keep almost indefinitely. A bit of red food coloring may be added to the syrup to make it more enticing. This is especially helpful in establishing new feeders, as they are likely to be more quickly located by feeding birds. The honey syrup can be fed from any home-made or commercially manufactured hummingbird feeders.

A more elaborate hummingbird food is used in aviaries where the birds are entirely dependent upon prepared mixtures. The formula used in the New York Zoological Park is as follows:

    2 teaspoons Mellen's Food
    1 teaspoon condensed milk
    3 teaspoons honey
    2 teaspoons Ledinac (Lederle's Liver Protein Hydrolysate)
    8 drops Vi-penta
    4 inches beef extract (Measured from tube. Purchased from
        Difco Laboratories, Inc., 920 Henry Street, Detroit, Michigan)
    Add water to make one pint.

As this formula produces a balanced diet for captive birds, there is no reason to believe that it wouldn't be equally attractive to wild birds if presented in feeders about our gardens.

Hummingbird Feeders

There are many and varied types of feeders available for hummingbirds. Most of these can be purchased from garden centers, pet shops, or hardware stores. If they are not available locally, consult the list of dealers in bird-attracting equipment in the appendix, and write for their catalogs. Some feeders are so simple in design that they can be easily made at home from materials at hand.

One of the most practical designs for hummingbird feeders incorporates the principle of an inverted container with a small feeding hole at the bottom. As the syrup is eaten, a partial vacuum is created in the container which prevents the loss of syrup when the feeder is not being used. This type of feeder has the added advantage of less encroachment from ants, honey bees, and other insects than the open-top styles.

Attractive and practical feeders can be made from vials, test tubes, pill bottles, chemists' bottles, individual cream bottles like those used in restaurants, and similar small glass containers. The bottle-type feeder can be made more attractive by rimming the top with an artificial flower made from tin or plastic and painted a bright red. A bow of red ribbon tied about the neck of the bottle is often sufficient enticement to encourage the use of new feeders. Attach the completed feeders on individual stakes and place them in flower beds about your garden. If possible, place one or more feeders so they can be observed from indoors.

If ants become a serious problem about your feeders, spray the bottom foot or so of the stakes periodically with an insect repellent. Open-top feeders can be protected from honey bees and the larger insects by covering the openings with a coarse (⅛-inch) wire or plastic screening. Hummingbirds will feed through the screens.

FIGURE 34.   HUMMINGBIRD FEEDERS.

(A) Commercial type available from Audubon Novelty Co., Box 22, Rochester 16, N. Y.; (B) chemists' bottle; (C) small restaurant-

type cream bottle; (D) test tube with rubber stopper and two curved
pieces of glass tubing; (E) stained glass feeder available from Winthrop Packard, Salem 3, Mass.

Hummingbird Gardens

The surest way of attaining success in attracting hummingbirds is
to plant a section of your garden for this specific purpose. One or
two flower beds, a corner plot, or a border section will provide
sufficient space for this hummingbird garden. The garden, through
the selection and management of plants, should have a continuous
blossom from spring until fall. Plants can be selected from those
listed in this chapter. The addition of one or two artificial feeders
will make the garden more attractive.

The following planting plan for a hummingbird garden is presented as a suggestive guide. Your particular plan will, of course,
have to be based on the amount of space available and adapted to
your specific geographic location.

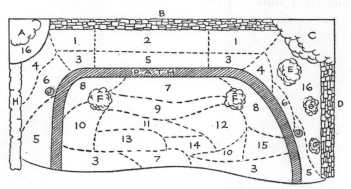

FIGURE 35.   SUGGESTED PLANTING PLAN FOR HUMMINGBIRD GARDEN.

A Japanese flowering quince (*Chaenomeles japonica*)
B Fence or stonewall: trumpet vine (*Campsis radicans*); trumpet honeysuckle (*Lonicera sempervirens*); clematis (*Clematis texensis*)

C　Beautybush (*Kolkwitzia amabilis*)

D　Trellis, side of building, or fence: Goldflame honeysuckle; clematis (*Clematis texensis*)

E　Tree: mimosa (*Albizzia julibrissin*)

F　Butterflybush (*Buddleia sp.*)

G　Weigela (*Weigela sp.*)

H　Hedge: Tatarian honeysuckle (*Lonicera tatarica*); Siberian peashrub (*caragana arborescens*)

J　Artificial feeders

(1) Columbine (*Aquilegia sp.*)

(2) Hollyhocks (*Althaea rosea*)

(3) Coral bells (*Heuchera saguinea*)

(4) Sage (*Salvia sp.*)

(5) Pinks (*Dianthus sp.*)

(6) Larkspur (*Delphinium sp.*)

(7) Petunias (*Petunia sp.*)

(8) Flowering tobacco (*Nicotiana sanderae*)

(9) Gladiolus (*Gladiolus sp.*)

(10) Bee balm (*Monarda sp.*)

(11) Foxglove (*Digitalis sp.*)

(12) Scabiosa (*Scabiosa sp.*)

(13) Snapdragon (*Antirrhinum sp.*)

(14) Phlox (*Phlox sp.*)

(15) Spider plant (*Cleome spinosa*)

(16) Lawn

CHAPTER XI

ATTRACTING
GAME BIRDS

A Product of the Land

GAME BIRDS, like all forms of wildlife, are a direct product of the land. They are dependent upon plants for food, or upon other animals and insects that are dependent upon plants. The problem of maintaining or increasing wildlife populations, therefore, becomes one of properly managing our soil, water, and vegetation. Farmers, ranchers, and other private landowners control most of our nation's wildlife. The manner in which their land holdings are managed will largely determine the success or failure of wildlife populations.

Why Management Is Necessary

Today we are on the threshold of a rapidly increasing human population. We are at the beginning of an urban sprawl that flows across our land like silt across barren ground. Homes, shopping centers, industries, highways, and countless boundaries have so parceled our land that, in most cases, the remaining areas are too small to maintain a natural environmental balance. The land mass capable of supporting wildlife becomes smaller with each passing year.

Man's land-use policy during recent decades has been based

[135]

largely on his desire for a quick cash crop from every acre of available land. This has resulted in intensive cultivation, drained wetlands, and eroded soil — factors not conducive to wildlife survival. If the pheasant, ruffed grouse, quail, and other forms of wildlife are to be attracted and supported in any appreciable numbers, the land must be managed with a skill similar to that used in planning a field crop. Natural homesites must be retained or restored, and an ample food supply made available throughout the year. Game management can and should be well integrated with crop production and soil-erosion control.

Factors Determining Game-Bird Populations

Certain factors in every environment limit the number of game birds that can be supported by the land. The number of quail, pheasant, or ruffed grouse that can survive in a given area is limited by the amount of food available and the extent of adequate cover. Man's activities, weather conditions, diseases, and predators are other factors that to some degree limit all wildlife populations.

Of all these limiting factors, only certain ones can be controlled by man. Occasionally, man's own activities can be altered in a manner that will be of immediate benefit to existing wildlife. If plowing can be delayed, natural foods will be available for longer periods of time. The time of mowing can be changed, on occasion, to favor nesting birds. The use of flushing bars on all mowing machines will save the majority of quail and pheasants nesting in hay fields. Weather conditions are a fixed factor, and there is little we can do to control wildlife diseases. Fortunately, the two major factors in limiting game-bird populations — food and cover — can be managed successfully by man.

Providing Food and Cover

There are two basic approaches to providing additional food and cover for upland game birds. Existing vegetation can be managed to produce more effective results, and new vegetation, in the form of grasses, legumes, shrubs, and trees, can be established by new plantings.

Cover is generally classified as any thicket of grasses, weeds, vines, shrubs, or trees that provide shelter and protection for wildlife. Game birds need cover to protect them from severe weather and to provide them with a means of escape when pursued by their natural enemies, such as owls, hawks, and foxes. They need cover in which to nest, rear their young, and to protect them while they rest and sleep. These conditions require various types of plant growth. A uniform type of planting tends to limit the number of species, or the number of individuals, or both, whereas a variety of growth will often increase the number of species and individuals.

An unfailing food supply must be available during all seasons of the year. If food is lacking for one season, birds will abandon the area. A natural food supply is often abundant on farmlands during the summer and fall months, but winter and early spring are the critical periods for game-bird survival. The planting of trees and shrubs, particularly those species that bear fruits and berries that persist throughout the winter, is an excellent way to obtain this continuity in the supply of food. Any gain in food production from this type of planting will be permanent.

Almost any farm or sizable tract of land has areas unsuitable for cultivation. Eroded gullies, fencerows, woodlots, stony areas, and roadsides are all excellent places for wildlife plantings. In addition to providing food and cover for game birds, these areas will attract numerous species of insect-eating songbirds and other forms of wildlife. These same wildlife plantings can be used effectively as a means of controlling soil erosion.

WORKING WITH NATURE. The management of existing vegetation is often the simplest way of improving one's land for wildlife. This can be as simple as plowing strips of idle land and allowing them to seed naturally to ragweed, foxtail grasses, and smartweeds — three of our most valuable food-producing plants for upland game birds. Fencerows and waste areas can be left undisturbed when producing desirable cover. Food-producing trees and shrubs can be favored by the elimination of less desirable species that may be competing for sunlight and space. This can be done by cutting and then painting the stubs with a commercial brush-killer to prevent respouting. Protecting woodlots from grazing stock is often all that is necessary to greatly improve their wildlife value. Water areas, although not of vital concern to most upland game birds, can sometimes be managed to benefit the earth-probing woodcock.

PLANTINGS FOR GULLIES AND ERODED AREAS. Gullies, ravines, and eroded drainage areas are the results of poor land management. Such erosion conditions can ruin fertile land for cutlivation and greatly decrease property values. Erosion can be controlled through plantings that will hold and rebuild the soil. These plantings need to be selected so they provide food and cover for game birds and other wildlife.

Most eroded areas are partially sterile and dry because of the lack of vegetation to hold the moisture and topsoil. Species that will tolerate these conditions should be planted. The following woody plants are recommended for plantings in gullies and deeply eroded areas:

American elder	jack pine
autumn olive	persimmon
basket willow	Russian olive
bayberry	shrub bushclover
bittersweet	silky dogwood
blackhaw	snowberry
black locust	Tatarian honeysuckle
chokeberry	Thunberg barberry
coralberry	Virginia pine
gray dogwood	wild plum
Hall's honeysuckle	woodbine

PLANTING FIELD AND ROADSIDE BORDERS. The narrow strips of land along farm roadsides and fields are often unproductive from the farmers' point of view. These odd strips of land can be well utilized for the benefit of wildlife. If properly planted, they can provide food and cover, prevent erosion, and be used as protective travel lanes by pheasant and quail when traveling from one area to another.

Existing borders often need little more than some selective cutting to make them attractive to wildlife. If the undesirable plants are removed, the favored species have a better chance to mature. Trees or shrubs planted in the thinned spaces will complete the border.

Perennial grasses and legumes are desirable for eroded field borders and sloping hillsides. Field borders along woodlots often have little crop-producing value, owing to excessive shade and the loss from soil of the nutrients and moisture that go to the far-reaching roots of the forest trees. These woodland borders, planted with a mixture of grasses and legumes, turn waste areas into good game-bird cover.

Wider areas, of 20 to 30 feet, can be planted with a double border — a background of woody plants and an inner border of grasses and legumes. The following grasses and legumes are recommended by the United States Department of Agriculture. While most of these plants are adaptable to the region covered by this book, your local county agent or the local office of the U. S. Soil Conservation Service should be consulted as to the plants best suited for your immediate area.

> alsike clover (*Trifolium hybridum*)
> birdsfoot trefoil (*Lotus corniculatus*)
> common lespedeza (*Lespedeza striata*)
> corn (*Zea mays*)
> domestic ryegrass (*Lolium multiflorum* and *L. perenne*)
> Japanese millet (*Echinochloa crusgalli* var. *frumentacea*)
> Korean lespedeza (*Lespedeza stipulacea*)
> orchard grass (*Dactylis glomerata*)

partridge pea (*Chamaecrista fasciculata* or *C. procumbens*)
reed canarygrass (*Phalaris arundinacea*)
sericea (*Lespedeza sericea*)
Sudan grass (*Sorghum vulgare* var. *sudanense*)
sunflower (*Helianthus annuus*)
tall catgrass (*Arrhenatherum elatius*)
timothy (*Phleum pratense*)
white sweetclover (*Melilotus alba*)

FENCEROWS AND HEDGES.   Modern wire fences allowing close cultivation are fast replacing the old rail fence and the bush fencerow.
This practice gives the land a clean and well-groomed appearance.
It also accounts for the great depletion of upland game in many
sections of the eastern half of our country. The bushy fencerow
provided food, cover, and ideal nesting sites for pheasants, quail,
and songbirds. Clean sweeps of land, divided only by long stretches
of wire fencing, do not offer any enticement to game birds or other
wildlife.

In addition to providing food and cover for wildlife, woody fencerows and dense hedges conserve soil. Hedges planted on the contour
of the land help prevent excessive washing of good topsoil. Hedges
also serve as windbreaks, lessening the effects of drying winds and
helping the soil retain more moisture.

Plants that will produce desirable hedges include dogwoods,
Thunberg barberry, autumn olive, multiflora rose, bicolor lespedeza, Tatarian honeysuckle, bayberry, highbush cranberry, arrowwood, and numerous other viburnums.

The U. S. Soil Conservation Service and similar state conservation agencies now widely recommend the planting of "living"
fences, such as can be attained by the use of multiflora rose. This
shrub is adaptable to most soil conditions and will not spread beyond a width of 10 feet. It is a hardy shrub that can stand mass
planting in plowed furrows, or it can be planted by hand. For a
thick fence, place the plants about one foot apart. Mulching will

keep the weeds down, hold moisture, and speed up growth. The fence will be cattle-proof in four or five years. Plants can be obtained from state conservation agencies or most any garden nursery.

A mature fence of multiflora rose is ideal for wildlife. It offers the best type of escape cover and provides nesting sites for both game birds and songbirds. The haws of the rose are an excellent source of emergency winter food. They are particular favorites of wintering mockingbirds, bluebirds, robins, and waxwings. Pheasants and quail will feed on the haws quite readily when more desirable foods are covered with snow.

WINDBREAKS. A double row of evergreens conifers bordered by low-growing shrubs protects the soil from wind erosion and excessive drying. The conifers furnish excellent shelter for wildlife, and the shrubs provide a variety of desirable foods.

Any of the conifers that grow well in your locality may be used. Cedars, pines, spruces, and hemlocks make excellent windbreaks. A mixture of low-growing shrubs, such as barberry, bayberry, coralberry, snowberry, and hazelnut, will make an ideal border around the evergreens.

PLANTINGS FOR THICKETS AND WOODLOTS. Waste areas, such as sink-holes and rock outcroppings, which have little value to the owner, can be made more attractive both to mankind and to wildlife by thicket plantings. By the same measure, woodlots can be improved for wildlife by the planting of selected trees and shrubs.

The island type of thicket is ideal for isolated waste areas. The center of the area is planted with some tall-growing evergreens or other trees beneficial to wildlife. The center is then surrounded with a ring of large shrubs and with an outer ring of smaller shrubs. Plants such as roses and dogwoods will noticeably enhance the beauty of an otherwise unattractive area.

Planned management of the farm woodlot is one of the best ways the landowner has of attracting ruffed grouse and other upland game birds. Such management calls for protection against fire and grazing. A woodlot provides poor pasture, and grazing depletes the forest of ground cover, small reproduction trees, and food-bearing shrubs. Large woodlots and forested areas can be improved by creating openings at varying intervals throughout the tract. Established shrubs should be protected and additional ones planted. Occasionally, when space permits, these open areas can be partially seeded to perennial grasses and legumes. If these openings are established as food-producing areas, the woodlot will support a greater abundance and variety of wildlife. The following trees and shrubs are recommended for thicket and woodland plantings by the United States Department of Agriculture. The woodland plantings should be confined to the open areas and roadside edges where they can receive sufficient sunshine to assure reasonable growth.

LOW SHRUBS

American hazelnut	fox grape
bayberry	mapleleaf viburnum
black chokeberry	swamp rose
climbing bittersweet	Thunberg barberry
coralberry	woodbine

MEDIUM TO HIGH SHRUBS

American crabapple	gray dogwood
American elder	highbush cranberry
arrowwood	nannyberry
bear oak	silky dogwood
blackhaw	Tatarian honeysuckle
flowering dogwood	wild plum

TREES

hackberry	red pine
mountain ash	sugar maple
Norway spruce	Virginia pine
persimmon	white cedar
red mulberry	white oak
red oak	white pine

FOOD PATCHES. The planting of food patches or feed strips next to protective cover is an excellent way of providing a supplementary supply of winter food for pheasants, quail, and songbirds. These plantings are most practical in areas where food is a limiting factor in game-bird populations. The plantings, alone, should not be considered as being sufficient to guarantee the survival of more birds. Natural foods and escape cover are of primary importance. Along bushy fencerows, abandoned fields, and woodland borders are good locations for feed strips. Avoid heavily shaded areas.

As with all farm crops, the ultimate yield of any food patch will depend largely upon soil preparation and fertility. The seed bed should be plowed and disk-harrowed. This will loosen the soil and help eliminate competition from undesirable grasses. If the soil is highly acid, liming may be necessary for good grain production. A generous application of barnyard manure or commercial fertilizer will assure a better crop. The fertilizer, and the lime, if used, should be disked into the ground before seeding.

A good seed patch will provide food from fall until spring. This requires a seed mixture that will produce plants in varying growth habits and seeding periods. The seed formula will vary according to geographical locations and soil conditions; however, there are certain seeds that are basic in most mixtures recommended for planting in the East. The millets are particularly attractive to quail and songbirds. Lespedezas are widely used for quail in the southeastern states. Buckwheat attracts doves, while field corn and soy beans are preferred by pheasants. Wheat, barley, and oats are valuable additions to any mixture. Plants such as Sudan grass and sunflowers give support to weaker plants and help keep their seed heads above snow level.

June is the preferable month for planting, as this allows time for maturing before frost. The mixture may be spread with a small hand seeder and disked under with a harrow.

Note. The game commission or conservation department of most states recommend food-patch formulas that have been tested and proved within their respective states. They will also give assistance regarding liming, fertilizing, amount of seed required per acre, and other information pertinent to your area. A request for their assistance will save you time and experimentation.

The following food-patch mixtures are those recommended by five representative states. Success will not necessarily depend upon strict adherence to these formulas, but they will serve as a basis or guide in planning your food patch.

RHODE ISLAND

golden millet	15 pounds
Sudan grass	5 "
rape	3 "
buckwheat	20 "
oats	15 "
amber cane	10 "
kafir corn	10 "
soy beans	10 "
vetch	10 "
sunflower	2 "

VIRGINIA

brown top millet	5 pounds
German millet	5 "
Brabham cow peas	9 "
iron cow peas	9 "
Korean lespedeza	20 "
Plainsman combine milo	20 "
buckwheat	10 "
dwarf Essex rape	2 "
Loredo soy beans	10 "
yellow mammoth soy beans	10 "

PENNSYLVANIA

(quail and songbirds — 1 acre)

broom corn millet, Japanese millet, or German millet	3.5 pounds
broom corn or Midland grain sorghum	2.5 "
amber sorghum	2.5 "
sunflower	1.5 "

NEW JERSEY

(late planting)

buckwheat	15 pounds
German millet	15 "
Sudan grass	15 "
soy beans	25 "
cow peas	25 "
rape	5 "

GEORGIA

One part each (by weight) of the following:
Korean lespedeza
brown top millet
partridge peas
Florida beggar seed, sorghum, or millet
cow peas or soy beans

Winter Feeding and Artificial Shelters

Winter feeding is one of the most effective ways of attracting and maintaining a permanent game-bird population. In areas lacking an adequate supply of natural food, or where deep snow covers the natural supply, artificial feeding during the winter months will enable the land to support a larger number of birds and may actually save many of them from starvation. Food put out for game birds needs to be protected from rain and snow and placed near escape cover.

GAME-BIRD FEEDERS.   The main purpose in using feeders is to keep
the grain off the ground so that it does not become moldy or con-
taminated. Also, the grain is better protected from rain or snow
and is less likely to be wasted. There are several types of feeders
that can be used for this purpose; the hopper-type feeder is best
for loose grains, and the spike-board is a simple method of providing ear corn.

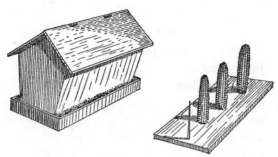

FIGURE 36.   GAME-BIRD FEEDERS.
hopper type for loose grains and spike-board for ear corn.

Hopper feeders can be made from boards as illustrated above, or
from nail kegs, barrels, or other sizable containers. Mash feeders
used by poultrymen are obtainable from most hardware stores and
feed dealers. Many of these are practical for feeding game birds.
Wire baskets make a practical container for feeding ear corn. They
can be made of chicken wire, but a more durable basket can be had
by using the wire-type trash burner available at hardware stores.
WHAT TO FEED.   In most sections of the United States, common
field corn is the ideal grain for winter feeding of upland game birds.
Corn is preferred by pheasants and, in the central and western
states, by prairie chickens and sharp-tailed grouse. It is also a good
winter food for quail and Hungarian partridges, particularly in the
finer cracked form. Corn can be fed in open, unhusked shocks that
provide a natural shelter, or from feeders placed under artificial
shelters.

Buckwheat is a proved favorite of game birds. It can be fed in

man-made feeders, or unharvested grain can be left in food patches
for winter foraging. Other grains acceptable for winter feeding include wheat, barley, rye, kafir, millet, and popcorn. These grains
may be fed as a mixture. A few visits to the feeding shelter will
soon reveal which grains are favorites. Place some grit or fine
gravel under the shelters in areas subject to prolonged periods of
ice and snow.

ARTIFICIAL SHELTERS. Regardless of the feed or feeder used, they
should be placed under protective shelter. In most instances the constructed shelter is most practical. Artificial shelters can be an effective conservation measure if they are properly constructed and
tended. This is especially true in northern areas where natural
shelter is rarely dense enough to protect grain from blowing and
drifting snow.

FIGURE 37.   LEAN-TO SHELTER FOR WILDLIFE COVERED WITH CORN
FODDER AND BRUSH.

In the construction of artificial shelters, consideration ought to
be given to the nearness of good protective cover and to the ease
with which birds can escape when pursued by enemies. Shelters
should never form a trap that makes quick escape impossible. The

food supply must be constant, as birds will become dependent upon it during periods of emergency.

Shelters may vary in type and design. An easily constructed shelter can be made by leaning shocks of corn fodder against the top wire of a fence. Corn fodder may also be used to form a shelter by placing it over the top of a small thicket of low shrubs. A lean-to shelter with three sides open provides good protection and at least two emergency exits. The top of the lean-to may be covered with brush, evergreen boughs, corn fodder, or straw.

Stocking Game Birds

The landowner with few game birds on his property may wish to release some initial breeding stock. This stock may be purchased from game farms or, in some states, may be procured through co-operation with the state game commission.

Stocking during the warm months when there is an ample supply of natural food is most successful. This procedure also gives stocked birds time to acclimate themselves to their surroundings before the severity of winter weather.

Actually, in most cases, stocking is not necessary and is apt to have only a small degree of success. If the food supply and cover available cannot support an increase in birds under natural conditions, it is unlikely that much of an increase will result from stocking additional birds. The easiest and most economical way to increase the game-bird population of an area is to manage the land so as to increase the natural food supply and desirable cover. This can be done through planting and other measures previously described in this chapter.

Assistance through Available Agencies

The landowner desiring to improve his property for the benefit of game birds and other wildlife can obtain valuable information and assistance through a number of agencies. Following is a list of agencies through which this information can be obtained:

local county agents
local office, U. S. Conservation
   Service
state game commissions

state agricultural colleges
U. S. Department of Agriculture
Wildlife Management Institute

CHAPTER XII

ATTRACTING WATERFOWL

THE COLOR AND LIFE of breeding or migrating waterfowl enhance the beauty and value of any stream, pond or marshland. Attracting waterfowl depends largely upon managing watered areas and adjacent lands in much the same way as land is managed for the benefit of game birds. Waterfowl have definite and distinctive requirements for food, nesting sites, brooding areas, and protective shelter. The nearer we can come to meeting these demands, the greater success we shall have in attracting ducks and geese to our favorite pond.

Ponds for Waterfowl

Before making any major changes in existing ponds, or before constructing new ponds, investigate your state laws concerning water rights. Most states have laws designed to protect the public against floods, dam failures, loss of water for grazing cattle, and so on. The state agency authorized to enforce these laws should be consulted and the necessary permits obtained for your particular type of proposed construction. This action may save you from future legal entanglements with your neighbors. This state agency may also be able to furnish you with valuable information concerning the construction and maintenance of ponds.

When planning for improvement or building of a pond, consider the requirements of the species most likely to be attracted. Plan to make the pond particularly enticing to the species known to inhabit or migrate through the region. In the eastern United States we do not have the large concentrations of numbers or species that are found in the western half of our country. In the East, the principal nesting species on inland ponds are the black duck, wood duck, and a scattering of mallards. There are other species, however, that will nest in the East, particularly in New England and coastal areas. A larger variety of species can be attracted during the migration season, when flocks come down to rest and feed.

Waterfowl traveling to or from their nesting or wintering grounds follow rather definite travel lanes. A great variety of shore birds, also, follow these same general routes and are attracted to pond areas for feeding and resting. In the East, the two main routes of travel are designated as the Atlantic flyway and the Mississippi flyway. There are many lesser flyways that lead into these two main arteries of travel, so that virtually all the eastern half of our country, with the possible exception of the mountain ridges, has, in varying degrees, spring and fall migrations of waterfowl and shorebirds. While most migrating species follow quite definite patterns of travel, there is rarely a season passes in any area that the unexpected or "rare" find does not add to the excitement of bird watching.

In general, local species will be attracted to areas that provide good nesting sites with ample space and food for rearing their young. Migrating flocks and individual birds will be attracted to areas providing an abundance of food, resting areas, and protection from storms.

Features of a Good Waterfowl Pond

In most instances, ponds can be constructed for multiple uses. The real need for pond construction may be necessitated by erosion, flood control, insufficient water for livestock, or personal reasons. Whatever the cause may be, most ponds can be made attractive to waterfowl with some forethought and planning. The features of a good waterfowl pond are somewhat flexible and can be applied in varying degrees to most any pond.

MARGINS AND DEPTHS OF PONDS.   Most species of waterfowl prefer shallow ponds with adjacent areas of marsh or grassland where food and shelter are adequate. Deep ponds without borders of vegetation will be attractive to the diving ducks — mergansers and golden-eyes. On land, a variety of habitats attract a diversity of wildlife. And so it is on water areas — a pond with shallow borders, some deep areas, and surrounded by an abundance of marshy vegetation will be appealing to the greatest variety of waterfowl. Ponds with facilities for controlling water levels are desirable. Plant growth can be managed and silting lessened.

FIGURE 38.   IN THE EAST, MOST POND DUCKS ARE "DABBLERS" PREFERRING PONDS WITH SHALLOW FEEDING AREAS.

FOOD AND COVER.   Vegetation is necessary in any pond area designed to attract waterfowl. It serves as the main source of food and provides cover essential to nesting and protection. If, in addition to attracting waterfowl, the pond is to be used for fishing and other forms of recreation, a compromise may have to be reached on the amount of vegetation that can be tolerated. Excessive amounts of vegetation provide easy escape for fingerlings and often result in ponds becoming overpopulated with stunted fish.

Perhaps cover is most important to waterfowl during the brood-ing period. Young ducklings are subject to easy predation unless they can be concealed quickly. Plants such as rushes, cattails, and pickerelweed will supply almost constant protection for the young until they are grown and ready to fend for themselves.

NESTING SITES. Black ducks and mallards prefer to nest on land. In the East, their first choice is the grass marshes along the coastline and along the many inland ponds and streams. If marsh grasses and plants are not available for nesting sites, they will seek a protective brush or woodland area. Small, brushy islands in ponds or streams are favorite locations.

Wood ducks nest in tree cavities, but their natural nesting sites are becoming increasingly scarce, and now they will nest readily in man-made nesting boxes (see Chapter 9). Other cavity-nesting ducks of the Northeast which have been known on occasion to use nesting boxes include hooded mergansers, American golden-eyes, and buffle-heads.

Canada geese prefer to build their nests on small, grassy islands. These small islands can sometimes be made more enticing by add-ing one or two cut evergreens for temporary nest protection.

FIGURE 39. LOAFING AREA
black ducks and mallards prefer sandbars; wood ducks will use partially submerged trees and logs.

LOAFING AREAS. Sandbars, partially submerged logs, and small islands are used extensively by waterfowl as a place to loaf and preen their feathers. Much of their time is spent there when they are not feeding. Any pond planned as a duck-breeding area should include a number of these loafing places. Islands may be left or built during the digging if they are above the proposed flood level. Sandbars can be constructed in shallow areas by the use of fill and gravel. In addition to waterfowl, sandbars and exposed edges will attract a variety of shore birds.

Pond Management

PROTECTION. One of the foremost essentials in pond management for nesting and migrating waterfowl is adequate protection for the pond and its watershed. Mainly, this means the prevention of excessive grazing and trampling of vegetation by livestock and avoiding silting of the pond by controlling erosion on run-off areas.

Ponds subject to constant use by cattle can be damaged in a number of ways, all detrimental to waterfowl management. Border vegetation is eaten or trampled to the ground, leaving the bare flanks exposed to wave action and erosion. Water is frequently kept turbid by wading cattle, thus preventing the growth of certain aquatic plants valuable as waterfowl food. Nests and nesting cover are destroyed. For these reasons, ponds in grazing areas should be fenced whenever possible. Allow ample space within the fenced area for nesting and feeding. Watering places can usually be developed along the overflow below the pond. If livestock must use the pond to obtain water, a small corner may be fenced off for this purpose.

Land erosion on the watershed will result in muddy waters and filling the pond with silt. Sound farming and forestry practices are the only ways of controlling this problem. All drainage land should be stabilized with a complete vegetative cover.

The following watershed practices will retard run-off waters and prevent excessive pond siltation.[1]

1 Your County Agent or Soil Conservation Service representative will assist you with these practices.

1. Keep areas immediately surrounding the pond covered with grasses, legumes, or shrubs. Do not cut or burn.
2. Plant a windbreak on the prevailing wind side of the pond. This will reduce wave action and provide a lee for waterfowl.
3. Avoid plowing on drainage slopes. When necessary, plow and plant on the contour.
4. Plant winter cover crops on cultivated areas.
5. Don't use steep slopes for grazing — plant with trees.
6. Plant all ditches and gullies with soil-binding plants.[2]
7. Terrace slopes, if necessary.

NATURAL FOOD AND COVER. Our concepts of wildlife management are based too often upon artificial practices — planting, feeding, and stocking. While these practices do have advantages and may be necessary in certain areas, wise management of existing resources will frequently produce more satisfactory results. This is particularly true regarding vegetation.

In the case of ponds and adjacent areas, enough natural vegetation is frequently available so that the need for artificial propagation becomes unnecessary. Keeping cattle from grazing around pond borders may be all that is needed to permit the growth and spread of plants already established.

Most farm ponds have a relatively permanent water level. Fortunately, where the margins are not too deep, this type of pond will support an abundance of aquatic food plants. Ponds with a controllable water level, however, can be more efficiently managed for waterfowl. Any new pond constructed for the purpose of attracting waterfowl should contain a device permitting flexibility in water level maintenance. Some of the best natural duck foods, such as smartweed and wild millet, thrive in areas that are flooded during part of the year. The water level is lowered in early summer and

---

[2] For a list of plants for planting ditches and gullies, see Chapter 11, "Attracting Game Birds."

then flooded to a shallow depth in the fall when the plants are ripe with seed.

PLANTING FOR WATERFOWL.   Planting affords the advantage of getting the specific plants desired established in a minimum length of time. The water level — whether it is permanent or controllable — will be a major factor in determining species to be planted. Before undertaking any extensive planting, analyze the pond area and find answers to these questions. What plants are already established? Are they beneficial to waterfowl? Is the water soft or hard? What is the natural range of the species to be planted? A preliminary survey of this kind will prove both timesaving and economical.

> *Note.* Most states have a Department of Natural Resources with one or more aquatic biologists on its staff. They are interested in waterfowl improvement projects and can provide valuable assistance in construction and management practices.

Plantings for inland ponds may be classified generally in eight divisions according to their growth habits and their benefit to waterfowl. The following figure and accompanying classifications are based on recommendations of the United States Department of Agriculture.

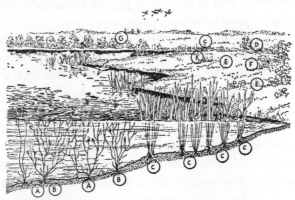

FIGURE 40.   PLANTINGS FOR THE POND AREA.

A Principally submerged plants, such as horned pondweed.

B Floating-leaved species of plants, such as longleaf pond-weed, act as oil does in reducing wave action.

C Rushes hold sediment and form vegetation on shorelines.

D Woody plants in the upper parts of the inlet and in gullies halt the flow of silt into the pond.

E A ground cover of grasses or legumes protects the upland adajcent to the pond and provides nesting sites for water-fowl.

F Small clumps of trees and shrubs are used by wildlife for shelter, and the fruits provide food.

G The windbreak protects the pond by reducing wave action and also provides shelter for wildlife.

Include two or more species of plants for each division illustrated. This will allow for variation in growth habits or maturing dates and provide food and cover over a longer period of time. Most marsh and aquatic plants spread quite rapidly when planted in a suitable environment; therefore avoid overplanting, particularly in the pond itself. Dense plantings may be necessary to control shore erosion or the flow of silt.

In general, conditions favorable for planting for waterfowl would include fertile bottom soils and moderately hard water with some movement. Stagnant or polluted waters are unfavorable. Deep ponds with steep wooded banks have little attraction for waterfowl. Ponds that can be drained are more easily planted than those that maintain a constant water level. If there are fish in the pond, the pond may be partially drained and still retain the fish. Plant the wet bottom immediately with the desired seeds or plants, and keep it moist. Occasional flooding may be necessary during prolonged periods of drought.

When it is necessary to plant directly in the water, confine the planting to shallow areas not exceeding 3 or 4 feet in depth. When the water is too deep for ordinary methods of planting and a boat must be resorted to, wrap the root masses in clay balls or burlap. A small pebble may be included as an anchor, or they can be pinned down with forked sticks.

Seeds planted in water need to be thoroughly soaked so they will sink immediately and not be washed away with the current.

WEED CONTROL. The question of what constitutes a weed or a desirable plant is often a matter of personal opinion. However, from the pond-management point of view, there are a number of plants which spread rapidly and have comparatively little wildlife value which can be rightfully classified as weeds. Cattail, buttonbush, water-hyacinth, and water-chestnut are notable examples of plants in this category. Better waterfowl habitat can often be developed by the elimination of dense weed stands and replanting the area with more desirable species. New plantings cannot compete successfully with established stands of natural weed materials. The predominance of these materials is the result of conditions ideal for climactic growth.

There are a number of ways to control or eliminate objectionable pond and marsh plants. Most plants that emerge to heights above the water level can be eliminated by flooding. This is undoubtedly the easiest method in areas where control structures make it feasible. One or more growing seasons may be necessary to accomplish the desired results. Plants such as the cattail, spadderdock, and cutgrass can be controlled by mowing, preferably at the latter part of the flowering season.

A variety of chemicals are now used to control aquatic vegetation. Their extensive use is not recommended without the guidance of a competent wildlife technician. There is no doubt that certain chemicals are effective weed-control agents; however, it is equally important that we consider the over-all effect upon the ecology of our environment. Your State Game or Conservation Department will help with this analysis.

ENEMIES OF WATERFOWL. On inland ponds, the greatest enemy of waterfowl is the snapping turtle. They inhabit most ponds throughout the East, but their presence is often difficult to detect. Their toll upon young waterfowl is undoubtedly far greater than is suspected.

These large turtles can be removed from ponds by special traps and baited trotlines. Most local game wardens have a supply of turtle traps and will co-operate in eliminating these predators from waterfowl breeding areas.

As with all forms of wildlife, nesting and brooding waterfowl are subject to a certain amount of natural predation. Crows, hawks, cats, mink, foxes, raccoons, and snakes, in addition to snapping turtles, prey, in varying degrees, upon waterfowl. Occasional control measures may be necessary to keep this depredation within reasonable limits.

Plants for Ponds and Pond Areas

The following list of plants represents some of the more common and successful species of the eastern United States as tested and proved by government agencies and private landowners.

FIGURE 41.

ARROWLEAF (*Peltandra virginica*)

The seeds of arrowleaf are eaten by many species of waterfowl, but are a particular favorite of wood ducks. The projecting leaves provide shelter and aid in reducing wave action on shorelines. The plant may be propagated in the spring or fall by roots, plants, or seeds.

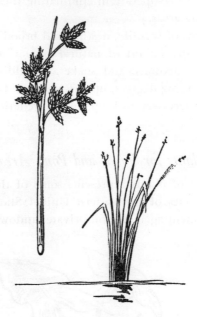

FIGURE 42.

BULRUSHES (*Scirpus*)

Common three-square *S. americanus:* The common three-square rush is one of our most valuable marsh plants. It provides excellent food and cover for waterfowl. The natural range of this plant includes all Eastern United States. Root stocks or plants are best set out in spring or fall.

Hard-tem *S. acutus:* One of the best plants for the protection of eroding dams and shorelines. This rush stands well in the winter. It provides good food, cover, and nesting sites for waterfowl and shore birds. Does well in northern areas.

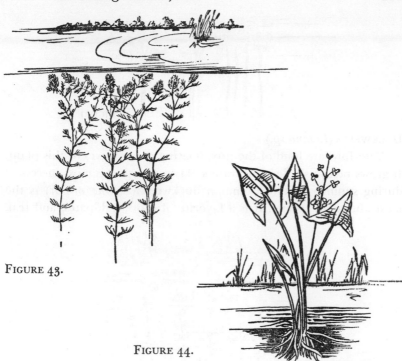

FIGURE 43.

FIGURE 44.

COONTAIL (*Ceratophyllum demersum*)

The underwater parts of this plant harbor small aquatic life valuable as food for waterfowl. Coontail may be introduced by planting masses of the bushy tips directly on still water during the summer months. It spreads rapidly and should not be allowed to crowd out other valuable species. Avoid overplanting.

DUCK POTATO (*Sagittaria heterophylla, S. Cuneata, S. latifolia,* and *S. platyphylla*)

The tubers of the duck potato are known to be eaten by sixteen kinds of ducks. Varieties of this plant can be found throughout most of the country. The range of the Delta duck potato (*Sagittaria platyphylla*) is confined to the South and Southeast. Tubers may be planted in the spring or fall.

FIGURE 45.

DUCKWEEDS (*Lemna sp.*)

Waterfowl are fond of the tiny, floating green leaves of this plant. It grows best in shaded still waters. Transplanting is most successful during summer or fall. Common duckweed (*Lemna minor*) is the most abundant species. It is a favorite of coots, baldpates, and teal.

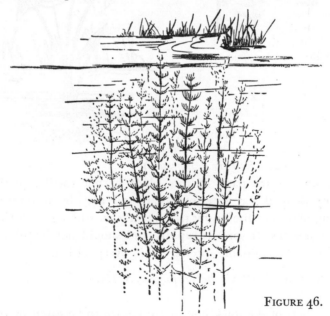

FIGURE 46.

MUSKGRASSES (*Chara sp.*)

The muskgrasses are recommended for use in water with a high lime content. They are usually classified with the algae and are a favorite waterfowl food, especially when bearing an abundance of minute sporelike reproductive structures. Plant masses may be moved in summer or fall.

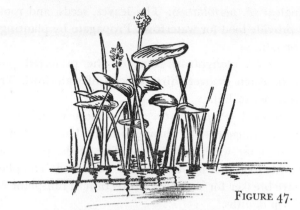

FIGURE 47.

PICKERELWEED (*Pontederia cordata*)

The range of the pickerelweed is confined chiefly to the eastern states. The seeds are eaten by at least ten varieties of ducks. This plant can be introduced into a pond by seeds, roots, or plants. It spreads rapidly and should be planted in moderate amounts.

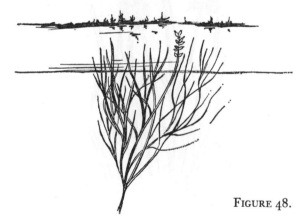

FIGURE 48.

PONDWEEDS (*Potamogeton sp.* and *Naias flexilis*)

Bushy pondweed (*Naias flexilis*): A shallow-water plant adaptable to a wide variety of soil and water conditions. Twenty species of ducks are known to feed on the seed masses. Transplant before the seeds disappear.

Claspingleaf (*P. perfoliatus*): The leaves, seeds, and roots of this plant all provide food for waterfowl. Propagate by planting roots in summer or fall.

Ribbonleaf (*P. epihyrdrus*): One of the preferred pondweeds, known to be eaten by over thirty species of waterfowl. Transplant roots in summer or fall.

Sago pondweed (*P. pectinatus*): The most valuable of all the pondweeds. Its range extends throughout the United States and it is adaptable to most water conditions. The seeds, plants, and rootstocks provide food that is sought by all waterfowl. The plant is also a good wave-breaker for shoreline protection. Transplant roots during the warm months.

FIGURE 49.

REEDS (*Phragmites communis*)

Reeds are excellent plants for holding silt at pond inlets. Their range extends over the entire country. The dense growth provides good cover. Reeds spread rapidly and will crowd out other valuable plants if not controlled. Transplant rootstocks in summer or fall.

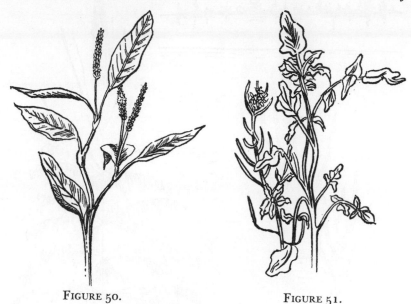

FIGURE 50.   FIGURE 51.

SMARTWEEDS (*Polygonum sp.*)

There are many varieties of smartweeds found throughout the United States. They grow in moist areas — some species in alkaline soils, others in soil that are predominantly acid or brackish. Smartweeds are particularly valuable as producers of food for waterfowl. The better species include: dotted (*P. punctatum*): largeseed (*P. pennsylvanicum*); marsh (*P. muhlenbergii*); nodding (*P. lapathifolium*); water (*P. amphibium*).

Smartweeds may be started by planting seeds or by transplanting clumps of growing plants. They can often be found growing naturally on freshly flooded land.

WATERCRESS (*Sisymbrium nasturtium-aquaticum*)

Watercress thrives best in the cool, shallow, spring waters of northern areas. Waterfowl are fond of the small, tender green leaves. Also eaten by upland birds. It is best introduced by transplanting the entire plants.

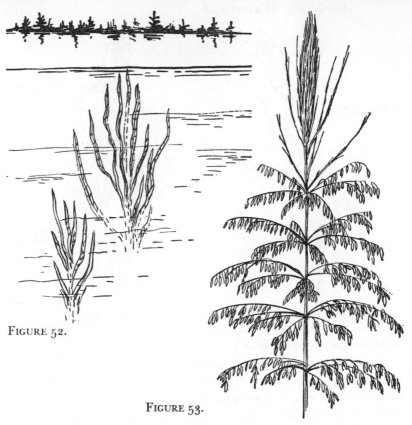

FIGURE 52.

FIGURE 53.

WILD CELERY (*Vallisneria spiralis*)

This is one of the better plants for the north-central and north-eastern states. The submerged foliage, tubers, and roots are avidly eaten by many kinds of ducks. It grows best in water with a slight current. Wild celery may be introduced by planting seeds, winter buds, or rootstocks.

WILD RICE (*Zizania aquatica*)

This plant does well in shallow lakes and fresh-water streams throughout the East. It is an excellent duck food and provides good cover. For best results in propagation, the novice planter should purchase seeds from a commercial grower. The fertility of seed stock is maintained through proper moisture and temperature control.

Grasses and Legumes for Pond Areas

Freshly graded areas, bare earthen dams, and the upland immediately adjacent to a pond must be planted with a thick vegetation if the pond is to be kept free of silt. The following grasses and legumes are recommended for this purpose:

GRASSES: bluegrasses (*Poa sp.*); timothy (*Phleum pratense*); orchard grass (*Dactylis glomerata*); reed canarygrass (*Phalaris arundinocae*).
LEGUMES: lespedezas (*Lespedeza sp.*); vetch (*Vicia sp.*); clovers (*Trifolium sp.*); partridge peas (*Chamaecrista sp.*) (southern areas).

CHAPTER XIII

BIRDS IN
THE SMALL GARDEN

A GARDEN CAN BE attractive to birds without sacrificing beauty or formality. Although the gardener's primary purpose may be to create an effectual style of landscape, a little thought as to the requirements of birds will add color, life, and song to his garden. Regardless of the style of development, there are many plants that will fulfill the gardener's needs and at the same time provide food and homes for birds. Garden accessories used for contrast and design may well include a birdbath or fountain where birds may drink or bathe. Posts, arbors, trellises, and pergolas provide ideal locations for nesting boxes and feeding trays.

A Plan for Your Garden

Many people find that much of the real fun and excitement in attracting birds is to be found in the planning and management of their gardens for this specific purpose. Obviously, feeding, planting, and providing nesting boxes will attract additional birds, but the results will be much more gratifying if these projects are based on a predetermined plan.

While planting to provide food and cover is the most essential part of any extensive bird-attracting program, there are many other factors that should be given consideration in the development of your plan. These would include: facilities for an adequate water supply for drinking and bathing purposes; a variety of properly designed and placed nesting boxes; a continuous winter feeding program; and trails or observation points from which your endeavors can be enjoyed.

Perhaps the best way to start your plan would be to take an inventory of the plants, nesting boxes, water facilities, etc., that already contribute to your objective. These can be spotted on a scale map and used as a basis for future planning. Once this is accomplished, then you can decide just how you would like to develop each section of your garden.

You will soon discover that your map is primarily a planting diagram. This is the time to decide on the location of future paths and observation points so that planting can be planned accordingly. The locations of birdbaths, nesting boxes, and feeding stations can be changed periodically as the planting mature.

Planting

Of all the endeavors we can make to attract birds to a small garden, the most effective is planting. Plants provide nesting sites, food, and cover and often trap enough water for drinking and bathing.

The variety of trees, shrubs, vines, or flowers selected for garden planting will depend upon the size and location of the land and upon the style of landscaping planned by the gardener. Often in this choice the concern of birds is a secondary matter. With a beautiful garden as the desired result, plants are chosen according to size, shape, color of foliage, flowers, or fruit, and their over-all contribution toward the desired result. Therefore the plants recommended in this chapter are species that can be used effectively in garden landscaping and at the same time be inviting to birds.

Trees and shrubs need not be berry- or fruit-bearing types in order to be attractive to birds. For example, the lilac provides little in the way of food other than the insects it attracts, but it serves as an ideal nesting place for robins and catbirds. This is true of many plants found in our gardens. Fortunately, many of the ornamental species so widely used in gardening provide food, cover, and desirable sites for nesting.

The plants included in the following lists are arranged according to their value to the gardener; but all plants listed are in some way beneficial to birds.

Plants for Dry Soils

DECIDUOUS TREES

box elder (*Acer negundo*)
gray birch (*Betula populifolia*)
hackberry (*Celtis occidentalis*)
red oak (*Quercus rubra*)
scarlet oak (*Quercus coccienea*)
wild cherry (*Cerasus serotina*)

EVERGREEN TREES

black spruce (*Pisea nigra*)
pitch pine (*Pinus rigida*)
red cedar (*Juniperus virginiana*)
red pine (*Pinus resinosa*)
white pine (*Pinus strobus*)

DECIDUOUS SHRUBS

bayberry (*Myrica carolinensis*)
beach plum (*Prunus maritima*)
buckthorn (*Rhamnus cathartica*)
bush clover (*Lespedeza bicolor*)
coralberry (*Symphoricarpos vulgaris*)
huckleberry (*Vaccinium corymbosum*)
panicled dogwood (*Cornus paniculata*)
snowberry (*Symphoricarpos racemosus*)

EVERGREEN SHRUBS

bearberry (*Arctostaphylus uva-ursi*)
common juniper (*Juniperus communis*)
Japanese spurge (*Pachysandra terminalis*)

Plants for Moist Soils

TREES

American elm (*Ulmus americana*)
larch (*Larix leptolepis*)
pin oak (*Quercus palustris*)
river birch (*Betula nigra*)
sour gum (*Nyssa sylvatica*)
striped maple (*Acer pennsylvanicum*)
weeping willow (*Salix babylonica*)
white spruce (*Picea canadensis*) (*alba*)

SHRUBS

arrowwood (*Viburnum dentatum*)
black chokeberry (*Pyrus nigra*)
elderberry (*Sambuccus canadensis*)
inkberry (*Ilex glabra*)
red chokeberry (*Pyrus arbutifolia*)
red osier (*Cornus stolonifera*)
silky cornel (*Cornus sericea*)
spicebush (*Laurus benzoin*)
winterberry (*Ilex verticillata*)
withe rod (*Viburnum cassinoides*)

Plants for the Seashore

DECIDUOUS TREES

beach plum (*Prunus maritima*)
honey locust (*Gleditsia triacanthos*)
scarlet oak (*Quercus coccinea*)
white poplar (*Populus alba*)

EVERGREEN TREES

American holly (*Ilex opaca*) (south of New Jersey)
jack pine (*Pinus banksiana*)
pitch pine (*Pinus rigida*)
red cedar (*Juniperus virginiana*)
red spruce (*Picea rubra*)
Scotch pine (*Pinus sylvestris*)
Thayer's yew (*Taxus cuspidata thayerae*)

SHRUBS

bayberry (*Myrica carolinensis*)
buffaloberry (*Shepherdia argentea*)
common privet (*Ligustrum vulgaris*)
Japanese rugosa (*Rosa rugosa*)
sand cherry (*Cerasus pumila*)
wild rose (*Rosa lucida*)

Trees and Shrubs with Colored Fruits

RED FRUITS

bird cherry (*Cerasus pennsylvanica*)
cockspur thorn (*Crataegus crusgalli*)
common barberry (*Berberis vulgaris*)
flowering dogwood (*Cornus florida*)
hawthorn (*Crataegus nitida, C. punctata*)
highbush cranberry (*Viburnum opulus*)
Japanese barberry (*Berberis thunbergi*)
Japanese rose (*Rosa rugosa*)
meadow rose (*Rosa glanda*)
mountain ash (*Sorbus americana, S. aucuparia*)
scarlet haw (*Crataegus mollis*)
scarlet thorn (*Crataegus coccinea*)
Tatarian honeysuckle (*Lonicera tatarica*)
Washington thorn (*Crataegus cordata*)
winterberry (*Ilex verticillata*)

BLUE FRUITS

arrowwood (*Viburnum dentatum*)
blueberry (*Vaccinium corybosum, V. pennsylvanicum*)
honeysuckle (*Lonicera coerulea, L. villosa*)
sheepberry (*Viburnum lentago*)
silky cornel (*Cornus sericea*)
withe rod (*Viburnum cassinoides*)

WHITE FRUITS

common red osier (*Cornus stolonifera*)
red-twigged dogwood (*Cornus alba*)
snowberry (*Symphoricarpos racemosus*)
white-fruited dogwood (*Cornus candidissima*)

BLACK FRUITS

black chokecherry (*Pyrus nigra*)
black haw (*Viburnum prunifolium*)
buckthorn (*Rhamnus cathartica*)
common privet (*Ligustrum vulgaris*)
elderberry (*Sambucus canadensis*)
inkberry (*Ilex glabra*)
maple-leaved viburnum (*Viburnum acerifolium*)
wayfaring tree (*Viburnum lantana*)

YELLOW FRUITS

buffaloberry (*Shepherdia argentea*)
goumi (*Elaeagnus longipes*)
oleaster (*Elaeagnus augustifolia*)
small-flowered honeysuckle (*Lonicera minutiflora*)
yellow-fruited honeysuckle (*Lonicera Ruprechtiana xantho-carpum*)
yellow-fruited Tatarian honeysuckle (*Lonicera tatarica fructo lutea*)
yellow-fruited viburnum (*Viburnum Opulus xanthocarpum*)

Plants with Attractive Autumn Foliage

TREES

American beech (*Fagus ferruginea*)
flowering dogwood (*Cornus florida*)
oak (*Quercus sp.*)
red maple (*Acer rubrum*)
sour gum (*Nyssa sylvatica*)
sugar maple (*Acer saccharum*)
sweet gum (*Liquidambar styraciflua*)
Washington thorn (*Crataegus cordata*)

SHRUBS

alternate-leaved dogwood (*Cornus alternifolia*)
blueberry (*Vaccinium corymbosum, V. pennsylvanicum*)
burning bush (*Euonymus atropurpureus*)
chokeberry (*Pyrus nigra, P. arbutifolius*)
flowering currant (*Ribes aureum*)
Japanese barberry (*Berberis thunbergi*)
panicled dogwood (*Cornus paniculata*)
viburnums (*Viburnum sp.*)

City and Suburban Gardens

If you live in or near the city and are fortunate enough to have sufficient land for a small garden, you, too, can share in the joy of bird watching. Your garden may appear as a green oasis to migrant flocks in the spring and fall as they wing their way over barren acres of streets and buildings. Thrushes will pause in their southward journey to feed upon the red berries of the flowering dogwood or mountain ash as fall flights of warblers busy themselves about the coloring foliage. In the spring, visiting warblers and vireos will feast upon insects about shrubs and flowers; robins will probe the lawn in search of earthworms; and from the trees will come the spring song of new and strange visitors.

A shrubbery border or bushy corner may entice a variety of species to stay and rear their families in your garden. Catbirds, brown thrashers, song sparrows, chipping sparrows, cardinals, and yellow warblers are fond of such places. The garden border will make a more inviting home if it is not too even and formal in appearance. A variety of garden shrubs, including forsythia, lilac, barberry, viburnum, hydrangea, mock orange, privet, spiraea, and others, makes an attractive informal border that is especially appealing to birds. The following illustration shows an informal border designed for immediate effect and succession of bloom. An occasional small tree adds contrast and helps accent the sky line.

If planting a complete border is not practical, a similar arrangement can be made in one or more corners of the garden. Two or three trees with contrasting foliage, surrounded by shrubs of varying heights, will make a corner attractive to man and birds.

Adverse growing conditions are sometimes encountered in city areas. Where there is poor soil, lack of water, and a prevalence of smoke, dust, and gases, only the most hardy species of plants will survive. Where such conditions are encountered, plants selected from the following list will assure a greater degree of successful growth:

Plants Tolerant of City Conditions

DECIDUOUS TREES

Cockspur thorn (*Crataegus crusgalli*)
Crabapple (*Pyrus floribunda, P. baccata*)
English hawthorn (*Crataegus oxycantha*)
Hackberry (*Celtis occidentalis*)
Horsechestnut (*Aesculus hippocastanum*)
Mulberry (*Morus alba, M. tatarica*)
Norway maple (*Acer platanoides*)
Pin oak (*Quercus palustris*)
Tree of heaven (*Ailanthus glandulosus*)
White ash (*Fraxinus americana*)

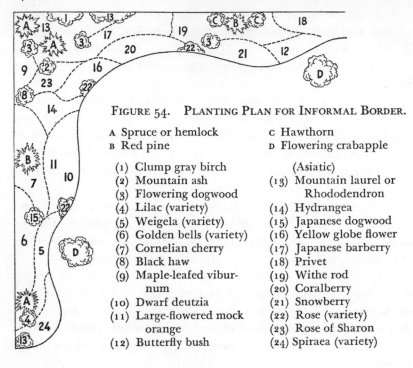

FIGURE 54. PLANTING PLAN FOR INFORMAL BORDER.

A Spruce or hemlock   C Hawthorn
B Red pine   D Flowering crabapple

(1) Clump gray birch   (Asiatic)
(2) Mountain ash   (13) Mountain laurel or
(3) Flowering dogwood   Rhododendron
(4) Lilac (variety)   (14) Hydrangea
(5) Weigela (variety)   (15) Japanese dogwood
(6) Golden bells (variety)   (16) Yellow globe flower
(7) Cornelian cherry   (17) Japanese barberry
(8) Black haw   (18) Privet
(9) Maple-leafed vibur-   (19) Withe rod
     num   (20) Coralberry
(10) Dwarf deutzia   (21) Snowberry
(11) Large-flowered mock   (22) Rose (variety)
     orange   (23) Rose of Sharon
(12) Butterfly bush   (24) Spiraea (variety)

EVERGREEN TREES

Arborvitae (*Thuja occidentalis*)
Austrian pine (*Pinus austriaca*)
Blue spruce (*Picea pungens kosteri*)
Colorado spruce (*Picea pungens*)
Japanese yew (*Taxus cuspidata capitata*)
Red cedar (*Juniperus virginiana*)
Scotch pine (*Pinus sylvestris*)

SHRUBS

Amur honeysuckle (*Lonicera maacki*)
Coralberry (*Symphoricarpos vulgare*)
Dwarf deutzia (*Deutzia gracilis*)
Golden bell (*Forsythia fortunei, F. intermedia, F. suspensa*)

Gray dogwood (*Cornus racemosa*)
Highbush cranberry (*Viburnum trilobum*)
Japanese barberry (*Berberis thunbergi*)
Privet (*Ligustrum sp.*)
Red osier (*Cornus stolonifera*)
Snowberry (*Symphoricarpos racemosus*)
Tatarian honeysuckle (*Lonicera tatarica*)
Weigela (*Weigela sp.*)
Withe rod (*Viburnum cassinoides*)
Yellow globe flower (*Kerria japonica*)

Country Gardens

Country gardens are often larger than those in suburban areas and usually have the advantage of being surrounded by land not too densely settled. In the fields, meadows, and woodlands bordering the country garden many kinds of birds feed, build their homes, and rear their young. Many of these bird neighbors can be attracted to a garden that has been planned to provide them with food, water, cover, and the kinds of places in which they like to nest.

The environment surrounding a country home lends itself well to the use of a wider variety in planting. In addition to the trees and shrubs recommended for city and suburban use, more native or "wild" species can be used. More and larger-growing trees can be included.

The viburnums are excellent shrubs to include in borders or other types of group plantings. They produce an abundance of fruit that lasts well into the winter months. One of the most common varieties, maple-leaved viburnum (*Viburnum acerifolium*), is also one of the most attractive and beneficial species in the group. It produces clusters of dark-blue berries relished by many birds, and adds varying shades of lavender and purple to the autumn foliage. The black haw (*Viburnum prunifolium*) produces large clusters of blue-black fruit favored by robins and cedar waxwings.

The seemingly translucent red berries of the highbush cranberry (*Viburnum trilobum*) are also excellent winter provender for the waxwings. Arrowwood (*Viburnum dentatum*) and nannyberry (*Viburnum lentago*) are good food-producing varieties. Species of birds known to eat the fruits of viburnums include the cedar waxwing, robin, flicker, hermit thrush, bluebird, ruffed grouse, catbird, purple finch, and rose-breasted grosbeak.

One or more varieties of the hawthorns (*Crataegus sp.*) should be included in every country garden planned to attract birds. In addition to producing fruits liked by nearly all song and game birds, the spiny branches provide well-protected nesting sites. Birds that are particularly fond of making their homes in these small trees include the catbird, brown thrasher, mourning dove, and cuckoo.

Large shade trees are a part of the landscape in nearly every country garden. One of the most graceful and beautiful of these trees is the American elm (*Ulmus americana*). In the spring, warblers will flit tirelessly among the branches, devouring quantities of tiny insects. In May the Baltimore oriole will be content to build its nest on the tip of an outermost branch. The birches (*Betula sp.*) bear cones containing tiny seeds that are eagerly sought by wintering goldfinches, redpolls, and pine siskins. The graceful form and light-colored bark of the white birch (*B. alba*) and the gray birch (*B. populifolia*) add a pleasing contrast to the surrounding green foliage. Generally the black birch (*B. lenta*) is not preferred as a garden tree; it does, however, produce quantities of the tiny seeds valuable as winter food. The yellow birch (*B. lutea*) grows best along the bank of a pond or stream.

Formal Gardens

The formal garden is usually designed for the primary purpose of obtaining a desired form of beauty through the use of flowers, shrubs, and trees. Although this design often eliminates the natural

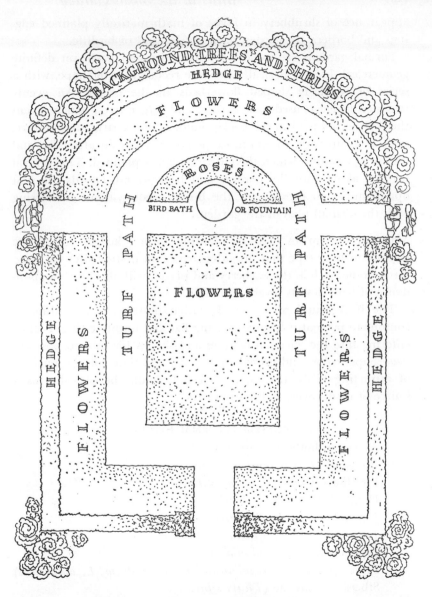

FIGURE 55.   DESIGN FOR FORMAL GARDEN.

appearance of shrubbery in favor of mathematically planned edgings and borders, the garden need not be void of birdlife.

Formal gardens are usually small in size and based on definite geometrical designs. Basically they are rectangular in shape, with a series of regularly shaped flowerbeds in the center. An evenly trimmed hedge is used as a border, and larger trees, which accent the skyline, are used in the background. A center structural feature, such as a birdbath, fountain, or pergola, makes an attractive and useful axis around which the entire design is planned. This central feature, along with the borders and background, affords the best opportunities to provide for the birds' needs without interfering with the over-all plan of the garden.

Many of the shrubs used in planting formal hedges are of the thick-branching type that provides cover and nesting sites for songbirds. Some, such as the barberry and privet, will also bear an abundance of fruit despits severe trimming.

The background of a formal garden must vary in outline or contour to prevent it from appearing flat and uninteresting. Factors entering into the selection of trees and shrubs for this purpose are size, shape, color, and growth habits. In addition, for the purpose of attracting birds, the plants selected should be of value as a source of food, cover, and nesting sites.

PLANTS FOR FORMAL HEDGES

American holly (*Ilex opaca*)
Boxwood (*Buxus sempervirens*)
Firethorn (*Crataegus pyracantha*)
Hemlock (*Tsuga canadensis*)
Japanese barberry (*Berberis thunbergi*)
Japanese bush yew (*Taxus cuspidata*)
Japanese quince (*Cydonia japonica*)
Privet (*Ligustrum regelianum, L. ovalifolium, L. amurensis*)
Siberian arbovitae (*Thuja sibirica*)
Small-leaved pea tree (*Caragana microphylla*)

TREES AND SHRUBS FOR BACKGROUND PLANTINGS

Arborvitae (*Thuja occidentalis*)
Arrowwood (*Viburnum dentatum*)
Flowering dogwood (*Cornus florida*)
Lombardy poplar (*Populus nigra fastigiata*)
Mountain ash (*Sorbus americana, S. aucuparia*)
Red cedar (*Juniperus virginiana*)
Sassafras (*Sassafras officinale*)
Scotch pine (*Pinus sylvestris*)
Sheepberry (*Viburnum lentago*)
Sour gum (*Nyssa sylvatica*)
Wayfaring tree (*Viburnum lantanum*)
Weeping mulberry (*Morus alba pendula*)
White birch (*Betula alba*)

Summary

Our success in attracting birds to a small garden will depend largely on how well we have provided for their needs. Food, cover, and water must be available for their use. These essentials can be provided adequately through the following five projects:

1. PLANTING. Planting provides food, cover, and nesting sites. Additional information on how and what to plant can be found in Chapter 6, "Attracting by Planting," and in Chapter 7, "Plants Attractive to Birds."

2. PROVIDING WATER. Birds need water for drinking and bathing. Chapter 5, "Attracting with Water," gives complete details on the use of birdbaths and fountains.

3. NESTING BOXES. A few well-placed nesting boxes in your garden will provide homes for some of the cavity-nesting species. For information concerning the selection and use of nesting boxes, see Chapter 8, "Helping Birds at Nesting Time," and Chapter 9, "Home for Birds."

4. WINTER FEEDING. Feeding stations will keep your garden "alive" during the winter months. Many kinds of winter birds that would

otherwise go unnoticed can now be observed at close range. For the various types of feeders and what to feed, see Chapter 4, "Feeding Songbirds."

5. PROTECTION.   Your garden should offer birds means of protection from their enemies. While dense growths of shrubbery usually provide adequate protection from natural predators, the presence of cats may require the use of protective guards about nesting boxes and feeding trays. Details for the use and construction of these guards can be found in Chapter 16, "Predators."

CHAPTER XIV

BIRDS ON FARMS
AND ESTATES

THE FARM or country estate, where land is measured in numbers of acres, presents virtually unlimited possibilities for attracting birds and providing for their needs. Here, from among the woodlands, fields, and orchards, songbirds and game birds may choose the type of environment they like best. Ponds, streams, and swamplands, if available, will provide food and shelter for nesting and migrating waterfowl. Thus the country place with more and varied types of lands will support a larger number and variety of birds. Although nearly every sizable tract of land in rural areas does support some birdlife, wildlife populations can be increased in any area through the proper use and development of the land.

If you are one who owns property in the country, you may be wondering: "How can I improve my land for the benefit of birds and other wildlife? Where do I start?"

Let us take your tract of land and develop it with the objective of increasing bird and wildlife populations. Perhaps the best approach would be through a series of projects — projects that would make the land increasingly valuable to you and to wildlife. The following are suggested as those being most generally adaptable to any sizable tract of country land.

PROJECT NO. 1. *Take an inventory of your property.*

Before you begin the actual work of improving your property so that it will support more birds and wildlife, you will need to know just what your land now offers in the way of food, cover, and water. Also, determine the areas that can be improved by planting, refencing, clearing, and similar projects. Plotting all this information on a rough map of your land is an interesting way of keeping your inventory.

Indicate on the map such areas as cultivated fields, woodlands, swamps, fences, steep banks, ditches, gullies, brier patches, brush plots, ponds, streams, and so on. These are the areas that will figure largely in the plan for improving your property. You may also want to show on your map, or on a chart accompanying the map, an estimate of the number and variety of birds now on your land.[1] A new map or chart made each year will indicate the progress of your endeavors. You will find that as the vegetation changes, so will the bird population, both in species and numbers.

Aerial photos are a big help in planning your map and improvement projects. These are often on file in township or county tax offices and are available for use by property owners. They are also available in the local Soil Conservation Service office if you are a farm co-operator. Once the map is completed, it will help you plan the type and location of additional projects that are needed.

PROJECT NO. 2.   *Start with what you have.*

A survey of your land may reveal that certain areas need little more than some selective cutting to increase their value for wildlife. Woodland borders, bushy fencerows, and steep slopes often contain many wild shrubs that will provide food and cover for birds. These shrubs must be given ample room and sunlight, however, if they are to mature properly. This can be done by cutting out dense shade trees and undesirable species. Paint the stumps with a solution of 2, 4, 5-T to prevent resprouting. Shrubs and small trees can often be eliminated without cutting by painting the boles with this same solution.

If you own a farm, the fencing of cattle out of woodlands, brush patches, and eroded hillsides is often all that is needed to give

[1] See Chaper 18, "Aids to Bird Study," on how to take a nesting census.

these areas a chance to produce natural food and cover. Further improvements can be made by removing the unproductive plants and by planting more desirable species.

You can start your program by transplanting some of the smaller specimens of native trees and shrubs. Chances are, a number of the viburnums, hawthorns, and dogwoods are already growing in scattered areas about your property. Some of these plants can be moved to the more desirable locations under development. The smaller ones can be moved quite easily and will often grow more vigorously as a result.

PROJECT NO. 3. *Make use of eroded and waste areas.*

Few country properties are entirely free of gullies, ditches, or eroded hillsides and remote sections that cannot be cultivated. Both the landowner and wildlife will benefit from the development of these waste areas. Planting will check erosion and save valuable topsoil. It will also serve as a means of providing food, cover, and nesting sites for numerous species of birds.[2] Have the local Soil Conservation Service supervisor check your eroded areas. You may have a good location for a drainage-type farm pond.

Frequently, waste areas may be reclaimed so that they will serve a multiple purpose. For example, the black locust is a good tree to use as a soil binder in checking erosion. It grows rapidly and produces durable wood ideal for making fence posts. Its seed pods drop to the ground in fall and winter and provide a staple source of food for wintering quail. Steep banks, rocky fields, and similar areas unsuitable for cultivation will often support a planting of evergreen trees that can eventually be harvested for their lumber. In the meantime they will provide food and shelter for birds.

PROJECT NO. 4. *Use strip cropping for a better harvest and more birds.*

Strip cropping is a method of planting field crops in a way that will minimize water and wind erosion. They are planted in long,

[2] For a list of plants especially recommended for the planting of ditches and gullies, see Chapter 11, "Attracting Game Birds."

narrow strips that follow the general contour of the land. Narrow bands of tilled crops such as corn, sorghum, wheat, millet, mixed food patches, and other small grains, are alternated with strips of hay or other close-growing erosion-resistant plants.

This type of farming is promoted vigorously by the U. S. Soil Conservation Service. It conserves the farmer's valuable topsoil and prevents many areas from eventually becoming useless. If you are not already a co-operator with the SCS, call your local supervisor and ask how he can help. He will be glad to provide valuable assistance in both farming techniques and wildlife management.

PROJECT NO. 5. *Plant field borders.*

If you have fields adjacent to a woodlot, the shaded edges are probably unproductive so far as crops are concerned. The long roots of the taller forest trees may extend well into the cropland and absorb valuable moisture needed by your field plantings. These barren edges can be reclaimed so as to benefit both the farmer and wildlife.

Field borders planted with grasses or legumes will provide food and cover for birds, help prevent erosion, increase fertility, make a good turning area for farm machinery, and help prevent seedlings from spreading into your croplands.

In eastern states south of New York and southern Michigan, the deep-rooted perennial *Lespedeza sericea* makes an ideal border planting. In the more northern states, timothy, orchard grass, tall oatgrass, birdsfoot trefoil, or clover may be used.

A mixed hedge of berry-bearing shrubs growing between the woodlot and border plantings will also provide additional food and nesting places for birds.

PROJECT NO. 6. *Plant hedges and fencerows.*

A large span of open land affords little enticement to bird life. Fencerows that consist of nothing more than a barbed-wire fence are equally unattractive. Hedges planted on the contour in conjunction with strip cropping have many values that cannot be overlooked by the progressive farmer. They make permanent field boundaries, reduce soil erosion, serve as windbreaks, and provide food, cover, and nesting sites for birds in areas previously void of all wildlife.

One of the best plants for hedge planting is the multiflora rose (*Rose multiflora*). It grows rapidly and will produce a cattle-proof fence in a period of five years. It also provides the best kind of protective cover for wildlife and produces an abundance of food in the form of haws, which make excellent winter provender for both game birds and songbirds. Birds will spread the seeds, and sproutings may have to be controlled in uncultivated areas. Other thick-growing shrubs suitable for hedge planting include the bayberry, highbush cranberry, silky dogwood, Tatarian honeysuckle, autumn olive, and, in areas south of Pennsylvania, bicolor lespedeza.

PROJECT NO. 7. *Improve your woodlot.*

Uniform growths of timber appeal to a limited number of bird species. Thrushes, vireos, some woodpeckers, and certain kinds of warblers prefer the dense shade of woodlands, but the majority of our songbirds like open, sunny areas. Large woodlots can be made more attractive to birds and other wildlife by occasional clearings that will permit the sunlight to enter and encourage the growth of food-bearing shrubs. These clearings can be made in areas with few productive trees or in areas where trees are ready for harvesting. Paths, trails, and wood-roads will also help in this respect.

If, on the other hand, your woodlot is sparcely covered, owing to grazing or extensive cutting, some planting may be necessary to provide sufficient food and cover. Pines, spruces, and firs planted in areas not too deeply shaded will produce excellent cover and furnish food for siskins, finches, grosbeaks, crossbills, and other songbirds. Hemlocks will tolerate more shade and are equally attractive.

PROJECT NO. 8. *Build brush piles for emergency cover.*

When you are cutting undesirable trees and shrubs from fence-rows, woodlots, and waste areas, don't be in a hurry to burn the brush. If heaped in large piles, it will provide homes and emergency cover for birds and small game. Fence corners, eroded areas, and rock heaps are good locations for brush piles.

Start your brush pile by placing two or three of the larger limbs over a stump or protruding rock. This will give rabbits and game birds a chance to get underneath and will also keep the brush from rotting and settling too rapidly.

PROJECT NO. 9.   *Improve or build a pond for waterfowl.*

If you are fortunate enough to have a pond on your property, or have sufficient water to warrant the construction of a new one, waterfowl and shore birds can be added to the variety of wildlife found on your farm or estate. Existing ponds often need little more than a planned planting project to make them attractive to migrating or nesting ducks and geese. This planting should provide food, cover, and safe nesting places.

Before you start the construction of a new pond, make sure you understand the laws of your state concerning the impounding of water. Also, plan your pond for the species of waterfowl known to inhabit your section of the country. For more complete details concerning the construction and planting of ponds, see Chapter 12, "Attracting Waterfowl."

PROJECT NO. 10.   *Put up nesting boxes for cavity-nesting birds.*

This is one project that will produce results immediately. You will be surprised by the number of bluebirds, tree swallows, and house wrens that will use the boxes the first year they are erected. Along stone walls, fencerows, and orchard borders are good locations to erect houses intended for bluebirds and tree swallows. Place the houses on posts or poles 5 to 10 feet in height. Be sure they are free from any surrounding foliage.

House wrens are quite sociable and will nest in boxes placed about the lawn or garden and other areas adjacent to your buildings. Boxes located in orchards and pastures and along woodland borders will attract chickadees, nuthatches, crested flycatchers, woodpeckers, tufted titmice, screech owls, and other species. Wood duck boxes placed about ponds or marshes will help increase your waterfowl population. The additional birds attracted by the use of nesting boxes will be of real economic worth to you. While they are rearing their families, they will free your land of thousands of insects.

More detailed information concerning the use, selection, and construction of bird houses can be found in Chapter 9, "Homes for Birds."

PROJECT No. 11. *Plan your garden for birds.*

The lawns and gardens adjacent to your house should be a definite part of your estate or farm plan. These will be the areas where you will do much of your bird-observing. Appropriate landscaping combined with other techniques will attract many birds from adjacent areas.

Actually, the plan for your garden need be little more than a miniature version of your over-all plan. Many of the same features are needed, only on a lesser scale. A year-round food supply, ample water for drinking and bathing, and adequate cover for protection and nesting — these are the essentials that will make your garden a haven for birds.

Much of the information you will need can be found in the preceding chapter, "Birds in the Small Garden." More complete details concerning planting, providing water, supplementary feeding, and furnishing cover can be found in other chapters devoted mainly to these subjects.

PROJECT No. 12. *Provide extra food for winter birds.*

Winter is often a critical season for birds. When the ground is covered with snow or ice for long periods of time, the food supply of ground feeding birds is virtually inaccessible. Some well-sheltered feeding stations about your country place may save many quail, pheasants, and songbirds from starvation during severe winter weather.

Although your land may furnish an abundance of food during the spring and summer months, the actual number of birds it will support may be limited by the amount of *available* food during the more critical winter periods. This is particularly true of quail and pheasants.

An extra supply of winter food can be furnished for game birds in a number of ways. Corn left standing in shocks or uncut will keep the grain above snow level. Corn may also be fed from hopper feeders placed under constructed shelters. Food patches of mixed grains planted next to protective cover will supply additional winter food for both songbirds and game birds.[3]

Living in the country provides an ideal opportunity to observe many winter songbirds. They can be observed most easily by attracting them to your lawn or garden by the use of one or more feeding stations. Suet, peanut butter, sunflower seeds, and mixed grains will attract a variety of both insect-eating and seed-eating species.

The farm illustrated below includes the following features beneficial to wildlife:

Fencerows, to furnish food, cover, and protected lanes along which qauil, pheasants, and other wildlife can travel safely.

Gullies and stream banks, planted to prevent erosion and provide food for wildlife.

Food patches, planted near protective cover.

Brush piles, to provide emergency cover for game girds and small animals.

Feeding stations, to provide additional winter food for game birds and songbirds.

Woodlands, fenced against pasturing.

A pond, built and planted to attract waterfowl.

Cattle fenced from the main pond area. They get drinking water in pastures below the pond.

3 For food-patch mixtures, see Chapter 11, "Attracting Game Birds."

Rocky waste areas, protected from pasturing and allowed to grow up in briers and underbrush.

Hedges, to serve as fences, provide food and cover, and help hold valuable topsoil.

Windbreaks, to protect the pond, orchard, and buildings.

Bird boxes, to attract cavity-nesting species.

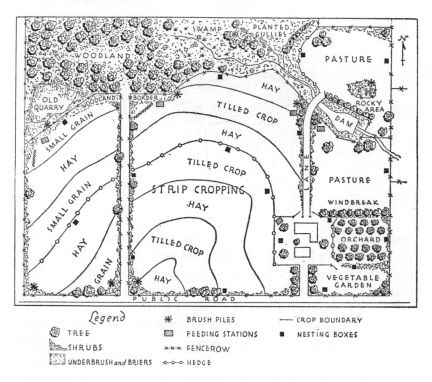

FIGURE 56. A FARM PLANNED TO ATTRACT BIRDS AND OTHER
FORMS OF WILDLIFE

CHAPTER XV

CARE OF YOUNG
AND WOUNDED BIRDS

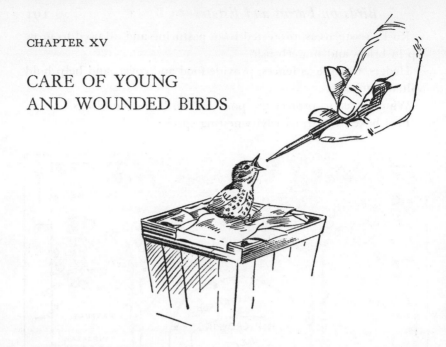

ONCE YOU BECOME known as one who feeds and loves birds, you are also likely to be known as the bird doctor of your neighborhood. Children and adults will come to you for advice, bring you birds that are too young to feed for themselves or are sick or injured. You will have to assume the role of diplomat or doctor.

The best advice you can give is to *leave the young birds where you find them.* Our desire to help the young, chirping fledgling in the grass often leads to disaster. The chances are that the bird is not lost or injured, but merely telling its parents: "Here I am, and I'm hungry." Birds found in this predicament should not be disturbed unless there is immediate danger from a cat or other predator. In such cases place the bird on a high perch in dense cover where it will be comparatively safe. The parent birds will find the chirping fledgling quite easily.

Occasionally young birds will fall from the nest prematurely or become orphans because of some disaster to their parents. Cases of this sort warrant your kindness and help. Fledglings that have fallen from the nest should be returned so their parents can care for them. Young birds that have lost their parents often can be reared successfully.

The Care and Feeding of Young Birds

SUBSTITUTE NESTS AND CAGES. Once you have assumed the role of foster parent, a bit of ingenuity and resourcefulness will be most helpful. A quart fruit box padded and lined with facial tissues makes a good substitute nest. Larger birds, such as crows or hawks, would need a larger box. If the birds are old enough to perch, they can be put in cages — the larger the better. The cages need not be elaborate structures. A cardboard box with a screen covering makes a satisfactory temporary cage. A more permanent cage can be made from wood and hardware cloth. Young birds need to be kept warm and protected from drafts. The nest boxes should be covered with a cloth at night. Fledglings require a certain amount of sunshine but must not be exposed to the midday sun. Avoid excessive handling and keep the nest boxes and cages clean.

 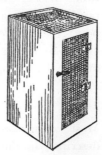

FIGURE 57. A SUBSTITUTE NEST AND REARING CAGE.

Food for Young Birds

Feeding young birds requires considerable patience and time. They have insatiable appetites and require feeding every fifteen or twenty minutes. Food requirements vary somewhat according to species, but all birds require a reasonable balance in their diet to assure healthy growth.

A good mixture for very young songbirds is equal parts of dry baby cereal (Pablum) and the yolk of hard-boiled egg. These ingredients should be thoroughly mixed and moistened with raw egg white or milk, and occasionally with cod-liver oil. Fine bread crumbs may be substituted for the baby cereal if it is not readily available. As the bird grows older, other mixtures may be substituted. Insect-eating species will accept a combination of one part scraped raw beef and two parts grated carrot. Some finely chopped greens may be added to provide needed calcium and vitamins. Bits of fine gravel, charcoal, and crushed seeds are needed by seed-eaters to aid digestion. These can be added occasionally to the softer mixtures.

Basic diets can be supplemented with other foods, such as canned dogfood, earth worms, bits of suet, and insects. Meal worms are good and can be found in most pet shops. In certain areas they can also be acquired from dealers in fishing baits. Insects can be obtained around outdoor lights at night. Soft fruits in the diet will fulfill the need for water. Bits of strawberries, cherries, mulberries, raspberries, bananas, dates, and raisins are excellent for this purpose. *Never force a bird to drink,* as this is virtually a sure way of killing it. Young birds get sufficient water from their food. As they mature, fresh water should be available in their cages.

Feeding Various Species

Most young songbirds can be started safely on the basic foods described in the preceding section. However, certain species will thrive better if this diet is supplemented or eventually replaced with foods closely resembling their natural supply. The following listing will serve as a guide to feeding many of our common species.

ROBINS AND THRUSHES. Earthworms are a staple source of food. They can be found by digging, under stones in damp areas, and on your lawn at night, particularly after heavy rains.

Cooked cereal, small pieces of cooked spaghetti, insects, and meal worms are good supplementary foods. Bits of soft fruits should be included in their diet.

CATBIRDS AND THRASHERS. Wild fruits constitute a good portion of their normal diet. If these are not available, you may substitute pieces of washed, dried fruits — raisins, currants, dates, apricots, and peaches. Portions of cherries, apple, or berries are good because of their moisture content.

In addition to fruit, you may include the beef-carrot mixture, insects, and meal worms.

ORIOLES AND TANAGERS. For very young birds, mix a small amount of mashed, ripe banana to the basic formula of Pablum and yolk of hard-boiled egg (see page 194). Tanagers are quite partial to bananas, and small pieces may be added to the daily menu as the birds begin to grow. Orioles are fond of bits of orange, tangerine, and white grapes. Fledglings will pick at these when placed in their cages.

SPARROWS. To the Pablum-egg mixture, add small amounts of any of the following: corn meal, crushed seeds, crushed dog meal, or peanut hearts. Soft insects, meal worms, and bits of fruit may be substituted occasionally. Parakeet food is a good source of seeds for older birds.

STARLINGS. Starlings are omnivorous and will thrive on almost any diet. Supplement the basic diet of Pablum-egg yolk, or raw beef and carrot, with any of the following: softened whole-wheat bread, crushed nuts, seeds, fruit, or canned dogfood.

BLUE JAYS. Young jays will thrive well on the basic Pablum-egg mixture. Small amounts of corn meal may be added occasionally for variety. When the young birds start to feed themselves, seeds and nuts will be accepted readily. At this point, keep some para-keet gravel and a small amount of charcoal in the cage. Release young jays as soon as possible.

WOODPECKERS. Young woodpeckers can be reared successfully on a softened mixture of dry dogfood, suet, and yolk of hard-boiled egg. Meal worms make an excellent addition to this diet.

HUMMINGBIRDS. Your chances of getting a young hummingbird are quite remote. Owing to their peculiar feeding habits, it is most difficult to feed the young birds. However, adult birds that have been stunned or injured may be fed temporarily on a mixture of equal amounts of honey and water. This will be accepted best from a glass vial resembling a flower placed on the side of the cage. For more complete details on keeping hummingbirds in captivity, see Chapter 10, "How to Attract Hummingbirds."

HAWKS AND OWLS. The natural food of hawks and owls consists of meat — meat with fur and feathers on it to aid digestion. Good substitute foods are frozen horsemeat warmed to room temperature, ground beef, and strips of liver. Some chicken feathers and a few drops of cod-liver oil should be added occasionally. Older birds may be kept in cages or jessed to a perch (see illustration, page 199). Food for older birds can often be supplemented by road kills — birds, chipmunks, squirrels, rabbits, etc. Young hawks and owls need feeding three or four times during the day. Once a day is sufficient for adult birds. Avoid overfeeding captive hawks, as an accumulation of excess fat can be fatal. A daily piece of horsemeat about the size of a golf ball will keep a red-tailed or red-shouldered hawk in good physical condition.

How to Feed

Very young birds need feeding frequently and at regular intervals during daylight hours. Once every fifteen or twenty minutes is gen-erally conceded to be sufficient. If the bird's eyes are not yet open, tap gently on the nest box or cage and they will open their mouths for food instinctively. With a match stick or small paint brush, place bits of food well back in the bird's throat. You may repeat the process once the food is swallowed. When the bird has had a sufficient amount for the current feeding, it will refuse to accept more food. FORCE FEEDING. Caged fledglings and sick or injured birds are sometimes too frightened to accept food. Forced feeding then becomes necessary until they are used to their new foster parent. To do this, place your hands gently down over the bird's back and let it clasp your little finger with its claws. This will hold the wings in position and permit you to use your thumb and index finger to open the bird's mouth. Apply slight pressure to either side of the mandibles, and the bird will open its mouth. Be prepared to insert the food with the other hand.

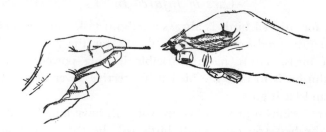

FIGURE 58.   HOW TO HOLD A BIRD FOR FORCED FEEDING.

Caring for Sick Birds

Your sympathetic neighbors will occasionally bring you a "sick" bird — a bird showing no visible injury, but apparently unable to care for itself. Attempts to help such a bird are usually futile and often hasten its death. Perhaps the best you can do, weather permitting, is return the bird to some protective cover and hope that nature will aid its recovery. If you must keep the bird temporarily, keep it warm and free from drafts. A dark cover over the cage will help provide warmth and tend to keep the bird still.

Caged birds are sometimes subject to constipation or diarrhea.

This is usually attributable to improperly balanced diets. Constipation can often be corrected by increasing the amount of fruit in the diet. If necessary, one or two drops of castor oil can be added to the food mixture. In cases of diarrhea, reduce the fruit intake and substitute dry bread and tiny balls of dry peanut butter.

Young birds just out of the nest are often infested with lice and mites. These can be eliminated by dusting the bird with an insect powder and spraying the cage thoroughly with one of the many commercial bug sprays now on the market.

Perhaps the best cure for ill birds is a preventative one. Always keep the cages clean, dry, warm, and free from drafts. Try to keep a reasonable balance in diets.

Care of Injured Birds

Caring for injured birds is always a tedious task and one that very infrequently produces satisfactory results for the amateur. In the case of birds, nature has remarkable healing powers. Often the best solution is to take the bird to protective cover near available water and let it go.

Where serious injury is obvious, you will have no alternative but to do the best you can. Small birds will be the most difficult to help. If the bird must be transported before assistance can be given, carry it in a way to prevent movement of injured parts. The wings should be closed in a natural position and the legs extended downward and held by the fingers.

Bleeding can often be stopped by applying a few of the bird's own breast feathers over the wound. If the position of the wound permits, apply a small pressure bandage.

In the case of a badly injured leg, amputation may be necessary to prevent the bird from eventually becoming entangled and perhaps starving to death. If a wing is damaged to the extent that you are unable to mend it, you have no alternative but to put an end to the bird's painful existence. A bird without the use of both wings would soon starve or be caught by some predator.

With laregr birds, where the actual bone positions can be determined, broken bones can sometimes be mended successfully. Set the bones by pulling them into position and then apply small protective splints. Wrap the splints once or twice with a bit of soft cloth and then fasten them firmly in place with fine, soft copper wire. Fasten the wings down with Scotch tape until after healing takes place. The tape can then be removed with a sponge and warm water. Keep the bird in a darkened cage except during feeding periods if it is inclined to be too active.

Larger birds, such as hawks and owls, can be kept less active by jessing them to a perch rather than giving them the freedom of a large cage. They soon learn that they are jessed fast and will cease attempting to escape.

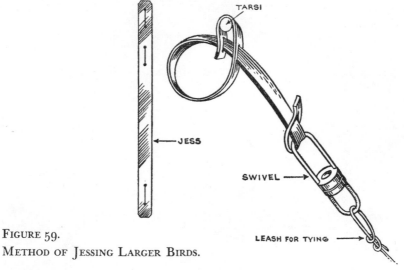

FIGURE 59.
METHOD OF JESSING LARGER BIRDS.

Jesses are made of strong, soft leather that will not chafe the bird's leg. They are approximately ½-inch wide and 10 inches long. The distance between the end cuts is determined by measuring the diameter of the leg. The fit should be loose but small enough to prevent the bird from pulling its foot through the loop.

When Birds Grow Up

Birds reared by humans often become household pets. As it is illegal to keep most birds in captivity without a special permit, all birds should be released as soon as they are able to care for themselves. They can do a much better job of it than we can, and their chance for survival will be greatly increased.

Sometimes young birds hesitate to leave once they have been released. They may also have some difficulty in learning to capture their own food. This transition to the outdoors can be made easier by placing their food on the ground in a safe place. This will help them learn to feed in a natural environment. They will soon learn to hunt and pick at natural foods and become quite independent.

CHAPTER XVI

PREDATORS

PEOPLE WHO FOR ONE reason or another are interested in wildlife are prone to consider as harmful any bird or animal that tends to encroach upon or interfere with the project of their immediate interest. Too often the chicken farmer will shoot the soaring hawk or trap the "thieving" owl as a menace to his business. Actually, that same hawk or owl was probably feeding upon the mice and rats that were eating the grain intended for the farmer's chickens. Cattle raisers wage a relentless campaign against coyotes despite the fact that in certain areas where they have been eliminated, jack rabbits and rodents consume or destroy pasture worth far more than the occasional cattle lost to the coyotes. Hunters of upland game blame the fox for the scarcity of ruffed grouse, quail, or rabbits. In reality, the fox aids the sportsman by eliminating the weak and diseased individuals, thus keeping the remaining stock healthy, vigorous, and alert — the very essentials that make the sport so appealing.

Thus, through misunderstanding, our interference with nature's balance often accentuates the very problem we seek to solve.

The Balance in Nature

Each season of the year presents some spectacle in nature which causes us to look upon it with an aesthetic appreciation of its beauty and magnitude. It may be the northward flight of geese in the

[201]

spring, the summer bloom of wild flowers, the colors of autumn, or the magic of a snow scene in winter. These, and similar scenes of outdoor life and beauty, are the result of a balance in nature — a balance so delicate that every living plant and animal contributes to its maintenance.

Maintaining nature's balance is a circuitous process. Plants store energy from the sun and combine it with compounds from the soil to produce proteins, fats, starches, and other substances. One group of animals, classified as herbivorous, feed upon these plants. Another group, known as carnivorous, feed upon the herbivores and upon each other, thus enlarging and keeping the circle intact. Through excrement, decay, and death, these substances that support life again enter the soil to combine with the sun's energy in producing more plant life.

The killing of one animal by another is therefore a normal function necessary in maintaining nature's balance. Nevertheless, it is difficult to convince mankind that this process is a natural one. The aggressor is immediately labeled a "predator" and, as such, becomes subject to all the inventions and schemes that can be devised by an equally predacious mankind.

Man, in the process of changing his environment or safety, comfort, and personal gain, has brought about many changes affecting the stability of nature's balance. These changes often produce a new environment less beneficial to man's endeavors. Rich prairie lands give way to barren deserts; closely deforested watersheds fail to hold water, and we suffer from flood and drought. Despite the vast changes, nature maintains stability by introducing new plants and new wildlife.

How Nature Stays in Balance

The necessity of nature to maintain this stability is of paramount importance. The diagram below illustrates how nature stays in balance. One nesting pair of bluebirds has a reproduction capacity of two broods, or ten new bluebirds, each nesting season. On the average, the rate of survival will be such that the total population will remain approximately the same. If every bird reached maturity and produced an equal number of new birds the following year, and the year after, we would soon be overrrun with bluebirds. This would be true of any species of wildlife.

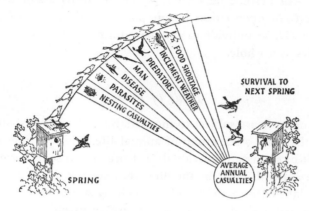

FIGURE 60.   HOW NATURE STAYS IN BALANCE.

Understanding Predators

To all of us who would attract birds to our garden, or in any other way become involved with the habits of wildlife, there will come a time when we need to form an opinion about predators. This opinion should be arrived at with the full realization that without depredation mankind could not exist in his present environment. This is difficult to believe when we see a hawk prey upon one of our favorite chickadees, yet a little realism in our thinking will help us prove to ourselves that this is so.

A pair of field mice are capable of producing a million descendants in one year. At this rate of reproduction, they would soon overrun the earth if it were not for such limiting factors as disease, food shortages, and particularly depredation by carnivorous animals. In brief, the predator's function in nature is to maintain a limit on the species that feed upon plants and grain.

As our attitude toward predators develops, we begin to realize that most predatory birds and mammals are particularly beneficial to the welfare of mankind. Occasionally, however, an individual predator will become dependent upon the birds about our feeding stations, or upon chicks in our poultry yard, as an easy source of supply. These individuals can be eliminated without injury to the species as a whole.

Birds of Prey

Hawks and owls are subject to more abuse and wanton destruction by man than any other group of animal life. This attitude is often the result of seeing an individual bird prey upon some form of life looked upon with favor by the observer. Every hawk and owl then becomes labeled as a thief and, as such, is subject to destruction. When we see a single act of predation, we rarely stop to realize that perhaps a dozen more birds of prey are at the same time maintaining a check upon the insects and rodents about our property.

There are many species of hawks and owls, each with its own peculiar feeding habits. Individual species are often difficult to identify and are casually referred to as just another "hawk" or "owl." The Cooper's hawk, sharp-shinned hawk, goshawk, and great horned owl are generally conceded to be the most destructive among our birds of prey. The actions of these few, usually individuals of the species, should not be cause for wholesale destruction to be waged against our entire population of hawks and owls. We should give thoughtful consideration to the facts concerning our local areas. What are the native species of hawks and owls? What are their feeding habits? How do they fit into the over-all pattern of nature relationships? An intelligent answer to these questions will prove beneficial, not only to the hawks and owls concerned, but to mankind as well.

	INSECTS	RATS and MICE	FROGS SNAKES ETC.	AQUATIC	SMALL BIRDS	POULTRY	GAME BIRDS	RABBITS and SQUIRRELS
RED-SHOULDERED HAWK	32	28	25	5.3	6.0	1.4	.9	.9
RED-TAILED HAWK	10.5	55	6.1	1.5	9.2	6.3	2.1	9.3
ROUGH-LEGGED HAWK	6.5	72	2.1	2.2	4.3		4.3	8.6
BROAD-WINGED HAWK	39.7	23	30.9	2	3.4		.5	.5
SPARROW HAWK	63.5	20.3	7.8		8.4			
SHARP-SHINNED HAWK	.7	2.6	.1		96.4	.1		.1
COOPER'S HAWK	3.3	17	1		55	10	12	1.7
MARSH HAWK	3.3	33	4.1	.1	41	2.3	7.2	9

FIGURE 61.   WHAT HAWKS EAT.[1]

Cats and Dogs as Predators

What should be our attitude toward cats and dogs that hunt from instinct, or because they are homeless? They, too, kill rodents, and in other ways attain man's affection.

Of the two, cats present the more serious problem. They are known to capture many young birds still in the nest, or to capture the parent and leave the young to die of starvation. Homeless cats are the worst offenders, and their presence in sanctuary areas should not be tolerated. On the whole, the destruction of bird life by cats is comparatively negligible in relation to the toll taken by extreme weather conditions, disease, and starvation. Nevertheless,

[1] The information presented in this chart is based on studies made by the U. S. Department of Agriculture, covering the contents of 5,185 hawk stomachs. All figures indicate percentage.

their maraudings about feeding stations and nesting areas should not be condoned.

Cats are often most destructive during the night and early morning hours. If they were locked in an outbuilding for the night, many birds would be saved from needless destruction.

Feeders and nesting boxes mounted on poles can be protected from cats and squirrels by guards, as illustrated. These guards are made of smooth tin or sheet metal. If you use them around trees, do not tighten them, as they may scar or retard the tree's growth.

Dogs rarely harm birds, because of their inability to catch them. They should not be allowed to range unattended during the nesting season, however. The eggs and young ground-nesting species can be easily found and destroyed.

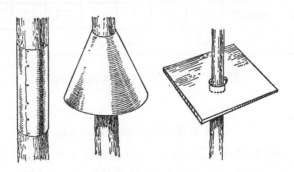

FIGURE 62.   POLE GUARDS PROTECT FEEDERS AND NESTING BOXES
collar-type, 2 feet long; inverted cone, 2 feet in diameter; flat-type for use around metal pipe, 2 feet square. cut hole in center of metal sheet so it fits loosely around pipe and will tilt easily in any direction. metal sheet rests on collar clamped or tapped to pipe.

Predatory Wild Animals

Songbirds suffer little from predacious wild animals. Some nests are destroyed by foxes, raccoons, opossums, weasels, and snakes. This is a natural loss in the cycle of maintaining nature's balance.

Certainly, all such animals cannot be exterminated in the hope of aiding bird life. The maraudings of red squirrels sometimes includes the destruction of eggs and nestlings. An excessive number of red squirrels in a comparatively small area may be a serious deterrent to a successful nesting season. Control measures are warranted when such conditions exist within bird-attracting areas.

Game birds and waterfowl suffer some loss, particularly from foxes and raccoons. Control measures can be effective only where there are dense populations, as in game refuges or waterfowl breeding areas. Time spent in providing adequate food and shelter will prove much more profitable than time spent trying to control predators.

Starlings and English Sparrows

Whether we do or do not want starlings and English sparrows to occupy our feeders and nesting boxes is purely a matter of personal opinion. Some people look upon these aliens with as much admiration and respect as they do upon our native species; others look upon them as greedy, aggressive, and obnoxious.

A flock of English sparrows crowding about a bird feeder gives little cause for admiration. Their feeding habits often earn them the just title of "greedy" or "aggressive." They consume enormous quantities of bird food and wage a constant battle to maintain possession of the feeder. Starlings occasionally visit our feeding stations in large flocks, but they are not likely to be so persistent and habitual as the English sparrow.

Flocks of English sparrows attracted by winter feeding persist until the spring nesting season when they are prone to forcibly occupy natural nesting cavities and bird boxes intended for other species. If we permit them to occupy our nesting facilities, we are certainly depriving the more valuable species of good home sites. House wrens, bluebirds, tree swallows, and flickers are more attractive and beneficial to have around our gardens.

Both starlings and English sparrows are gaining favor in public sentiment because of their aid in controlling the Japanese beetle. English sparrows are known to consume quantities of the actual beetles, while starlings are partial to the grubs.

For those desiring to limit the numbers of these two species about their property, the following suggestions are recommended: destroy all nesting sites and actual nests in the spring; and trap the English sparrows during the winter months. There is little value in trapping starlings, as their range is so wide as to permit others immediately to replace those trapped. Specially designed sparrow traps can be purchased through advertisments in nature and outdoor magazines.

Other Birds as Predators

There is a certain amount of natural predation among birds. These acts of aggression sustain life as life is being destroyed. Along with other factors, they assist in maintaining reasonable stability in our bird populations.

Crows and blue jays are known to raid the nests of songbirds. These acts are somewhat difficult to condone when they occur within our gardens unless we are aware of their significance in relation to our over-all bird density. We must remember, too, that both crows and blue jays are extremely sensitive to the imminence of danger. Their alertness and raucous cries protect many songbirds from becoming easy prey for other predatory wildlife. In fact, the blue jay's alertness and warning cries have earned him the just title of "alarm clock of the woods."

We admire the house wren for its bubbling song and busyness about our gardens; yet on occasion, it can be one of our most aggressive songbirds. During periods of competition for nesting sites, it will not hesitate to enter a box occupied by bluebirds and pick the eggs or kill the nestlings. Again, we must evaluate the order of survival within our environment. When we do, we will certainly continue to welcome the house wren as a valuable neighbor.

Shrikes are sometimes attracted by an abundance of birds about winter feeding stations. Through our acts of kindness, we have inadvertently provided a feeding station for them, also. Shrikes will attack and kill small songbirds, particularly during the winter months when their favorite diet of grasshoppers and mice is most difficult to procure. Usually, predation of this kind is by an individual and may warrant control measures. Live-trapping and removal to a distant area is usually a satisfactory way of solving this problem.

The Proper Attitude—and Abundant Wildlife

In view of the facts presented, what should be the proper attitude toward predators in relation to the maintenance of abundant wildlife?

Attitudes toward predators are formed individually. Collectively, they form the basis for public opinion. If any appreciable progress is to be made toward the growth and preservation of an abundant wildlife population, this opinion must be an understanding one, based on proved biological facts.

The land can support only so many individuals of a species. The average rate of survival is constant, with disease, starvation, and other natural causes limiting the surviving population to a number that can be supported by the land. Our greatest contribution, therefore, is to improve the land so that it will provide more food, water, and cover for a larger wildlife population. All increases will include both prey and predator — nature must stay in balance.

CHAPTER XVII

BIRDS AND THE LAW

Birds, being "animals of nature" in the legal sense, belong to the people. In the United States, the state is the political body representative of collective ownership on behalf of its people; therefore, birds and other forms of wildlife are conceded to be the property of the state. For the most part, the adoption and enforcement of bird-protection laws become the responsibility of the state.

State Laws

Although our early colonists enacted certain laws regarding the taking of game birds, not until the middle of the nineteenth century was there any apparent concern regarding the protection of songbirds. Connecticut and New Jersey were pioneers in establishing legal status for non-game species. Other states followed their lead on a gradual basis.

Most of the early laws protecting songbirds were initiated in recognition of the birds' value to the farmer. Today, realizing the aesthetic as well as the economic import of songbirds, all states provide them a certain degree of protection varying in scope from only those protected by federal law to complete blanket coverage.

Hawks and owls have not fared so well. This has been due to

controversial concepts regarding their place and value in the out-door community. They have long been subject to the pressures of hunting on the pretense of their being harmful to game populations. Most states have been slow to recognize that it is basically unsound to label any one species or form of wildlife as "harmful." Fortunately, during the past decade ecological concepts have become an increasingly important part of biological teachings. More and more people understand that all species contribute to the functioning of a healthy wildlife community. This new interpretation of values has motivated numerous states to pass "model laws" relative to the protection of hawks and owls.

The essence of these laws consists of state statutes specifying that hawks and owls may be destroyed only by the farmer or landowner, and then only when they are in the act of damaging property on the land he owns or occupys. This type of law is generally conceded to be the most practical for state adoption. It provides greatly needed protection for our birds of prey; but at the same time, it does not deny the farmer or landowner the right to protect his property from the depredations of individual birds.

Our states also have laws regarding the capture and confinement of wild birds. Most states require special permits in order to collect or keep wild birds and mammals in captivity. Specific regulations for your state can be had by writing to the appropriate state department listed in the appendix.

Federal Laws

One of the most significant enactments of federal law relative to the protection of wild birds was the passage of the Tariff Act of 1913. This measure prohibited the importation, sale, and exportation of wild bird feathers. Prior to this time tens of thousands of birds were slaughtered annually for the millinery industry. Egrets and grebes suffered tremendous losses. Even the skins of tiny hummingbirds were highly prized in the London market. With the signing of the 1913 Tariff Act by President Woodrow Wilson, American markets disappeared and world markets declined. Millions of unhatched birds were saved from a future of certain destruction.

Birds, of course, are not aware of state and national boundaries. Migratory species hatched and reared in one area were potentially susceptible to persecution in another. This fact was readily recognized by the governments of North America countries.

On August 16, 1916, a Convention between the United States and Great Britain was signed providing protection for migratory birds in the United States and Canada. After ratification of the Convention by both countries, it was proclaimed by President Wilson on December 8, 1916. The Convention became effective in this country with the approval of the Migratory Bird Treaty Act on July 3, 1918.

Article I of the Convention between the United States and Great Britain provides that: "The high contracting powers declare that the migratory birds included in the terms of this convention shall be as follows:

1. Migratory game birds:

(*a*) Anatidae or waterfowl, including brant, wild ducks, geese, and swans.

(*b*) Gruidae or cranes, including little brown, sandhill and whooping cranes.

(*c*) Rallidae or rails, including coots, gallinules, and sora and other rails.

(*d*) Limicolae or shorebirds, including avocets, curlews, dowitchers, godwits, knots, oyster catchers, phalaropes, plovers, sandpipers, snipe, stilts, surf birds, turnstones, willet, woodcock, and yellowlegs.

(*e*) Columbidae or pigeons, including doves and wild pigeons.

2. Migratory insectivorous birds: Bobolinks, catbirds, chickadees, cuckoos, flickers, flycatchers, grosbeaks, hummingbirds, kinglets, martins, meadowlarks, nighthawks, or bull-bats, nuthatches, orioles, robins, shrikes, swallows, swifts, tanagers, titmice, thrushes, vireos, warblers, wax-wings, whippoorwills, woodpeckers, and wrens, and all other perching birds which feed entirely or chiefly on insects.

3. Other migratory nongame birds: Auks, auklets, bitterns, fulmars, gannets, grebes, guillemots, gulls, herons, jaegers, loons, murres, petrels, puffins, shearwaters, and terns."

On February 7, 1936, a Convention between the United States and Mexico was signed in Mexico City. This Convention provided protection for migratory birds and game mammals in both countries. This Convention was ratified by both countries and proclaimed by President Roosevelt on March 15, 1937.

Article IV of the Convention states: "The high contracting parties declare that for the purpose of the present convention the following birds shall be considered migratory:

Migratory game birds:
 Familia Anatidae
 Familia Gruidae
 Familia Rallidae
 Familia Charadriidae
 Familia Scolopacidae
 Familia Recurvirostridae
 Familia Phalaropodidae
 Familia Columbidae
Migratory nongame birds:
 Familia Cuculidae
 Familia Caprimulgidae
 Familia Micropodidae
 Familia Trochilidae
 Familia Picidae
 Familia Tyrannidae
 Familia Alaudidae

 Familia Hirundinidae
 Familia Paridae
 Familia Certhiidae
 Familia Troglodytidae
 Familia Turdidae
 Familia Mimidae
 Familia Sylviidae
 Familia Motacillidae
 Familia Bombycillidae
 Familia Ptilogonatidae
 Familia Laniidae
 Familia Vireonidae
 Familia Compsothlypidae
 Familia Icteridae
 Familia Thraupidae
 Familia Fringillidae

Others which the Presidents of the United States of America and the United Mexican States may determine by common agreement."

The Migratory Bird Treaty Act was amended by an Act of Congress to cover these additional provisions. It was approved on June 20, 1936.

This Act also authorizes the Secretary of the Interior to adopt regulations relative to the hunting and possession of migratory game birds.

"The Secretary of the Interior annually adopts hunting regulations to permit a reasonable harvest of migratory game birds and leave an adequate breeding stock for subsequent years. To provide a sound basis for the regulations, each year considerable information is assembled on current populations of birds and on numbers available for harvesting. Four surveys are made of migratory waterfowl: (1) During the hunting season, a hunter-success survey by questionnaires to determine the number of birds taken; (2) a survey of wintering grounds to find out how many birds are left after the hunting season; (3) after the northward migration in spring, a survey of nesting grounds across the continent to measure size and distribution of breeding populations; and (4) a later breeding-ground survey to estimate production of broods. With a year's accumulation of data, the Secretary sets up a framework of proposed hunting regulations, including season lengths, bag and possession limits, and the earliest opening and latest closing dates within which the State game departments recommend hunting seasons best suited to conditions in their States."[1]

Why Laws Are Necessary

Man has been slow in recognizing the importance of birds in his daily life. For too many generations he has looked upon all wildlife as a personal possession — a possession that could be admired, ignored, or destroyed. Unfortunately, this phase of man's history has been one of little admiration, much ignorance, and wanton destruction.

The struggle to protect birds for their own rights, and for their economic and aesthetic values to mankind, has been a slow and arduous one, championed by a minority of individuals, institu-

[1] U S. Fish and Wildlife Service Regulatory Announcement 61. Issued September 1959.

tions, and organizations. By means of a persistent educational program, the eyes of the general public are being opened — gradually, but with a view that admonishes concern and action. Surely this action cannot expend itself upon any problem greater than that of protecting our natural resources. Seemingly, in view of current social standards, this must be done by laws — at least until we realize that the future of human welfare will be measured by the duration of our soil, plants, water, and wildlife.

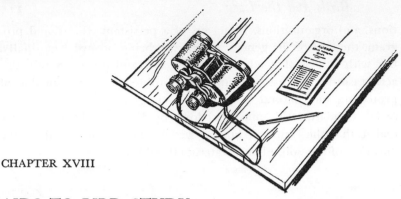

CHAPTER XVIII

AIDS TO BIRD STUDY

You will find that much of the joy in attracting birds is learning to know and understand them better once they have accepted your garden or estate as a place of refuge. As they flit tirelessly about your hedges and feeding stations, bright new colors and ecstatic songs will prompt you to wonder "What bird is that?" This is where the real fun begins. The challenge of identification and the excitement of finding new species help make the sport of bird study a fascinating and pleasurable experience.

As your interest in birding progresses, the chances are you will not be content merely to observe the birds from your kitchen window or the confines of your garden. New horizons — forests, fields, swamplands, and shorelines — may lure you on in search of still more exciting discoveries. The dawn chorus on a June morning may lead you afield before sun-up. If this be so, you are truly a bird student.

The sport of bird study requires few rules and a minimum of equipment to make it a pleasurable experience. A small notebook and pencil will come in handy for jotting down notes and sketches of birds not immediately identified. A good binocular and a reference book to aid in identification are essential items for any extensive field work. About the only rule you need to abide by —

and this will have to be self-enforced — is to identify positively all species recorded. There is much more satisfaction in *knowing* you did or did not see a certain bird than there is in *thinking* you saw it.

Books Helpful in Identifying Birds[1]

One of the most important aids to identification is a good reference book or field guide. Several of the smaller pocket-sized books now on the market are excellent for this purpose. The following books are generally conceded to be best for the identification of birds in the eastern half of the United States.

A Field Guild to the Birds by Roger Tory Peterson. This is the most widely accepted field guide on the market today. It is commonly referred to as "The Bird Watchers' Bible." The illustrations include both colored plates and a series of black-and-white patterns. In both, distinctive "field marks" are pointed out, thus making positive identification possible by comparing one species with another. For example, the fall warblers of similar colors and patterns are illustrated on a single page with the attention drawn to the individual differences of the birds shown.

The effects of light and distance often make the distinguishing of colors difficult, especially in waterfowl, where we have to contend with reflections from the water. To aid in situations of this sort, Peterson uses the black-and-white patterns to present the bird as it would actually appear to us.

Audubon Bird Guide by Richard H. Pough. This is another excellent manual for use in the field. Forty-eight full-page color plates illustrate more than 400 different land-bird plumages. The text includes a full discussion of each of the species, describing the significant points of identification, voice, range, nesting, and food habits.

A companion book, *Audubon Water Bird Guide,* by the same

1 Complete names and addresses of publishers are listed in the appendix.

author, includes the water birds, game birds, and larger land birds such as the hawks, buzzards, eagles, and falcons. There are 623 illustrations of 258 species, 485 in full color by Don Eckelberry and 138 in black and white by Earl L. Poole.

These two volumes cover the birds in the area of eastern and central North America from southern Texas to central Greenland.

A Pocket Guide to Birds by Allan Cruickshank. This is a compact paper-back edition that is exceptionally good for the beginning bird student. Its approach to identification is through the recognition of family groups. The book includes 72 natural-color photagraphs and 78 representative drawings.

How to Know the Birds by Roger Tory Peterson. This is another paper-back manual specifically written to simplify bird recognition. It emphasizes body shapes, flight patterns, characteristic habits, and similar aids to field identification. It includes a special section on habitats and indicates the species most likely to be found in each. Peterson has illustrated more than 200 species in this book — 72 in color and over 400 black-and-white drawings indicating identifying characteristics and silhouettes.

Bird Songs and Calls

Many of our songbirds are heard more often than seen. For this reason a knowledge of their songs and call notes is of the utmost importance in bird recognition.

The beginning student will experience some difficulty in distinguishing one song from another. A good approach to learning bird songs is actually to *watch the bird sing*. Watch the more common species, the ones you can identify instantly by sight, and then make some mental or written notations concerning the song you hear. A notebook will come in handy at this point. Jot down *your* impressions of the song. Perhaps you can associate words with the different notes. Your impression of a towhee's song may be recorded something like this: *see* ↘ *heee*. A chickadee's call

tow

could be recorded as: *chick* ↘ *dee-dee-dee*. The notes and calls

a

of many birds can be recorded in this way. Once you know a few songs, others can be learned easily by comparison.

A book written by Aretas A. Saunders entitled *A Guide to Bird Songs* presents a unique method recording bird voices by the use of various diagrams. If you are musically inclined, Schuyler Mathew's *Field Book of Wild Birds and Their Music* may be more helpful, as it is based on a series of musical notations.

A more recent aid to the identification of bird songs has been the release of several fine recordings. The actual songs of the birds of America's woods, gardens, fields, prairies, and shorelines have been recorded in the birds' natural environment. A list of these recording may be found in the appendix.

Binoculars

A good binocular is the bird students' most helpful piece of equipment. It is also likely to be the most expensive. However, the importation of Japanese optical items has made it possible for many birders to own good binoculars at a fraction of the cost of comparable American quality. Most of these imported glasses have such desirable qualities as central focusing and coated optics.

The task of selecting a binocular for bird study is sometimes confusing. What you want is a glass that will locate the bird easily and bring it close enough for observation and identification. To do this, you will need at least a six-power (6x) glass. The symbol "6x" means that the instrument magnifies an object six times its natural size. In other words, the distance between you and a bird is divided by six. When the bird is sixty feet away, it appears to be only ten feet away. Other glasses of seven, eight, nine, and ten power reduce the apparent distance to an object in proportion to their respective powers.

The higher the power of the binocular you use, the more difficult it will be to hold it steady. Every slight motion you make will be magnified in proportion also. The second figure (30) in a 6x, 30 binocular means that the objective lens (the large one) is 30 millimeters in diameter. This measurement is important in that it determines the amount of light which can be collected by the glass. For all-around use in bird work, the diameter of the objective lens should be about five times the power of the glass. Thus a 6x, 30, 7x, 35, or 8x, 40 would be a good binocular for this purpose.

Another important factor to consider in the selection of a binocular is "the field of view." A manufacturer who indicates his glass as have a field of 150 yards at 1,000 yards means that at a distance of 1,000 yards the observer would see an area 150 yards wide. If the object under observation is closer than 1,000 yards, the field of view is proportionately narrower. In bird study, binoculars are often used to view small objects at comparatively short distances. For this reason it is important that a bird glass have the widest field of view possible.

Keeping Bird Records

Many students keep records of their observations on field trips for birds. Such information as the number and kinds of species observed, location, behavior, and other aspects of bird life is carefully recorded. Records of this type become increasingly interesting and useful as they accumulate over a period of years. They will also prove useful to future students who may have access to them.

One indispensable item of equipment for use in the field is a small pocket notebook. Notations and sketches of birds not immediately identified can be referred to upon completion of the trip. Then, with the use of one or two good reference books, accurate identification can usually be made. Your notebook may also be used to make temporary recordings concerning migration, habits, or any other special study in which you may be interested.

For daily lists and field trips, you will find that the pocket-sized check lists are most convenient. The National Audubon Society publishes an inexpensive check list of this type covering all the birds occurring in North America east of the Mississippi River. This field card also provides space for recording locality, date, time, weather, and other pertinent information.

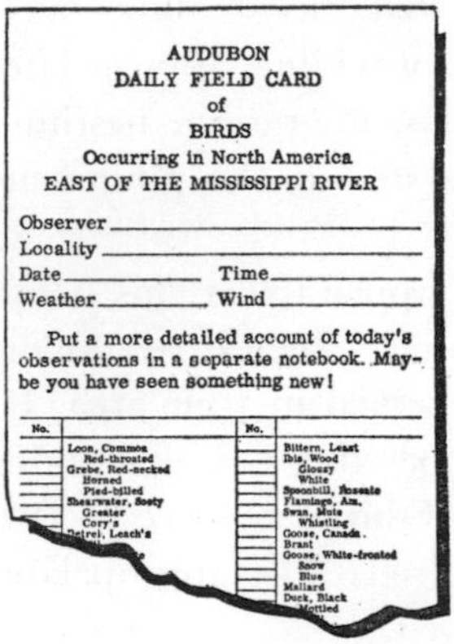

AUDUBON
DAILY FIELD CARD
of
BIRDS
Occurring in North America
EAST OF THE MISSISSIPPI RIVER

Observer ____
Locality ____
Date ____ Time ____
Weather ____ Wind ____

Put a more detailed account of today's observations in a separate notebook. Maybe you have seen something new!

No.		No.	
	Loon, Common		Bittern, Least
	Red-throated		Ibis, Wood
	Grebe, Red-necked		Glossy
	Horned		White
	Pied-billed		Spoonbill, Roseate
	Shearwater, Sooty		Flamingo, Am.
	Greater		Swan, Mute
	Cory's		Whistling
	Petrel, Leach's		Goose, Canada
			Brant
			Goose, White-fronted
			Snow
			Blue
			Mallard
			Duck, Black
			Mottled

FIGURE 63.
AUDUBON DAILY FIELD CARD
PUBLISHED BY
THE NATIONAL AUBUDON SOCIETY,
1130 FIFTH AVE.,
NEW YORK 28, N. Y.

You will undoubtedly want to keep a permanent record of the information accumulated on your daily field trips. A larger notebook or filing sytsem is ideal for this purpose. A simple form for recording dates and species observed can be ruled off as follows: First, list the species common to your locality along the left margin of the page. Then fill the remainder of the page (to the right of the species listed) with a series of vertical lines approximately half an inch apart. Allow space at the top of the columns to insert the date of each trip. A series of horizontal lines separating the species will keep all check marks and numbers in proper alignment. Several sheets may be necessary to list all the species found in your locality. A glance at this form, once it has been filled in, will reveal such information as the number and kinds of birds seen on a particular day or the dates on which a certain species was most abundant.

If you are interested in a special phase of bird study, you may have need for other forms. Be sure to plan all such forms so they require a minimum amount of bookkeeping and so they can be interpreted easily.

The National Audubon Society publishes an excellent record system called "Birdfile." It consists of 250 cards, 5 inches by 7 inches in size. Each card is imprinted with the common name and the scientific name of a single species found in the eastern United States. A few cards without names are included so that "accidentals" may be added. Each card is ruled and labeled, providing appropriate spaces for information regarding observations, migration, nesting, and other pertinent data. This is a compact system for keeping neat and accurate records.

The "Check List of Eastern Birds" in the appendix of this book was included for your convenience in keeping a handy record of the total number of species attracted and observed in your area. It can be made more informative by an accompanying key that indicates the location as well as the number of birds observed — (P) pond; (B) birdbath; (F) feeders; (N) nesting; etc. The appropriate letter can be entered with the number observed.

Bird Photography

Bird photography is becoming increasingly popular. At one time or another, nearly every bird student is tempted to test his skill with a camera. New and better types of cameras are making it possible for both amateur and professional to obtain more satisfactory results. The subject of photography and cameras is so large that, rather than attempt to present all the details involved, the more general aspects of this popular hobby will be covered in the hope that they will serve as a guide to the reader.

Cameras now on the market vary in price from a few dollars to several hundred dollars. Although acceptable pictures can be taken with the cheaper cameras, more consistent satisfactory results can be attained through use of the better equipment. The actual selection of a camera for bird photography will, of course, depend upon the amount of money available for investment and the type of pictures desired. Many photographers prefer color transparencies while others still adhere to black-and-white prints.

The 35-millimeter cameras are most popular for color work. They are compact, easily transported, very adaptable, and the color film is relatively inexpensive compared to that required by the larger cameras. There are many makes of this size camera on the market. They vary considerably in price, lens quality, focusing, and features included. The single-lens-reflex design has the advantage of through-the-lens focusing. This permits critical focusing through any attached lens, even on extremely close subjects. Any 35-millimeter camera selected for bird photography should be so designed as to permit the adaptation of a telescopic lens.

Color films preferred for bird photography include the standard daylight Kodachrome and the comparatively new High Speed Ektachrome. Kodachrome has an exposure index of 10; the newer Ektachrome, an exposure index of 160. The latter permits photographing in less light, faster exposures for action shots, and smaller apertures resulting in a greater depth of field.

For black-and-white pictures, most of our country's outstanding bird photographers use the Graflex or Reflex type of camera. These cameras have longer focal lengths and permit focusing up to the instant exposure is desired. This is an important feature, especially when pictures of birds in flight are being taken. These cameras are necessarily rather large. One size takes a 4-by-5-inch negative; another, a 3¼-by-4¼-inch negative. Of the two, the 3¼ by 4¼ is the lighter in weight and more easily transported.

A certain amount of extra equipment is necessary regardless of the type of camera you may use. A supplementary lens or a telephoto lens is essential for taking close-up views. This permits photographing from a distance that is less likely to frighten birds. A sturdy tripod will eliminate any unnecessary movement of the camera during exposure and afford a better opportunity for desired picture composition.

A flash attachment is extremely useful for taking bird pictures.

Nests, feeders, and likely perches are often in subdued light. A synchronized flash will supplement the natural light, resulting in more detailed pictures. With a flash it is also possible to continue photographing on dull, cloudy days.

On many of the newer cameras, the flash and exposure can be synchronized with a remote-control device. This permits the camera to be located and focused on a predetermined perch. Exposure can then be made from a considerable distance. While many good pictures are taken in this manner, it is quite difficult to get the desired composition. Most bird photographers prefer to use a blind and a magnifying lens.

One of the simplest home-made blinds employs the use of an old lawn or beach umbrella and some burlap. The pole should be firmly

FIGURE 64.   BLINDS FOR PHOTOGRAPHIC AND OBSERVATION PURPOSES (A) *Home-made type using lawn or beach umbrella and burlap;* (B) *commercial pop-up type.*

fastened in the ground and the burlap pinned to the top edges of the umbrella. The pieces of burlap (opened bags) can be easily pinned together with nails. The bottom edges should be staked to the ground to prevent movement in the wind. The entrance (or closure) can be faced in any direction with a slit left for camera use.

Portable blinds are available commercially. The relatively new pop-up type consists of a folding aluminum frame covered with cloth. This blind can be set up quickly and is easily transported. It is highly recommended for extensive field photography.

Much fun and satisfaction are to be had when you are recording your birding experiences on film. As your interest increases and you approach the professional stage, the task of selecting the ideal camera for your purposes will not be so difficult. Likewise, the use of remote-control devices, flash equipment, blinds, and other tricks of the trade will become common knowledge as you pursue this fascinating hobby.

Special Study Projects

BIRD-BANDING. Every year bird students co-operating with the United States Fish and Wildlife Service place tiny numbered bands about the legs of many thousands of our wild birds. The results of this work are the basis for much of the known information about the habits of many species. Such interesting facts as where birds migrate, what routes they follow, how long they live, whether the numbers of a certain species are increasing or decreasing, and the answers to other innumerable questions can be proved accurately.

Banders catch the birds in various types of traps that have been designed so as not to injure the trapped birds. The birds are then banded and released immediately. The bander records such pertinent information as the species of the bird banded, number of the band, date, location, type of trap, age (adult, juvenile, or nestling), and sex when known. This information is recorded on special forms and forwarded periodically to the United States Fish and Wildlife Service. When other banders retrap these same birds, they also record and forward similar information to this agency. The original bander then receives a report of when, where, and by which his bird was recovered. The bander making the recovery also receives information as to when, where, and by whom the bird was originally banded. Many numbers are also reported by persons finding bands on dead birds and by hunters of waterfowl and other game birds.

Bird-banding is a fascinating hobby that contributes much valuable information to the scientific study of our North American birds. If you are interested in becoming a bird-bander, you must first secure a special federal permit that allows you to trap and band wild birds. These permits are not issued freely to everyone who applies. The following points will help you decide whether you can qualify for such a permit:

1. Applicants must be at least eighteen years of age.
2. Applicants must be thoroughly competent to identify positively all the local species of birds.
3. The foregoing must be vouched for by three recognized ornithologists or banders.
4. The program is a voluntary one. The bander donates his time and pays for his equipment and receives no compensation or reimbursement from the government. The Service, however, provides at no cost to the bander, the bands, report forms, and flanked envelopes.
5. Application blanks are obtainable from the Bird Banding Office, Patuxent Research Refuge, Laurel, Maryland.

NESTING CENSUS.   An abundance of birds about one's property is often the inspiration for field work and ornithological studies. A nesting survey of a given area is one of the most fascinating and rewarding of all birding adventures. It takes one afield throughout the months of spring — the time of greatest activity in the lives of birds. This is the season of singing, mating, nest-building, and the rearing of young.

In addition to the pleasure afforded the observer, an accurate nesting survey can frequently provide information of scientific value. There is still much to learn about nesting in relation to specific habitats, plant succession, range requirements, and similar ecological problems.

The size of the survey area chosen should not be too large for complete and accurate coverage. A fifty-acre field area is considered about maximum for one observer. In heavily wooded sections, this figure should be about halved. Marshes, swamps, and river areas requiring the use of a boat will reduce the amount of space that can be adequately covered.

A simple and accurate system of conducting a nesting census is known as the "quadrant method." A map of the area to be studied is essential. If a map is not available from the property owner, one is usually on file in the local tax or agricultural offices. For con-

venience in using, the map should be scaled to fit on a standard
8½-by-11-inch sheet of typing paper. The property is divided into
imaginary quadrants, each 50 yards square. With an appropriate
reduction scale, the same quadrants are drawn on the map. Each
quadrant is numbered on the map and in the field. A generous supply of complete maps can now be made by Mimeograph. Durable
and easily observed field markers can be made by painting can lids
yellow and numbering them with black enamel. They can then
be wired to a tree, post, or other prominent feature in respective
quadrants.

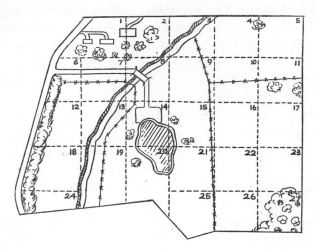

FIGURE 65.   NESTING BIRDS AND SINGING MALES CAN BE PLOTTED
    ACCURATELY ON A MAP DIVIDED INTO EQUAL QUADRANTS.

The census should be started by mid-March in order to include
owls, hawks, and other early-nesters. Late-nesting species such as the
goldfinch cannot be completely recorded until mid-July.

The actual survey is made by an observer covering each quadrant,
preferably at one-week intervals. New nests are counted, of course,
but the basis of the survey depends upon the recording of all singing males. Each singing male is plotted (according to quadrant) on a

dated map. A male singing in the same area on a number of consecutive observations is then conceded to represent a nesting pair. Rough field notations can be transferred to individual maps for a nesting record of each species. A total map (showing all nesting species) will indicate the nesting density of specific sections within the area being surveyed.

The real value of a nesting census lies in annual (or at least periodic) repetition. In this way nesting densities can be compared with environmental changes and similar factors of ornithological significance.

MIGRATION STUDIES. The knowledge and mysteries of migrating birds have long stirred the imagination of bird watchers everywhere. Flights of thousands of miles, some starting and ending in our own backyards, arouse our curiosity concerning this seasonal phenomenon. There is a challenge to learn more of the ways and travels of these far-ranging migrants.

The arrival of the first bluebird or robin in the spring is a moment often remembered and recorded. This act is of little value unless it represents the beginning of a more thorough migration study. We need to know more about migration waves, the length of the period of maximum abundance, routes followed, the influence of weather, and similar allied factors.

A practical area study can be made by recording information on a sheet of ordinary graph paper, or on paper especially ruled for the purpose. The names of the birds are listed in a column along the left margin of the paper. Across the top, each column is dated — one day per column. When a species is first observed, an "X" (or the actual number of birds seen) is placed after its name under the appropriate date column. All succeeding observations are entered in a like manner. Over a period of time, observations recorded in this manner will reveal at a glance such information as arrival dates, migration waves, departure dates, and other comparative migration data.

LIFE-HISTORY STUDIES. You undoubtedly have a favorite bird — a particular species that appeals to you more than any other. This being the case, your special field of interest may be a life-history study of this favored species.

A study, to be of the most value, should be as thorough and complete as possible. Practical conclusions cannot be based on brief studies of a few birds. An outstanding example of a life-history study was conducted by Margaret M. Nice, of Columbus, Ohio. Her *Studies in the Life History of the Song Sparrow* is regarded as the outstanding reference work in this particular field of ornithological study. Your particular endeavor may not result in a publication of this importance; however, good reference material will be of considerable help in planning your study. In addition to the publication just mentioned, I recommend *A Guide to Bird Watching* by Joseph J. Hickey. This book contains an excellent outline for a life-history study.

MAKING RESULTS KNOWN. Regardless of what your special study project may be, it will be of little value if the results are not shared with others in your field of interest. If definite findings have been made and conclusions reached, perhaps the initial approach to publication should be through your local bird club or Audubon Society. If your findings are of regional or national interest, publications such as *Audubon Magazine, The Auk, The Condor,* or *The Wilson Bulletin* may be interested in publishing them.

CHAPTER XIX

SANCTUARIES FOR BIRDS

THE MEANING of the word "sanctuary" has many interpretations. One's concept of the term may be applicable to a backyard area; to another, it may indicate vast expanses involving thousands of acres. Regardless of the size or type of area so designated, each may fill an important niche in the protection and better understanding of our wildlife resources. The backyard sanctuary's contribution to the immediate protection of wildlife may be somewhat negligible. Perhaps its greatest asset is in the inspiration and enlightenment of the owner, whose initial interest is frequently expanded into a better understanding and more generous support of the over-all resource picture. In the case of larger sanctuaries, their greatest value may be the promotion of a community educational program or as the only means of preservation for certain species.

The role of the sanctuary becomes increasingly significant as the human population increases, exerting greater pressures for living space and recreational areas. The need for the preservation of resource areas is urgent. Those that are not saved now may never be saved.

Backyard Sanctuaries

Any backyard or garden may become a sanctuary in the eyes of its owner merely by his labeling it as such. However, its contribution to the protection of bird life will depend largely upon the manner in which it is managed. Rarely is the term "sanctuary" alone sufficient to provide any measurable degree of protection. For an area to be of any appreciable value to wildlife, it must in some ways fulfill the requirements of a natural habitat.

Every day bird habitats give way to the power of the bulldozer. Increased suburban development, industrial expansion, new and bigger highways, are factors that make the development and maintenance of sanctuaries more significant and important. The small sanctuary helps, in part, to offset this daily encroachment upon natural wildlife environment. In addition, it may also serve as a research and study area where the findings may provide the initial inspiration for a better understanding of conservation in relation to human welfare.

The development and management of a backyard sanctuary incorporates most of the principles described throughout this book. Adequate vegetation — the kind that provides food, cover, and nesting sites — is most important. Water is a necessity. Nesting boxes and supplementary feeding are extras that will help make the grounds adjacent to your home more attractive to birds.

Community Sanctuaries

Modern concepts of the values of a wildlife sanctuary as related to community life are far more inclusive than the single objective of protecting the wildlife within its borders. The most important function of a sanctuary, particularly the relatively small public one, is serving as an educational center. The sanctuary that teaches the citizens of a community, through inspiration and recreation, the needs and ways of good, sound conservation practices will in turn increase many times its own value as a community asset.

The physical features of a sanctuary may vary according to the type and amount of land available. A city lot, a municipal park, undeveloped town property, or a near-by farm or country estate can be developed as a sanctuary to serve the needs of children and adults within the community. The ideal area for sanctuary purposes is one that has a varied type of terrain — woodlands, open fields and meadows, brooks and ponds. We must remember that all land-owners do not possess such ideal conditions for wildlife, but nevertheless the land they do have can be made more attractive to wild-life through appropriate conservation measures. A sanctuary can often be most beneficial by teaching ways and means of developing areas that are not so ideal — they need it most. The real worth of a sanctuary can be measured best by its program, not by the physical characteristics of the land.

VALUES OF A COMMUNITY SANCTUARY. Many of our country's citizens are beginning to realize that their future standard of living depends largely on the wise use and development of our natural resources. Farmers are becoming more interested in contour farming and other soil-conservation measures; city dwellers are concerned over flood conditions, water shortages, and food supplies; more individuals and organizations understand the part that birds and other forms of wildlife play in the over-all picture of our economic welfare. A community sanctuary can contribute much toward the furthering of this understanding attitude. The means of accomplishing this end will provide inspiration and recreation for thousands of people.

The processes of nature are slow. Long periods of time are required to rebuild soil, grow new forests, and increase depleted wildlife populations. If any real progress is to be made toward accomplishing these necessities, it will have to be done through the education of the youth of our communities. The most valuable contribution to community life which can be made by a public sanctuary is to help our citizens develop a well-founded understanding of our natural resources — the resources upon which mankind must now and forever subsist.

STEPS OF ORGANIZATION. The procedures of organizing a community sanctuary will, of course, depend upon the sources of motivation and the facilities immediately available. An individual interested in establishing a nature- and-conservation education center for his community, and possessing the physical and financial means of developing and maintaining such a center, may find it advantageous to contact the National Audubon Society, 1130 Fifth Ave., New York 28, N. Y. This organization maintains several educational centers throughout the United States, providing nature and conservation programs for tens of thousands of children yearly, coming by busloads with their teachers, scout, or youth leaders.

Occasionally, community-owned land and finances are available for outdoor education facilities. More often than not, the program in such cases is subject to rather liberal interpretations, and the land area is dedicated for "multiple use" purposes. It is most difficult and impractical, particularly in relatively small areas, to promote nature activities and conservation of resources amid picnicking, water skiing, and similar forms of recreation.

There is another type of community sanctuary that is gaining in popularity — one where the interested citizens form a corporate organization for the purpose of acquiring land and promoting their desired program. It is with this kind of community sanctuary that the remainder of this section is mainly concerned.

CREATE PUBLIC INTEREST. You may decide that a sanctuary would be a fine asset to your community; but unless you can create public interest in the project, your original idea will be of little worth. You must understand fully just how a sanctuary will benefit your community.

Most towns and cities have a nucleus of citizens who are interested in natural-history subjects. Garden clubs, Boy Scouts, Girl Scouts, sportsmen's clubs, and similar organizations have programs based on outdoor activities. Rotary, Lions, and Kiwanis are clubs organized primarily for the purpose of community service. Seek their help.

Lectures and motion pictures will also create public interest in wildlife. Many excellent films are available from the National Audubon Society and other agencies for nominal rental fees.

CALL A PUBLIC MEETING.   Once you have created interest in starting a community sanctuary, a public meeting is the next step. You should accomplish at least three things at this meeting. They are: (1) create further enthusiasm for establishment of a sanctuary by means of a good lecturer or motion picture; (2) decide on a definite date for the purpose of organizing; and (3) appoint the following committees: a publicity committee, a membership committee, a constitution and bylaws committee, a nominating committee, and a committee to investigate possible locations for the sanctuary.

The success of this meeting will depend largely on an inspirational program. If at all possible, secure a speaker who has had experience in developing wildlife areas. Naturalists from other sanctuaries, state or national parks, or state colleges are usually well versed in this subject.

The importance of appointing committees is to keep the project alive and before the public while much of the initial work is being done. Much of this responsibility rests with the publicity committee. Local newspapers and radio stations will help materially.

The committee selected to find a suitable site for the sanctuary would do well to seek the advice of professionally qualified personnel. Men from the local office of the U. S. Soil Conservation Service, or from the conservation department of a near-by college, are usually willing to help with this type of community endeavor.

The nominating committee will have the responsibility of selecting candidates for election to the board of trustees. To do this, they will have to work in conjunction with the bylaws committee so that candidates can be nominated in accordance with the adopted bylaws.

You will find several advantages, from the point of view of taxation, in forming a nonprofit corporation under the laws of your state. A lawyer interested in the sanctuary will be glad to work with the bylaws committee regarding any legal matters involved in this procedure.

The following Articles of Association and Bylaws are presented as a guide to be used by organizing committees. They are not necessarily technically correct under the laws of your state, nor are they intended to be all-inclusive in their provisions. Adjustments and additions will have to be made according to the requirements of each individual organization.

ARTICLES OF ASSOCIATION

Be it known, that we, the subscribers, do hereby associate ourselves as a body politic and corporate pursuant to the statute laws of the State of _____ regulating the formation and organization of corporations without capital stock, and the following are our articles of association:

ARTICLE I. The name of said organization shall be _____ Wildlife Sanctuary, Incorporated.

ARTICLE II. The purposes for which said corporation is formed are the following; to wit:

To maintain and operate a sanctuary for wildlife in the Township of _____, County of _____, and State of _____, and for such purpose to acquire, by purchase, grant, gift, or devise, real and personal property of every kind and description, and to hold, manage, remodel, alter, repair, develop, invest, sell, assign, mortgage, pledge, change, and reinvest the same at its discretion.

It shall have the power to make bylaws suitable for its government, which may include provision for establishing a membership of one or more classes in the corporation, for the fixing and collection of membership dues or fees, and, in general, for the orderly carrying out of the purposes of the corporation.

The membership, when so established, shall have the right to elect trustees of the corporation. The bylaws may provide that, by vote of the membership, the number of trustees may be altered by increase or decrease.

The corporation shall have perpetual existence, but in case it should be at any time dissolved or its existence terminated, none of its members shall acquire, or be presumed to acquire, receive, have, or enjoy, any financial or material profit or benefit out of, or to be derived from, the sale or disposal of its assets.

ARTICLE III.   The said corporation is located in the Township of ——, County of ——, and State of ——, and the location of the principal office is at —— in the said Township of ——, and the name of the agent upon whom process may be served is ——.

DATED at (city and state), this —— day of ——, 19——.

SIGNED (Signatures of incorporators).

BYLAWS

ARTICLE I
Name and Object

The name of this Association shall be the —— Wildlife Sanctuary, Inc., and its purpose shall be to promote an educational program in the field of conservation and to encourage the study and love of nature by acquiring, developing, and maintaining a wildlife sanctuary on the property of —— in the Township of ——, State of ——; by holding classes, lectures, or exhibits, issuing publications, and by other means approved by the trustees.

ARTICLE II
Membership and Dues

1. Any person interested in the purposes of this Association shall be eligible for membership.

2. Membership shall be divided into the following classes, based upon the payment of dues, but the rights and privileges of members of all classes shall be the same:

(*a*)   Regular Members: annual dues five dollars ($5).

(*b*)   Contributing Members: annual dues, ten dollars ($10).

(*c*)   Sustaining Members: annual dues, twenty-five dollars ($25).

(*d*)   Patron Members: annual dues, fifty dollars ($50).

(*e*)   Life Members: fee, one hundred dollars ($100).

3. (*a*)   Other organizations (churches, schools, chambers of commerce, clubs, fraternal orders, etc.) shall be eligible for Contributing

and Sustaining Memberships, and shall be entitled to name one or two delegates, respectively.

(*b*) Junior organizations (Boy and Girl Scouts, 4-H Clubs, classes in schools) shall be eligible for a special Junior Membership, annual dues three dollars ($3), and shall be entitled to name one delegate.

(*c*) Delegates of member organizations shall enjoy all rights and privileges of regular members; but the rights of membership shall not accrue to the individual members of these affiliated organizations.

ARTICLE III
Meetings

1. The annual meeting shall be held on the (date) in _____ Township at such time and place as the trustees may designate.

2. Upon the call of the trustees, a special meeting for the transaction of business set forth in the notice of said meeting may be held upon ten days' notice in writing to all members, and such a meeting must be called upon written petition by twenty-five members.

3. At any regular or special meeting of this Association thirty members shall constitute a quorum and properly executed proxies, filed with the treasurer, shall be accepted.

ARTICLE IV
Management

1. The active management of the affairs of the Association shall be vested in the board of trustees, which is hereby empowered to delegate specific duties and powers to its regularly appointed committees.

ARTICLE V
Board of Trustees

1. The board of trustees shall consist of fifteen members, which shall be elected in the following manner: at the first meeting twenty candidates shall be regularly nominated and seconded by the members present, who shall then vote for fifteen; the three candidates

receiving the greatest number of votes to serve for five years, the three receiving the next greatest number of votes to serve for four years, and in this manner till fifteen are named, the last three to serve for one year. Thereafter a nominating committee of five, appointed by the trustees, shall present to each annual meeting three candidates, plus nominations from the floor, from whom three shall be elected to serve for five years.[1] After expiration of his term of office no trustee shall be eligible for re-election until one year shall have elapsed.

2. Vacancies in the board shall be filled temporarily by the trustees and by the members at the next annual meeting for the unexpired term.

ARTICLE VI
Meetings of the Trustees

1. The annual meeting of the board of trustees shall be held immediately following the annual meeting of the Association.

2. Regular quarterly meetings of the board shall be held in _____ Township on the (day) in (month) and at such time and place as the president shall designate.

3. Special meetings of the boards may be held at any time or place in the Township of _____, subject to the call of the president.

4. At all meetings of the board, six members shall constitute a quorum.

ARTICLE VII
Officers and Committees

1. At its annual meetings the board of trustees shall elect from among its members the following officers: President, Vice-President, Secretary, and Treasurer, who shall perform the duties usual and customary to these offices.

2. At its annual meeting the board of trustees shall appoint from

---

1 Most sanctuaries have found it advantageous to nominate the actual number of candidates that are to be elected. This makes the election of selected personnel more certain. It also eliminates the possibility of any ill will on the part of defeated candidates.

its members the chairmen of the following standing committees, which shall appoint their own committees:

Executive Committee of three members, one of whom shall be the president, which under the general direction of the trustees shall have active charge of the business of the Association.

Finance Committee of five members, one of whom shall be the treasurer, which shall present an annual budget for the approval of the trustees; and have charge of raising an endowment fund, and the investment of any funds available for this purpose.

Program Committee of five members to have charge of planning and executing an educational and recreational program, including lectures, classes, exhibits, entertainments, publications, and such other activities of similar character as it deems proper and expedient.

Junior Activities Committee of five members, which shall plan and direct a junior program of education and recreation in co-operation with the schools and the member junior organizations.

Public Relations Committee of five members to promote the objects of this Association through the newspapers, radio, and any other suitable media of publicity.

The trustees may appoint such other committees as they deem necessary.

ARTICLE VIII
Amendments

1. These bylaws may be changed or amended at any regular or special meeting of the Association by a majority vote of the members present, provided that a copy of the present clause and the proposed change or amendment be mailed to all members two weeks in advance of said meeting.

The duty of the membership committee is to enroll members in the new sanctuary. If appointed on a regional basis, all areas of the community can be thoroughly canvassed. Membership fees based on a graduated scale will enable all income groups to help provide financial support.

The organizing committees of the Pequot-sepos Wildlife Sanctuary in Mystic, Connecticut, adopted a unique plan that assured a minimum income for the first three years. They enrolled a definite number of Founders and Charter Members, each of whom signed a pledge of support (in the form of membership dues) for a minimum period of three years. Annual membership fees were set at three dollars for Charter Members and ten dollars for Founders. This plan assured the sanctuary of a definite annual income for the first three years of its existence. Every effort was made to re-enlist all members at the expiration of this period. Many new members were added by conducting annual membership drives.

HOLD AN ORGANIZATION MEETING. The next step in organizing your sanctuary is to call a meeting of all founders and charter members, the purpose of this meeting being to conduct the accrued business of the organization. The bylaws, as submitted by the committee, will be subject to amendment and adoption; other committees may have reports to make, and a board of trustees will have to be elected.

The importance of hiring a full-time professionally qualified director is another matter to be included on this meeting's agenda. If the sanctuary is to conduct an educational program for the benefit of the community, the services of a professional leader are necessary. The advantages of such leadership can be presented to the members in a convincing manner by a committee, or an individual, previously appointed to consider this matter. Once the members understand that professional direction of the sanctuary's activities is a necessity, a special committee can be appointed to engage a suitable director.

FINANCING. A bit of cautious judgment on the part of sanctuary personnel can eliminate most of the financial problems experienced by newly formed publicly supported groups. The essentials of a community sanctuary are flexible. The size may vary from a small lot to a tract of several hundred acres; the program can be expanded in proportion to the amount of funds available; and most of the activities can be held in the out-of-doors, thus eliminating buildings and similar items from the initial expenditures. In other words, if the land is available, any community can have a wildlife sanctuary.

Once your sanctuary is officially organized, an active educational and recreational program will prove the best means of gaining additional support from the citizens of your area. This type of program cannot be supported entirely on income from membership dues. Additional sources of revenue, including contributions from individuals, organizations, industries, and community welfare agencies, should be sought. The amount of success achieved in securing these contributions will depend on the type and value of the program available to the community.

PROGRAM ACTIVITIES. The activities of a sanctuary must provide fun and recreation for children and adults and not attempt to make them conservation experts. The most we can hope to do, especially with children, is to help develop an understanding attitude concerning the ways of nature. Once this interest is acquired, an intelligent understanding of conservation values will be well founded.

The following projects contain many opportunities for interesting nature activities:

SANCTUARY PROJECTS

Develop the sanctuary property.

Plant trees and shrubs attractive to birds and other wildlife.

Build or improve ponds to attract waterfowl.

Clear new trails so that all parts of the sanctuary are accessible.

Set up the following demonstrations:

Methods of erosion control

Feed strips

Wildlife shelters

Devices for winter feeding

Nesting boxes

Woodlot management

Plan a nature trail.

Put up descriptive signs and labels telling nature's story.

Start a trailside museum. Include exhibits of:

Nature pictures and charts

Habitat groups — scenes found on the sanctuary grounds

A collection of birds' nests

Minerals

Insects

Woods

Pressed plants

Sea shells

Live mammals

Electrical nature games for identification of birds, wild flowers, etc.

Mounted birds

Spatter prints of leaves and plants

Hold a Saturday-morning nature hour for children.

Motion pictures

Nature hikes

Instructional periods

Conduct a summer day camp for children.

Get volunteers to help with the program.

Invite school classes to visit the sanctuary.

Arrange for guided tours and instruction periods by the sanctuary's director.

Conduct a series of field trips for members.

Wild flowers

Geology

Trees

Bird migrations

Nesting surveys

Insects

Marine life

Astronomy

Make your program available for school use.

    Motion-picture programs

    Loan exhibits

    Winter feeding programs

    Bird-box projects

    Nature classes

Conduct a series of winter programs for members.

    Lectures

    Motion pictures

    Consider holding Audubon Screen Tour programs sponsored by the National Audubon Society, 1130 Fifth Avenue, New York 28, N.Y.

Private Sanctuaries

The population of America is growing at an increasingly rapid rate. With each new generation the momentum accelerates, exerting greater demands upon a given land mass. This seemingly bright symbol of prosperity may in itself be the means of its own undoing. As the public yields more land to the condemnation powers of local, state, and federal agencies, we are, without a doubt, placing an ever tightening noose about the very resources so vital to the survival of the growing multitudes.

As we understand the relationships within a single outdoor habitat, so must we respect the greater ecology that encompasses the natural resources of our land. We cannot exploit one resource — soil, water, plants, wildlife — without implicating the others. As shorelines and marshlands give way to housing developments, as woodlands fall before the forester's ax, as farmlands become ribboned with highways, so must our wildlife yield to the changing patterns of civilization. With the continuing loss of natural habitats, it has little recourse but to revert to substitute parcels of land — smaller parcels subject to the same pressures from which it has just escaped. The adaptability of most displaced species is so limited that few can permanently endure this continuous transition.

Some require very specialized habitat areas in order to survive. These areas must remain inviolate; otherwise, certain species of birds, plants, and mammals will become extinct. The private sanctuary is one of the best means of preventing this catastrophe.

Private ownership, by established conservation organizations with the knowledge and financial means of promoting a publicly acceptable program and sound management practices, presents the best opportunity of maintaining local respect and national good will regarding extensive land holdings. Foremost among such organizations is the National Audubon Society, which currently maintains thirty sanctuaries within the United States. They range in size from the 26,000-acre Rainey Sanctuary amid the coastal marshes of Louisiana, and the 6,020-acre Corkscrew Swamp Sanctuary in Florida, to numerous small water-bird sanctuaries of only a few acres each along the coasts of Florida and Texas. The contribution of the Society's sanctuary program to the preservation of American wildlife during the past fifty-five years is, indeed, a commendable one. In addition, and perhaps of greater significance, thousands of children and adults have gained a deeper appreciation of all our country's natural resources.

Public Sanctuaries

The history of public wildlife refuges (state and federal) in our country is comparatively recent. Not until greed and exploitation placed numerous species of birds and mammals on the brink of extinction was there any public concern or effort to seek protection for American wildlife.

In the year 1870 the state legislature of California created the first public wildlife refuge in our country. The area now known as Lake Merritt in Oakland was established as a waterfowl sanctuary. Although the city has grown up around the lake, it still provides refuge for thousands of migratory waterfowl each year. Two years later the first national wildlife refuge, Yellowstone Park, was created by action of the United States Congress. Since these first two enactments of wildlife protection, state and national land holdings have increased to the point where our country now supports the greatest wildlife refuge system in the world.

With several million acres of public land reserved for the protection of birds and other forms of wildlife, it would seem that the survival of all existing species is reasonably well assured; unfortunately, this is not the case. The early founders of our refuge system soon learned that the acquisition of impressive acreages alone was not necessarily sufficient to guarantee the survival and perpetuation of wildlife species. Land management became a necessity.

One of the primary problems of management is concerned with the fact that refuges are frequently too small to maintain sufficient ecological balance for a protected and expanding wildlife population. Complete protection may be cause for competition and overcrowding among species, resulting in the depletion of food supplies. Another problem, perhaps most serious and one that demands a more intelligent public approach, is the insistence of pressure groups for "multiple land-use." We have long known that certain species of birds and mammals cannot survive amid human encroachment.

Despite these limitations, our public sanctuaries and refuges are our most valuable asset in the preservation of today's wild life. They will become increasingly important as our population continues to expand, placing greater demands upon all public lands. They will continue to be effective so long as they have adequate support and remain inviolate to legal usurpation.

APPENDIX

Books That Will Help You

ATTRACTING BIRDS

Songbirds in Your Garden, by John K. Terres. Thomas Y. Crowell
Company, New York, 1953.

Birds in Your Back Yard, by Ted S. Pettit. New York: Harper &
Brothers; 1949.

Picture Primer of Attracting Birds, by C. Russell Mason. Boston:
Houghton Mifflin Co.; 1952.

Birds in the Garden and How to Attract Them, by Margaret
McKenny. New York: Reynal & Hitchcock; 1939.

IDENTIFYING BIRDS

A Field Guide to the Birds, by Roger Tory Peterson. Boston:
Houghton Mifflin Co.; 1947.

A Field Guide to Western Birds, by Roger Tory Peterson. Boston:
Houghton Mifflin Co.; 1941.

Audubon Bird Guide, by Richard H. Pough. New York: Doubleday
& Company, Inc.; 1949.

Audubon Water Bird Guide, by Richard H. Pough. New York:
Doubleday & Company, Inc.; 1956.

How to Know the Birds, by Roger Tory Peterson. New York: New
American Library, of World Literature, Inc.; 1957.

A Pocket Guide to Birds, by Allan Cruickshank. New York: Pocket
Books, Inc.; 1954.

BIRD WATCHING

A Guide to Bird Watching, by Joseph J. Hickey. Garden City, New
York: Garden City Books; 1953.

Watching Birds, by James Fisher. New York: Penguin Books, Inc.;
1951.

The Art of Bird Watching, by E. M. Nicholson. New York: Charles
Scribner's Sons; 1932.

BIRD STUDY

A Laboratory and Field Manual of Ornithology, by Olin S. Pettingill, Jr. Minneapolis: Burgess Publishing Company; 1956.

Natural History of Birds, by Leonard W. Wing. New York: The Ronald Press Company; 1956.

Fundamentals of Ornithology, by Josselyn Van Tyne and Andrew J. Berger. New York: John Wiley & Sons, Inc.; 1959.

Birds' Nests: A Feild Guide, by Richard Headstrom. New York: Ives Washburn, Inc.; 1949.

American Wildlife and Plants, by A. C. Martin, H. Zim, and A. L. Nelson. New York: McGraw-Hill Book Co. 1951.

The A.O.U. Check-List of North American Birds. Fifth Edition. American Ornithologists' Union. Baltimore: The Lord Baltimore Press, Inc.

BIRD SONGS

A Guide to Bird Songs, by Aretas A. Saunders. New York: Doubleday & Company, Inc.; 1951.

Field Book of Wild Birds and Their Music, by Schuyler Mathews. New York: G. P. Putnam's Sons; 1921.

BIRD FINDING

A Guide to Bird Finding (East), by Olin S. Pettingill, Jr. New York: Oxford University Press, Inc.; 1951.

A Guide to Bird Finding (West), by Olin S. Pettingill, Jr. New York: Oxford University Press, Inc.; 1953.

MISCELLANEOUS

Wings in the Wilderness, by Allan D. Cruickshank. New York: Oxford University Press, Inc.; 1947.

Wild America, by Roger Tory Peterson and James Fisher. Boston: Houghton Mifflin Co.; 1955.

1001 Questions Answered About Birds, by Allan and Helen Cruickshank. New York: Dodd, Mead & Co.; 1958.

Hawks Aloft; The Story of Hawk Mountain, by Maurice Brown. New York: Dodd, Mead & Co.; 1949.

Wildlife Conservation, by Ira N. Gabrielson. New York: The Macmillan Co.; 1959.

A Natural History of New York City, by John Kieran. Boston: Houghton Mifflin Co.; 1959.

Recordings of Bird Songs

A Field Guide to Bird Songs (33⅓ rpm). Houghton Mifflin Co., Boston. Recorded by the Laboratory of Ornithology, Cornell University, under the direction of Dr. Peter Paul Kellogg and Dr. Arthur A. Allen, in collaboration with Roger Tory Peterson. Includes songs and calls of more than 300 species of land and water birds of eastern and central North America. Songs and calls are arranged to accompany, page by page, Roger Tory Peterson's *Field Guide to the Birds.*

American Bird Songs (Two Volumes — 33⅓ rpm). Cornell University Press, Ithaca, N.Y. Recorded by Professors Peter Paul Kellogg and Arthur A. Allen, Laboratory of Ornithology, Cornell University. Songs and calls of 123 species.

Bird Songs of Dooryard, Field and Forest (Two Volumes — 33⅓ rpm), by Jerry and Norma Stillwell. Ficker Recording Service, Old Greenwich, Conn. Songs and calls of 107 species.

Warblers (33⅓ rpm), recorded by Dr. Donald J. Borror and Dr. William W. H. Gunn. Includes more than 400 warblers' songs representing 38 species of eastern North American warblers. Federation of Ontario Naturalists, 187 Highbourne Road, Toronto 7, Canada.

Wild Bird Songs (33⅓ rpm) by Ed and Ann Boyes, Detroit, Michigan. Songs and calls of 51 species of land birds.

Some Sources of Native Wildlife Plants

Massachusetts Audubon Society, 155 Newbury St., Boston 15, Massachusetts. A fine selection of shrubs and trees attractive to birds. Write for catalogue (25¢).

Dutch Mt. Nursery, Augusta, Michigan. A good source for species that are difficult to locate. Healthy, guaranteed plants. Write for listings.

Gardens of the Blue Ridge, Ashford, McDowell County, North Carolina. A large selection of native flowers, ferns, aquatic plants, bog plants, vines, shrubs, and trees. Write for catalogue.

Musser Forests, Inc., Indiana, Pennsylvania. An excellent source of evergreen seedlings and transplants. Some shrubs and hard-wood trees. Illustrated catalogue available.

Some Suppliers of Bird Items

Ardsley Woodcraft Products, Inc., 263 Douglas Road, Staten Island 4, N.Y. Bird feeders and other woodcraft products.

Audubon Workship, Box 67, Wonder Lake, Ill. Specializes in bird feeders. Free descriptive folder.

Bartlett Hendricks, Pittsfield 50-A, Mass. All types and prices of binoculars and telescopes.

Beverly Specialties Co., 10331 S. Leavitt St., Chicago 43, Ill. Portable sprays for birdbaths.

Dinah Dee, P.O. Box 6734, Dept. A9, San Antonio 9, Texas. Hummingbird feeders.

Hyde Bird Feeder Co., 56 Felton St., Waltham 54, Mass. Feeders, bird boxes, feed. Free catalogue.

Massachusetts Audubon Society, 155 Newbury St., Boston 15, Mass. Everything for bird attracting and bird watching. Write for catalogue.

Mirakel Optical Co., 14 W. First St., Mt. Vernon 2, N.Y. Everything in binoculars. Write for free catalogue.

National Audubon Society, 1130 Fifth Ave., New York 28, N.Y. The most complete stock of bird items available, including feeders, houses, birdbaths, books, prints, stationery, china, jewelry, etc. Write the Service Department for catalogue.

O B Enterprises, Box 21, Celina 1, Ohio. Field-guide carriers, indexes for Peterson Field Guides, plastic jackets for field guides.

Pecano Bird Feed Company, 110 West St., Albany, Georgia. Wild-bird feeds. Write for listings.

Prunty Seed & Grain Company, 620 N. Second St., St. Louis 2, Mo. Sunflower seeds and seed mixes. Write for price quotations on the quantity you want.

The Birdhouse, Plain Road, Greenfield, Mass. Write for catalogue listing feeders, houses, seeds, guides, binoculars, etc.

The Smith-Gates Corp., Farmington, Conn. Automatic water warmers for winter birdbaths.

Winthrop Packard, Plymouth 3, Mass. "Everything for wild birds."

Sources of Information and Help

State and Federal agencies are prepared to provide information and assistance for various conservation projects. Write them directly for the information you need; request the name and address of their nearest local representative.

FEDERAL AGENCIES

Bureau of Sports Fisheries and Wildlife (Regional Offices). Information on Federal laws and regulations pertaining to the protection of migratory birds and other species of wildlife.

Region 1 (California, Idaho, Montana, Nevada, Oregon, Washington): 1001 N. E. Lloyd Blvd. (P.O. Box 3737), Portland 8, Ore.

Region 2 (Arizona, Colorado, Kansas, New Mexico, Oklahoma, Texas, Utah, Wyoming): 906 Park Ave., S. W. (P.O. Box 1306), Albuquerque, N. Mex.

Region 3 (Illinois, Indiana, Iowa, Michigan, Minnesota, Missouri, Ohio, Nebraska, North Dakota, South Dakota, Wisconsin): 1006 West Lake St., Buzza Bldg., Minneapolis 8, Minn.

Region 4 (Alabama, Arkansas, Florida, Georgia, Kentucky, Louisiana, Maryland, Mississippi, North Carolina, South Carolina, Tennessee, Virginia): Peachtree-Seventh Bldg., Atlanta 23, Ga.

Region 5 (Connecticut, Delaware, Maine, Massachusetts, New Hampshire, New Jersey, New York, Pennsylvania, Rhode Island, Vermont, West Virginia): 59 Temple Place, 1105 Blake Bldg., Boston 11, Mass.

Region 6 (Alaska): P.O. Box 2021, Juneau, Alaska.

Hawaii: Fish and Game Division, Commissioner of Agriculture and Forestry, Honolulu.

Puerto Rico: Department of Agriculture and Commerce, Division of Fisheries and Wildlife, San Juan.

Soil Conservation Service (State Offices)

Information and assistance with soil and water conservation and land management for wildlife. Will supply publications, charts, motion pictures, and posters. Address your inquiries to the State Conservationist of your state.

Alabama: Soil Conservation Bldg., Alabama Polytechnic Institute Campus, Box 311, Auburn.

Alaska: Post Office Box F, Palmer.

Arizona: 223 New Post Office Building, Phoenix.

Arkansas: 323 Federal Building, Little Rock.

California: Tioga Building, Second Floor, 2020 Milvia Street, Berkeley 4.

Colorado: New Customhouse, Denver 2.

Connecticut: College of Agriculture Building, University of Connecticut, Box U-105, Storrs.

Delaware: 503 Academy Street, Box 418, Newark.

Florida: 35 North Main Street, Box 162, Gainesville.

Georgia: Old Post Office Building, Box 832, Athens.

Hawaii: Federal Building, Merchant and Mililand Streets, Honolulu.

Idaho: Annex B-Western Idaho, State Fairgrounds, Box 2709, Boise.

Illinois: Nogle Building, 605 South Neil Street, Champaign.

Indiana: 215 East New York Street, Indianapolis 4.

Iowa: Iowa Building, 505 Sixth Avenue, Des Moines.

Kansas: Public Utility Building, 114½ West Iron Street, Box 600, Salina.

Kentucky: Production and Marketing Building, 231 West Maxwell Street, Lexington.

Louisiana: Svebeck Building, 1517 Sixth Street, Alexandria.

Maine: University of Maine, East Annex Building, Orono.

Maryland: 228 Agriculture Building, University of Maryland, College Park.

Massachusetts: Cooks Block, 6 Main Street, Amherst.

Michigan: Michigan State College, Wells Hall, Unit E, East Lansing.

Minnesota: 517 Federal Courts Building, St. Paul.

Mississippi: Milner Building, Lamar and Pearl Streets, Box 610, Jackson 105.

Missouri: Federal Building, Sixth and Cherry Streets, Box 180, Columbia.

Montana: 26 East Mendenhall, Box 855, Bozeman.

Nebraska: 134 South 12th Street, Lincoln.

Nevada: 1485 Wells Avenue, Reno.

New Hampshire: 29 Main Street, Durham.

New Jersey: Feher Building, 103 Bayard Street, Box 670, New Brunswick.

New Mexico: Office Square Building, 1015 Tijeras Avenue, NW, Box 1348, Albuquerque.

New York: Byrns Building, 238 West Genesee Street, Syracuse.

North Carolina: 213 PMA Building, State College Station, Box 5126, Raleigh.

North Dakota: Professional Building, Fifth and Rosser Streets, Box 270, Bismarck.

Ohio: 222 Old Federal Building, Third and State Streets, Columbus.

Oklahoma: 2800 Southeastern Avenue, Box 1377, Oklahoma City.

Oregon: Ross Building, 209 Southwest Fifth Avenue, Portland.

Pennsylvania: Dauphin Building, 203 Market Street, Harrisburg.

Rhode Island: combined with Connecticut.

South Carolina: Federal Land Bank Building, 1401 Hampton Street, Columbia.

South Dakota: Knights of Columbus Building, 56 Third Street, SE Box 1357, Huron.

Tennessee: 561 United States Courthouse, Nashville.

Texas: First National Bank Building, 16-20 South Main Street, Box 417, Temple.

Utah: 222 Southwest Temple, Salt Lake City.

Vermont: 481 Main Street, Box 736, Burlington.

Virginia: 900 North Lombardy Street, Richmond.

Washington: 301 Hutton Building, South 9 Washington Street, Spokane 4.

West Virginia: Lazzelle Building, 178 Forest Avenue, Morgantown.

Wisconsin: 3010 East Washington Avenue, Madison 4.

Wyoming: Tip Top Building, 345 East Second Street, Box 699, Casper.

STATE AGENCIES

The type and amount of help available from state conservation agencies vary with each individual state. Most states offer information and assistance regarding wildlife management techniques, pond construction, winter feeding, etc. Will provide copies of state laws pertaining to the protection of birds and other species of wildlife.

Alabama: Director, Division of Game, Fish and Seafoods, Department of Conservation, Montgomery 4.

Alaska: Regional Director, Bureau of Sport Fisheries and Wildlife, P.O. Box 2021, Junea.

Arizona: Director, Game and Fish Department, Arizona State Building, Phoenix.

Arkansas: Director, Game and Fish Commission, Little Rock.

California: Director, Department of Fish and Game, 722 Capitol Ave., Sacramento 14.

Colorado: Director, Game and Fish Commission, 1530 Sherman Street, Denver 5.

Connecticut: Director, Board of Fisheries and Game, State Office Building, Hartford 14.

Delaware: Director, Board of Game and Fish Commissioners, Dover.

District of Columbia: Superintendent, Metropolitan Police, Washington.

Florida: Director, Game and Fresh Water Fish Commission, Tallahassee.

Georgia: Director, Game and Fish Commission, 401 State Capitol, Atlanta 3.

Hawaii: Fish and Game Division, Commissioner of Agriculture and Forestry, Honolulu.

Idaho: Director, Department of Fish and Game, Boise.

Illinois: Director, Department of Conservation, Springfield.

Indiana: Director, Division of Fish and Game, Department of Conservation, 311 West Washington Street, Indianapolis 9.

Iowa: Director, State Conservation Commission, East Seventh and Court Streets, Des Moines 9.

Kansas: Director, Forestry, Fish and Game Commission, Pratt.

Kentucky: Commissioner, Department of Fish and Wildlife Resources, Frankfort.

Louisiana: Secretary-Director, State Wildlife and Fisheries Commission, 126 Civil Courts Building, New Orleans 16.

Maine: Commissioner, Department of Inland Fisheries and Game, State House, Augusta.

Maryland: Director, Department of Game and Inland Fish, State Office Bldg., Annapolis.

Massachusetts: Director, Division of Fisheries and Game, 73 Tremont St., Boston 8.

Michigan: Director, Department of Conservation, Lansing 26.

Minnesota: Commissioner, Department of Conservation, State Office Building, St. Paul 1.

Mississippi: Director, Game and Fish Commission, P.O. Box 451, Jackson.

Missouri: Director, Conservation Commission, Farm Bureau Building, Jefferson City.

Montana: State Fish and Game Warden, Department of Fish and Game, Helena.

Nebraska: Director, Game Forestation and Parks Commission, Lincoln 29.

Nevada: Director, Fish and Game Commission, 51 Grove St., Reno.

New Hampshire: Director, Fish and Game Department, State House Annex, Concord.

New Jersey: Director, Department of Conservation and Economic Development, Division of Fish and Game, 230 W. State St., Trenton 7.

New Mexico: Director, Department of Game and Fish, Santa Fe.

New York: Commissioner, Conservation Department, Albany 7.

North Carolina: Executive Director, Wildlife Resources Commission, Raleigh.

North Dakota: Commissioner, Game and Fish Department, Capitol Building, Bismarck.

Ohio: Chief, Division of Wild Life, Department of Natural Resources, 1500 Dublin Road, Columbus 12.

Oklahoma: Director, Department of Wildlife Conservation, State Capitol Building, Room 118, Oklahoma City 5.

Oregon: State Game Director, State Game Commission, P.O. Box 4136, Portland 8.

Pennsylvania: Executive Director, Pennsylvania Game Commission, Harrisburg.

Rhode Island: Chief, Division of Fish and Game, Department of Agriculture and Conservation, State House, Providence 2.

South Carolina: Director, Wildlife Resources Department, Box 360, Columbia.

South Dakota: Director, Department of Game, Fish and Parks, Pierre.

Tennessee: Director, Tennessee Game and Fish Commission, Cordell Hull Bldg., Nashville 3.

Texas: Executive Secretary, Game and Fish Commission, Austin.

Utah: Director, Fish and Game Commission, 1596 West North Temple, Salt Lake City 16.

Vermont: Director, Fish and Game Commission, Montpelier.

Virginia: Executive Director, Commission of Game and Inland Fisheries, P.O. Box 1642, Richmond 13.

Washington: Director, Department of Game, 600 N. Capitol Way, Olympia.

West Virginia: Director, Conservation Commission of West Virginia, Charleston.

Wisconsin: Director, Conservation Department, State Office Building, Madison 1.

Wyoming: State Game and Fish Commissioner, Wyoming Game and Fish Commission, Cheyenne.

Puerto Rico: Department of Agriculture and Commerce, Division of Fisheries and Wildlife, San Juan.

Check-List of Eastern Birds

The following check-list is based on the Audubon Daily Field Card published by the National Audubon Society, 1130 Fifth Ave., New York 28, N.Y. It is included as a convenient means of keeping a handy record of the total number of birds attracted and observed in your area. It can be made more informative by an accompanying key that indicates the location as well as the number of birds observed — (P) pond; (B) birdbath; (F) feeders; (N) nesting; etc. The appropriate letter can be entered with the number observed.

—— Loon, Common	—— Gannet
—— Red-throated	—— Cormorant, Great
—— Grebe, Red-necked	—— Double-crested
—— Horned	—— Anhinga
—— Pied-billed	—— Frigate-bird, Magnificent
—— Shearwater, Sooty	—— Heron, Great White
—— Greater	—— Great Blue
—— Cory's	—— Egret, Reddish
—— Petrel, Leach's	—— Common
—— Wilson's	—— Snowy
—— Pelican, White	—— Heron, Louisiana
—— Brown	—— Little Blue

_____ Egret, Cattle

_____ Heron, Green

_____ Black-crowned Night

_____ Yellow-crowned Night

_____ Bittern, Am.

_____ Bittern, Least

_____ Ibis, Wood

_____ Glossy

_____ White

_____ Spoonbill, Roseate

_____ Flamingo, Am.

_____ Swan, Mute

_____ Whistling

_____ Goose, Canada

_____ Brant

_____ Goose, White-fronted

_____ Snow

_____ Blue

_____ Mallard

_____ Duck, Black

_____ Mottled

_____ Gadwall

_____ Widgeon, European

_____ American

_____ Pintail

_____ Teal, Common

_____ Green-winged

_____ Blue-winged

_____ Shoveler

_____ Duck, Wood

_____ Redhead

_____ Duck, Ring-necked

_____ Canvasback

_____ Scaup, Greater

_____ Lesser

_____ Goldeneye, Common

_____ Barrow's

_____ Bufflehead

_____ Oldsquaw

_____ Duck, Harlequin

_____ Elder, Common

_____ King

_____ Scoter, White-winged

_____ Surf

_____ Common

_____ Duck, Ruddy

_____ Merganser, Hooded

_____ Common

_____ Red-breasted

_____ Vulture, Turkey

_____ Black

_____ Kite, Swallow-tailed

_____ Mississippi

_____ Everglade

_____ Goshawk

_____ Hawk, Sharp-shinned

_____ Cooper's

_____ Red-tailed

_____ Red-shouldered

_____ Broad-winged

_____ Short-tailed

_____ Rough-legged

_____ Eagle, Golden

_____ Bald

_____ Hawk, Marsh

_____ Osprey

_____ Caracara

_____ Gyrfalcon

_____ Falcon, Peregrine

_____ Hawk, Pidgeon

—— Sparrow

—— Grouse, Spruce

—— Ruffed

—— Ptarmigan, Willow

—— Rock

—— Chicken, Prairie

—— Grouse, Sharp-tailed

—— Partridge, Gray

—— Bobwhite

—— Pheasant, Ring-necked

—— Turkey

—— Crane, Sandhill

—— Limpkin

—— Rail, King

—— Clapper

—— Virginia

—— Sora

—— Rail, Yellow

—— Black

—— Gallinule, Purple

—— Common

—— Coot, Am.

—— Oystercatcher, Am.

—— Plover, Piping

—— Plover, Snowy

—— Semipalmated

—— Wilson's

—— Killdeer

—— Golden

—— Black-bellied

—— Turnstone, Ruddy

—— Woodcock, Am.

—— Snipe, Common

—— Curlew, long-billed

—— Whimbrel

—— Plover, Upland

—— Sandpiper, Spotted

—— Solitary

—— Willet

—— Yellowlegs, Greater

—— Lesser

—— Knot

—— Sandpiper, Purple

—— Pectoral

—— White-rumped

—— Baird's

—— Least

—— Dunlin

—— Dowitcher, Short-billed

—— Long-billed

—— Sandpiper, Stilt

—— Semipalmated

—— Western

—— Buff-breasted

—— Godwit, Marbled

—— Hudsonian

—— Sanderling

—— Avocet, Am.

—— Stilt, Black-necked

—— Phalarope, Red

—— Wilson's

—— Northern

—— Jaeger, Pomarine

—— Parasitic

—— Long-tailed

—— Gull, Glaucous

—— Iceland

—— Great Black-backed

—— Herring

—— Ring-billed

_____ Black-headed
_____ Laughing
_____ Franklin's
_____ Bonaparte's
_____ Little
_____ Kittiwake, Black-legged
_____ Gull, Sabine's
_____ Tern, Gull-billed
_____ Forster's
_____ Common
_____ Arctic
_____ Roseate
_____ Sooty
_____ Least
_____ Tern
_____ Royal
_____ Sandwich
_____ Caspian
_____ Black
_____ Noddy
_____ Skimmer, Black
_____ Razorbill
_____ Murre, Common
_____ Thick-billed
_____ Dovekie
_____ Guillemot, Black
_____ Puffin, Common
_____ Pigeon, White-crowned
_____ Dove, Rock
_____ Mourning
_____ Ground
_____ Cuckoo, Mangrove
_____ Yellow-billed
_____ Black-billed
_____ Owl, Barn

_____ Screech
_____ Great Horned
_____ Snowy
_____ Hawk
_____ Burrowing
_____ Barred
_____ Great Gray
_____ Long-eared
_____ Short-eared
_____ Boreal
_____ Saw-whet
_____ Chuck-will's-widow
_____ Whip-poor-will
_____ Nighthawk, Common
_____ Swift, Chimney
_____ Hummingbird, Ruby-
       throated
_____ Kingfisher, Belted
_____ Flicker, Yellow-shafted
_____ Woodpecker, Pileated
_____ Red-bellied
_____ Red-headed
_____ Sapsucker, Yellow-bellied
_____ Woodpecker, Hairy
_____ Downy
_____ Red-cockaded
_____ Black-backed Three-toed
_____ Northern Three-toed
_____ Kingbird, Eastern
_____ Gray
_____ Western
_____ Flycatcher, Great Crested
_____ Phoebe, Eastern
_____ Flycatcher, Yellow-bellied
_____ Acadian

—— Traill's
—— Least
—— Pewee, Wood
—— Flycatcher, Olive-sided
—— Lark, Horned
—— Swallow, Tree
—— Bank
—— Rough-winged
—— Barn
—— Cliff
—— Martin, Purple
—— Jay, Gray
—— Blue
—— Scrub
—— Raven, Common
—— Crow, Common
—— Fish
—— Chickadee, Black-capped
—— Carolina
—— Boreal
—— Titmouse, Tufted
—— Nuthatch, White-breasted
—— Red-breasted
—— Brown-headed
—— Creeper, Brown
—— Wren, House
—— Winter
—— Bewick's
—— Carolina
—— Long-billed Marsh
—— Short-billed Marsh
—— Mockingbird
—— Catbird
—— Thrasher, Brown
—— Robin

—— Thrush, Wood
—— Hermit
—— Swainson's
—— Gray-cheeked
—— Veery
—— Bluebird, Eastern
—— Gnatcatcher, Blue-gray
—— Kinglet, Golden-crowned
—— Ruby-crowned
—— Pipit, Water
—— Waxwing, Bohemian
—— Cedar
—— Shrike, Northern
—— Loggerhead
—— Starling
—— Vireo, White-eyed
—— Yellow-throated
—— Solitary
—— Black-whiskered
—— Red-eyed
—— Philadelphia
—— Warbling
—— Warbler, Black-and-White
—— Prothonotary
—— Swainson's
—— Worm-eating
—— Blue-winged
—— Warbler, Brewster's
—— Lawrence's
—— Bachman's
—— Tennessee
—— Orange-crowned
—— Nashville
—— Parula
—— Yellow

_____ Magnolia
_____ Cape May
_____ Black-throated Blue
_____ Myrtle
_____ Black-throated Green
_____ Cerulean
_____ Blackburnian
_____ Yellow-throated
_____ Chestnut-sided
_____ Bay-breasted
_____ Blackpoll
_____ Pine
_____ Kirtland's
_____ Prairie
_____ Palm
_____ Ovenbird
_____ Waterthrush, Northern
_____ Louisiana
_____ Warbler, Kentucky
_____ Connecticut
_____ Mourning
_____ Yellowthroat
_____ Chat, Yellow-breasted
_____ Warbler, Hooded
_____ Wilson's
_____ Canada
_____ Redstart, Am.
_____ Sparrow, House
_____ Bobolink
_____ Meadowlark, Eastern
_____ Blackbird, Yellow-headed
_____ Redwinged
_____ Oriole, Orchard
_____ Baltimore
_____ Blackbird, Rusty

_____ Brewer's
_____ Grackle, Boat-tailed
_____ Common
_____ Cowbird, Brown-headed
_____ Tanager, Scarlet
_____ Summer
_____ Cardinal
_____ Grosbeak, Rose-breasted
_____ Blue
_____ Bunting, Indigo
_____ Painted
_____ Dickcissel
_____ Grosbeak, Evening
_____ Finch, Purple
_____ House
_____ Grosbeak, Pine
_____ Redpoll, Common
_____ Siskin, Pine
_____ Goldfinch, Am.
_____ Crossbill, Red
_____ White-winged
_____ Towhee, Rufous-sided
_____ Sparrow, Ipswich
_____ Savannah
_____ Grasshopper
_____ Le Conte's
_____ Henslow's
_____ Sharp-tailed
_____ Seaside
_____ Dusky Seaside
_____ Vesper
_____ Lark
_____ Bachman's
_____ Junco, Slate-colored
_____ Oregon

—— Sparrow, Tree   —— Fox
—— Chipping   —— Lincoln's
—— Clay-colored   —— Swamp
—— Field   —— Song
—— Harris'   —— Longspur, Lapland
—— White-crowned   —— Smith's
—— White-throated   —— Bunting, Snow

A NOTE ABOUT THE AUTHOR

THOMAS P. McELROY, JR., left a teaching career to become director of the famed Pequot-Sepos Wildlife Sanctuary at Mystic, Connecticut. He is presently Managing Director of the National Audubon Society's Aullwood Sanctuary and Nature Center at Dayton, Ohio. Mr. McElroy was born in Chester County, Pennsylvania, in 1914.

A NOTE ON THE TYPE

THE TEXT of this book was set on the Linotype in a type face called Baskerville, a facsimile reproduction of types cast from molds made for John Baskerville (1706-75) from his designs.

Composed by The Publishers' Composition Service, Inc., Brattleboro, Vermont. Printed and bound by The Plimpton Press, Norwood, Massachusetts. Paper manufactured by P. H. Glatfelter, Spring Grove, Pennsylvania. Typography and binding based on designs by W. A. Dwiggins.

8224